The Essential Catholic Handbook

A SUMMARY OF BELIEFS, PRACTICES, AND PRAYERS

Newly Expanded with a Glossary of
Key Terms and Cross-Referenced to the
Catechism of the Catholic Church

A REDEMPTORIST PASTORAL PUBLICATION

ONE LIGUORI DRIVE
LIGUORI MO 63057-9999
314.464.2500

Imprimi Potest
Richard Thibodeau, C.SS.R.
Provincial, Denver Province
The Redemptorists

Imprimatur
+ Edward J.O'Donnell, D.D.
Archdiocesan Administrator, Archdiocese of St. Louis

Library of Congress Cataloging-in-Publication Data

The essential Catholic handbook : a summary of beliefs, practices, and prayers : newly expanded with a glossary of key terms and cross-referenced to the 'Catechism of the Catholic Church' / foreword by John Cardinal O'Connor.

    p. cm. — (A Redemptorist pastoral publication)
  ISBN 0-89243-910-6
  1. Catholic Church—Handbooks, manuals, etc. 2. Catholic Church. Catechismus Ecclesiae Catholicae. I. Series.
BX842.E87 1997
282—dc21   96-48426

Contents

Contents

Contents

Foreword

The story of John the Baptizer is beautifully told in the first chapter of the Gospel of Saint John.

> There was a man sent from God, whose name was John. He came as a witness to testify to the light, so that all might believe through him. He himself was not the light, but he came to testify to the light. The true light, which enlightens everyone, was coming into the world (1:6–9).

Every person who is baptized into the Catholic Church bears the same awesome responsibility of the Baptizer himself: to be a witness to the Light. For indeed the Light has come into the world: Christ, the Son of God!

Our task as witnesses to Christ is complicated in an age filled with temptations toward self-aggrandizement and material desires. Much of the advertising and entertainment in our culture attempts to persuade us that our earthly life is all there is, so we should pursue the pleasures and successes of this world. The concept of heaven is ridiculed, and the idea of sin is dismissed as archaic.

The Catholic knows that he or she is not the Light, and that life on this earth is only a pilgrimage toward the life with God promised to those who believe, to those who are faithful witnesses to the Light. We need not despair in our efforts, for we have been given at least three important means of following the call of Isaiah that John the Baptizer made his own, "Make straight the way of the Lord" (1:23).

The first is constant prayer. Whether it be the prayer of the Church called the Divine Office, the rosary, the beautiful prayers to our Blessed Mother, or the simple prayers of meditation when we seek to do what our Lord himself asked, "Be still, and know that I am God" (Psalm 46:10), our conversations with God draw us to the Light, revealing him to each of us very personally. Prayer reawakens in us the recognition that Christ alone is the Light to the world.

The second gift we are given is grace, which comes to us through the sacraments of the Church. Frequent participation in the sacraments, especially the sacraments of penance and Eucharist, brings us the grace of the Light. It is this grace that strengthens us in our resolve to be faithful witnesses to Christ.

Finally, we are given the teachings of the Church. Timeless in their applicability, these teachings proclaim the primacy of the Light, who is the Alpha and the Omega. Those who are his witnesses are made in his image and likeness.

I am pleased to introduce *The Essential Catholic Handbook.* It is an easy-to-use guide to prayer, the sacraments, and the teachings of the Church. Indexed to the *Catechism of the Catholic Church,* the *Handbook* is an important and very usable companion for every Catholic. It is my hope that those who read the *Handbook* may be inspired to delve into the *Catechism* itself. Both will enable Catholics to meet the challenge to take their faith seriously, to comprehend it intelligently, and to demonstrate it passionately in their daily lives.

May this *Handbook* be used to help us fulfill our task, with John the Baptizer, to go forth as witnesses to testify to the Light.

JOHN CARDINAL O'CONNOR
ARCHBISHOP OF NEW YORK

Introduction

Our lifestyles, as well as our "faith-styles," have changed dramatically in the last generation. Scientific advances and streamlined communication methods have revolutionized not only our daily lives but also our understanding of the spiritual life. How we think and live influence the ways we relate to God and religion.

In 1962 Pope John XXIII, realizing that the Church needed to develop more meaningful ways of ministering in the modern age, called together the bishops of the world for the Second Vatican Council, or Vatican II. The renewal brought about by this historic assembly radically changed how Catholics understand and practice their faith today.

To be truly Catholic is to live according to the spirit and attitude launched by the Second Vatican Council. However, because the Catholic Church traces its origins back to Christ and the early Christian community, it treasures its centuries of tradition as well. To integrate the revered teachings of the past with the changes of modern times is the challenge Catholics face today. Whether you are Catholic by heritage or by a faith decision made later in life, you are called to live your baptismal commitment in every aspect of your life. The contemporary Catholic, in the midst of the complexities of modern life, shares an ancient historical legacy with a community of believers, accepts the insights of Vatican II, and forges ahead toward the future with hope.

The basic purpose of this *Handbook* is to provide information on the essentials of Catholicism and to enlighten all who wish to live out the teachings of Vatican II. Toward those ends, this edition of the *Handbook* has been fully indexed to the *Catechism of the Catholic Church.* Throughout the text, the numerical citations direct you to the sections or paragraphs of the *Catechism* where specific topics and subjects are explained.

Section One: Beliefs. What Catholics believe about God, the Trinity, Jesus, the Church, the sacraments, and other dogmas comprise the "sacred deposit of the Word of God." These truths express in human terms our understanding of who God is and what has been revealed through Jesus and the Church.

The Nicene Creed, which Catholics recite at the Sunday liturgy, summarizes our basic beliefs about God. In this section we discuss major Catholic doctrines not only as objective facts but as spiritual realities that are intimately connected to a lived-out faith life. They are "truths Catholics live by."

Section Two: Practices. The Ten Commandments are the moral norms for Catholics. Over the years the Church has developed the Precepts of the Church, time-honored observances to guide Catholics in living according to Church teaching. Section Two also contains practical points about the sacraments, the holy days, and other Catholic traditions.

Section Three: Prayers. Catholics firmly believe that a living faith includes communicating with God on a personal level. In Section Three we consider the basic prayer forms that are part of Catholic tradition. Catholics are encouraged to meditate on Scripture and inspirational writings for a well-rounded spiritual life.

Section Four: Living the Faith in the Spirit of Vatican II. In this expanded edition of the *Handbook*, Section Four has been added to provide an overview of insights and changes brought about by Vatican II. It discusses practical applications of post-Vatican II Catholicism regarding Scripture, liturgy and sacraments, ministries in the Church, life commitments, social responsibility, evangelization and the RCIA, and attitudes toward other religions.

"A Guide to Action for Today's Catholic" draws together important aspects of what it means to "Live in the Spirit of Vatican II."

Section Five: A Summary of the Documents of Vatican II. Since Vatican II provides guidelines for renewal, this section includes an outline of the sixteen Documents of Vatican II, which Pope Paul VI called "the great catechism of our times."

Section Six: A Dictionary of Essential Catholic Terms. This section provides a select yet comprehensive alphabetized list of essential Catholic terms, from *abba* to *zucchetto*. It is hoped that this listing, compiled by experienced pastors and catechists, will give a handy reference to those who do not have ready access to the larger dictionaries of Catholic words and phrases.

Section Seven: A Calendar of Catholic Saints. Finally, this *Handbook* provides a day-by-day listing of Catholic saints designed to acquaint readers more fully with the wide spectrum of saints honored by the Catholic Church. It serves also as a guide to celebrating one's name day rather than, or in addition to, a birthday; and finally it indicates patronages in order to increase devotion to and interest in those saints who have long been seen as intercessors for us in heaven.

THOMAS M. SANTA, C.SS.R.

SECTION ONE

Beliefs

1. You the Seeker, God the Seeker

YOU: A HUMAN BEING WHO SEEKS GOD

From the time you learned to talk, you asked questions—which reveals something absolutely basic about you: the fact that you have a questioning intellect.

Throughout your life, you have always wanted things, and you find yourself making constant decisions—saying yes to this, no to that. These experiences reveal something else very basic about you: the fact that you have a free will, the power to want and to choose. *(CCC 1–3)*

As time passes you are changing in bodily appearance, and your way of viewing life is shifting and deepening. But the basic you—the "I" behind your eyes—remains the same person. At your core you are constantly reaching out, seeking that for which you were created. This questing, spiritual core of your being has been called by many names. Common names for it are *soul*, *spirit*, or *heart*. *(CCC 27, 44–47)*

The Ultimate Reality you seek—which is present in everything you reach out to—has also been called by many names. The most common name for this Ultimate Reality is God. You are so bound to God that without him you would not live or move or have your being. You are so bound to God that if you did not sense his presence in some way, you would view life as pointless and cease to seek. *(CCC 43, 1701–1715, 1718)*

GOD: THE DIVINE LOVER WHO FOUND YOU

Meanwhile, as you seek God, God seeks you. The Vatican II Dogmatic Constitution on Divine Revelation expresses it this way: "The invisible God, from the fullness of his love, addresses men as his friends, and moves among them, in order to invite and receive them into his own company" (§2). *(CCC 1719)*

As a Catholic you are called to seek and find Christ. But you did not begin this quest on your own initiative. The initiative was all God's. All who follow Christ were once lost but were searched for and found. God first found you and made you visibly his in baptism. What he seeks now is that you seek him. In a mysterious way your whole life with God is an ongoing quest for each other by two lovers—God and you—who already possess each other. *(CCC 50–53, 521)*

2. Revelation, Faith, Doctrine, and Doubt

REVELATION AND FAITH

God seeks you—which is why, in the words of the Dogmatic Constitution on Divine Revelation, he has chosen to "manifest and communicate both himself and the eternal decrees of his will concerning the salvation of mankind" (§6). In revealing, God has not only communicated information; he has communicated himself to you. *(CCC 36–38, 50–64)*

Your personal response to God's communication of himself and his will is called *faith*. "By faith man freely commits his entire self to God, making 'the full submission of his intellect and will to God who reveals,' and willingly assenting to the Revelation given by him" (Dogmatic Constitution on Divine Revelation, §5). *(CCC 142–143, 153–164, 1814–1816)*

CATHOLIC DOCTRINE

The basic doctrines, or dogmas, of the Church are the verbal expression of what God has revealed to us about our relationship with him. The key characteristic of the Church's dogmas is that they agree with Sacred Scripture. The teachings spell out the unchangeable content of revelation, translating it into the changeable thought-forms and languages of people in every new era and culture. A dogma is a statement of truth, a formulation of some aspect of the Catholic faith. The purpose of each dogma is to bring Jesus Christ to our attention from a particular point of view. As a coherent set of teachings, Church dogma is a faithful interpretation of God's self-communication to humankind. *(CCC 84–100, 170–171)*

FAITH AND DOUBT

The Church's dogmatic formulas, however, are not the same thing as God's self-revelation; they are the medium through which Catholics place their faith in God. God unveils and communicates the hidden mystery of himself through Church teachings. The teachings are like sacraments through which you receive God. Through the medium of doctrinal formulas, you reach God himself in the personal act of faith. *(CCC 88–90)*

The life of faith is very personal and delicate—and ultimately mysterious. Faith is a gift of God and only God knows who has it. We can, however, presume that God is generous with his gift, and we should not presume that anyone lacks it. *(CCC 153)*

A person can lack faith through his or her own fault; we are free—even to reject God. But when a person doubts, we should not jump to conclusions. For example, there are people who remember their father as a man who inflicted pain on them. As a result these people cannot bring themselves to believe in God as their "good Father." This is not a lack of faith. It is a lack of memory images through which these persons can appreciate God as Father. Negative mental images can block a person from receiving God's self-revelation in a particular form. But such images cannot block out all forms in which people perceive and express God's mystery. God, who seeks us constantly, seeks us until we find him. *(CCC 215)*

A person who is seeking deeper insight into reality may sometimes have doubts, even about God himself. Such doubts do not necessarily indicate a lack of faith. They may be just the opposite—a sign of growing faith. Faith is alive and dynamic. It seeks, through grace, to penetrate into the very mystery of God. If a particular doctrine of faith no longer makes sense to a person, the person should go right on seeking. To know what a doctrine says is one thing; to gain an insight into its meaning through the gift of understanding is something else. When in doubt, "Seek and you will find." The person who seeks by reading, discussing, thinking, or praying eventually sees light. The person who talks to God even when God is "not there" is alive with faith. *(CCC 162)*

3. One God, Three Divine Persons

The Catholic Church teaches that the fathomless mystery we call God has revealed himself to humankind as a Trinity of Persons—the Father, the Son, and the Holy Spirit. *(CCC 238–248)*

THREE PERSONS, ONE GOD

The mystery of the Trinity is the central doctrine of Catholic faith. Upon it are based all other teachings of the Church. In the New Testament there is frequent mention of the Father, the Son, and the Holy Spirit. A careful reading of these passages leads to one unmistakable conclusion: each Person is presented as having qualities that can belong only to God. But if there is only one God, how can this be? *(CCC 199–202)*

The Church studied this mystery with great care and, after four centuries of clarification, decided to state the doctrine in this way: in the unity of the Godhead there are three Persons—the Father, the Son, and the Holy Spirit—truly distinct one from another. Thus, in the words of the Athanasian Creed: "The Father is God, the Son is God, and the Holy Spirit is God, and yet there are not three gods but one God." *(CCC 249–267)*

CREATOR, SAVIOR, SANCTIFIER

All effects of God's action upon his creatures are produced by the three divine Persons in common. But because certain effects of the divine action in creation remind us more of one divine Person than another, the Church ascribes particular effects to one or the other divine Person. Thus, we speak of the Father as Creator of all that is, of the Son, the Word of God, as our Savior or Redeemer, and of the Holy Spirit—the love of God "poured into our hearts"—as our Sanctifier. *(CCC 234–237, 257–260)*

To believe that God is Father means to believe that you are son or daughter; that God your Father accepts and loves you; that God your Father has created you as a love-worthy human being. *(CCC 238–240)*

To believe that God is saving Word means to believe that you are a listener; that your response to God's Word is to open yourself to his liberating gospel, which frees you to choose union with God and brotherhood with your neighbor. *(CCC 2716)*

To believe that God is Spirit means to believe that on this earth you are meant to live a sanctifying, supernatural life that is a created sharing in God's own nature—a life which is the beginning of life eternal. *(CCC 1691, 1703–1704)*

4. God, the Father of Jesus

The Book of Exodus records one of the most profound revelations in human history. The revelation is narrated in the story of God calling Moses to be the leader of his people. Speaking from a burning bush, which "though on fire, was not consumed," God called out: "Moses! Moses!" God then told Moses to organize the Israelites and persuade Pharaoh to let him lead that enslaved people out of Egypt. Hearing the plan, Moses was apprehensive. *(CCC 198–248)*

The dialogue goes as follows:

But Moses said to God, "If I come to the Israelites and say to them, 'The God of your ancestors has sent me to you,' and they ask me, 'What is his name?' what shall I say to them?" God said to Moses, "I AM WHO I AM." He said further, "Thus you shall say to the Israelites: 'I AM has sent me to you.' " *(CCC 446, 2575)*

God also said to Moses, "Thus you shall say to the Israelites: 'The LORD, the God of your ancestors, the God of Abraham, the God of Isaac, and the God of Jacob, has sent me to you.' "

Exodus 3:13-15

In this dialogue (and in others like it—see Judges 13:18 and Genesis 32:30) God does not really give himself a "name." He refuses to give himself a "handle" that could leave people the impression they "have a handle" on God. God says, in effect, that he is not like any of the many gods people worship. He conceals himself—thereby revealing the infinite distance between himself and all that we human beings try to know and control. *(CCC 205–208)*

But by telling Moses to say, "I AM has sent me to you," God also reveals something very personal. This God who "is," beyond all realities that come and go, is not unconnected with us and our world. On the contrary, this God who "is" reveals that he is with you. He does not tell what he is in himself. But he does reveal who he is to you. In this key moment recorded in Exodus (and developed further in Isaiah 40–45), God revealed that he is your God, the "God of your fathers"—the fathomless mystery who is with you through all time, with you beyond all powers of death and evil. *(CCC 214–221, 2810)*

The God who reveals himself in the Old Testament has two main characteristics. First, and most important, is the revelation that he is personally close to you, that he is your God. Second is the fact that this God who freely chooses a personal relationship with you is beyond all time and space. I AM is bound to nothing, but binds all things to himself. In his own words, "I am the first and I am the last; / besides me there is no god" (Isaiah 44:6). *(CCC 198, 212)*

Centuries after the revelation reflected in Exodus and Isaiah, the mysterious God of the burning bush did reveal his name—in Person. Shattering all human assumptions and expectations, God's Word "became flesh and lived among us" (John 1:14). In a revelation that blinds the mind with its light, Jesus spoke to I AM and said: "As you, Father, are in me and I in you...I made your name known to them, and I will make it known, so that the love with which you have loved me may be in them, and I in them" (John 17:21, 26). *(CCC 65, 260, 422–425, 820, 2750)*

I AM reveals his name in his Son. The burning bush draws you into its light. The God of Moses, revealed in Jesus, is love, is Father, is in you. *(CCC 211–221, 587–591)*

5. Jesus Christ

JESUS, GOD AND MAN

The second Person of the Blessed Trinity became a man, Jesus Christ. His mother was Mary of Nazareth, daughter of Joachim and Anne. Joseph, Mary's husband, was like a father to Jesus. Jesus' true and only Father is God; he had no human father. *(CCC 525–526)*

Conceived in Mary's womb by the power of the Holy Spirit, Jesus was born in Bethlehem of Judea, probably between the years 6 and 4 B.C. He died on Calvary (outside of Old Jerusalem) as a relatively young man, most likely in his early thirties. *(CCC 484, 487, 595–623)*

He is only one Person, but he has both a divine nature and a human nature. He is truly God, and he is also truly a human being. As God, he has all the qualities and attributes of God. As human, he has a human body, human soul, human mind and will, human imagination, and human feelings. His divinity does not overwhelm or interfere with his humanity—and vice versa. *(CCC 464–478)*

On Calvary he really died; he experienced the same kind of death that all human beings experience. But during his dying, at his death, and after his death, he remained God. *(CCC 595–623)*

After his death Jesus "descended to the dead." The older English translation of the Creed said "descended into hell"—which means the same thing: Hades, the nether world, the region of the dead, the condition of those who had passed on from this life. (This is clear from New Testament references such as 1 Peter 3:19 and following, 4:6; Ephesians 4:9; Romans 10:7; Matthew 12:40; Acts 2:27, 31.) Basically, therefore, "descended to the dead" means Jesus really died and entered among the dead as their Savior. Liturgically, Holy Saturday expresses this aspect of the mystery of salvation—the "death" or absence of God. *(CCC 631–637)*

The prayer of the dying Jesus—"My God, my God, why have you forsaken me?" (Mark 15:34)—finds its echo in the lives of many Christians. "Descended to the dead" expresses Jesus' outcry of agony—his experience of clinging to his Father in his moment of absolute anguish. It also expresses what many Catholics experience as God deepens their love of him by making them realize the hell life is without a sense of his presence.

Jesus rose from the dead on Easter morning. He is living today with his Father and the Spirit—and in our midst. He is still both God and man and always will be. *(CCC 638–658)*

He lives. And his passage from death to life is the mystery of salvation we are all meant to share.

CHRIST, THE REVELATION AND SACRAMENT OF GOD

By his preaching, and by his death and Resurrection, Jesus is both the revealer and the revelation of God. Who the Father is, is shown in his Son, Jesus. As the revelation of God, Jesus is both God's approach to humankind and our path to God. *(CCC 65–67, 73, 422–425)*

Jesus is the ultimate sign of God's salvation in the world—the center and means of God's encounter with you. Thus, we call him the original sacrament. The grace he communicates to you is himself. Through this communication of himself, you receive the total self-communication of God. Jesus is the saving presence of God in the world. *(CCC 519–520, 1113–1116)*

CHRIST, THE CENTER OF YOUR LIFE

Jesus comes to you, actively influencing your life in various ways. He comes to you in his Word—when the Word of God is preached to you or when you read the Scriptures with attentive reverence. He is also present to you in the seven sacraments—especially in the Eucharist. *(CCC 101–104, 1373)*

Another way you meet Jesus is in other people. As we read in the Final Judgment scene in the Gospel of Matthew, "Then the righteous will answer him, 'Lord, when was it that we saw you hungry and gave you food, or thirsty and gave you something to drink?'…And the king will answer them, 'Truly I tell you, just as you did it to one of these who are members of my family, you did it to me'" (25:37, 40). *(CCC 678, 1503, 1939, 2449)*

The Catholic Church believes that Jesus of Nazareth is the center of our lives and destiny. In the document Pastoral Constitution on the Church in the Modern World, Vatican II affirms that Jesus is "the key, the center and the purpose of the whole of man's history" (§10). With Saint Paul, the Church believes that "in him every one of God's promises is a 'Yes' " (2 Corinthians 1:20). *(CCC 65-73, 426–429)*

6. The Holy Spirit

THE INDWELLING SPIRIT

There is a common way in which God is present to all of creation. Saint Paul referred to this all-enveloping presence of God when he quoted a Greek poet who said, "In him we live and move and have our being" (Acts 17:28). *(CCC 28, 300)*

But there is another entirely personal presence of God within those who love him. Jesus himself speaks of it in the Gospel of John, where he says: "Those who love me will keep my word, and my Father will love them, and we will come to them and make our home with them" (14:23). *(CCC 260)*

This special presence of the Trinity is properly ascribed to the Holy Spirit, for as Saint Paul proclaims, "God's love has been poured into our hearts through the Holy Spirit that has been given to us" (Romans 5:5). This presence of the Spirit, God's gift of love within you, is called the divine indwelling. *(CCC 683–741)*

GIFTS OF THE SPIRIT

The Spirit is not only intimately present within you; he is silently but actively working to transform you. If you attune yourself to his silent promptings, then the gifts of the Holy Spirit become experienced realities in your life.

There are two kinds of gifts of the Spirit. The gifts of the first kind are intended for the sanctification of the person who receives them. They are permanent supernatural qualities that enable the graced person to be especially in tune with the inspirations of the Holy Spirit. They are wisdom (which helps a person value the things of heaven), understanding (which enables the person to grasp the truths of religion), counsel (which helps one see and correctly choose the best practical approach in serving God), fortitude (which steels a person's resolve in overcoming obstacles to living the faith), knowledge (which helps one see the path to follow and the dangers to one's faith), piety (which fills a person with confidence in God and an eagerness to serve him), and fear of the Lord (which makes a person keenly aware of God's sovereignty and the respect due to him and his laws). *(CCC 1830–1832, 1845)*

A second kind of gifts of the Spirit are called charisms. They are extraordinary favors granted principally for the help of others. In 1 Corinthians 12:6–11, nine charisms are mentioned. They are the gifts of speaking with wisdom, speaking with knowledge, faith, healing, miracles, prophecy, discerning of spirits, tongues, and interpreting speeches. *(CCC 688, 799–801, 809)*

Other passages of Saint Paul (such as 1 Corinthians 12:28–31 and Romans 12:6–8) mention other charisms. *(CCC 736, 1508, 2004)*

7. Grace and the Theological Virtues

GRACE: GOD'S LIFE WITHIN YOU

You are probably familiar with the distinction made between habitual grace (the state of sanctifying grace) and actual grace (divine help given for the performing of acts). These are two aspects of the life you live when you possess grace itself: the Spirit of God who is "poured into our hearts" (Romans 5:5). *(CCC 733, 1996–2005)*

Grace is the presence to you of God's living, dynamic Spirit. As a result of this presence, you live with a new, abundant inner life that makes you "become participants of the divine nature" (2 Peter 1:4), a son or daughter of God, and a brother or sister—a fellow heir—with Jesus, "the firstborn within a large family" (see Romans 8). *(CCC 357)*

As a result of the Spirit's presence, you live and respond to God in a totally new way. You live a "graced" life that is good, really pleasing to God. Under the Spirit's influence you live a life of love that builds up Christ's Body, the Church. Being "in the Spirit" with the rest of the Church, you live with others in such a way as to build a spirit of love and community wherever you are. *(CCC 1721, 1810)*

Grace—God's life within you—transforms the whole meaning and direction of your life. In grace, Saint Paul declared: "For to me, living is Christ and dying is gain" (Philippians 1:21). *(CCC 1010, 1698)*

Ultimately, grace—God's free gift of himself to you—is life eternal, a life that has already begun. Already, while you are still a pilgrim on this earth, grace is "Christ in you, the hope of glory" (Colossians 1:27). *(CCC 772)*

FAITH, HOPE, AND CHARITY

As a human being, you are capable of believing, trusting, and loving others. Grace transforms these ways you relate to others into the theological (God-directed) virtues of faith, hope, and charity—capacities to relate to God and others as one of his dearly loved sons and daughters. *(CCC 1810–1829)*

In the state of grace, you have faith: you believe in God, committing your total being to him as the personal source of all truth and reality and your own being. You have hope: you rest your whole meaning and future on God, whose promise to you of life everlasting with him is being fulfilled in a hidden manner even now through your graced existence. And you have charity: you love God as the personal All of your life and all persons as sharers in the destiny God desires for all—everlasting communion with himself. *(CCC 2086–2094)*

(If people alienate themselves from God by serious sin, they lose habitual grace and the virtue of charity. But this loss does not take away their faith or hope unless they sin directly and seriously against these virtues.)

LOVE FOR GOD, SELF, OTHERS

In this life, your love for God is bound together with your love of others—and these loves are bound together with your love of self. "Those who do not love a brother or sister whom they have seen, cannot love God whom they have not seen" (1 John 4:20). And by God's own commandment, you are to love your neighbor as yourself (Matthew 19:19; 22:39). *(CCC 2052, 2840)*

When it comes to practical, real-life terms, fulfillment of God's commandment to love begins with a proper self-love. In order to love God as he wills, you need to respect, esteem, and reverence yourself. *(CCC 2055)*

You increase your love of self by allowing yourself to realize, gradually and more deeply as the years go on, that God really loves you with a love that has no end. You are loved and you are lovable. Whenever you try to acquire or deepen this attitude about yourself, you are cooperating with the grace of God. *(CCC 2196)*

You also increase your love for self by trying to deepen your understanding of those around you—by listening and trusting, by loving and (what is more difficult) allowing yourself to be loved, by being truly forgiving and (what is most difficult) seeking true personal forgiveness, by widening your circle of compassion to embrace all living creatures and the whole of nature in its beauty. *(CCC 2842-2845)*

There is a basic principle in the New Testament writings of Saint John that goes: "Beloved, let us love one another, because love is from God; everyone who loves is born of God and knows God. Whoever does not love does not know God, for God is love" (1 John 4:7–8). You learn what love is by loving. By loving, you come to know God. *(CCC 214, 221, 773, 1828)*

8. The Catholic Church

THE CHURCH: FOUNDED BY JESUS CHRIST

The whole life of Jesus, the Word made flesh, was the foundation of the Church. *(CCC 514–521)*

Jesus gathered to himself followers who committed themselves completely to him and his mission. Praying beforehand, Jesus then chose his inner circle—the Twelve. To the Twelve he disclosed personal knowledge of himself, spoke of his coming Passion and death, and gave in-depth instruction regarding what following his way entailed. Only the Twelve were allowed to celebrate his Last Supper with him. *(CCC 1340)*

The Twelve were called apostles—that is, emissaries whose mission was to be Jesus' personal representatives. He gave these apostles the full power of authority he had from the Father. The fullness of that authority is indicated in the words of the Gospel: "Truly I tell you, whatever you bind on earth will be bound in heaven, and whatever you loose on earth will be loosed in heaven" (Matthew 18:18). *(CCC 75–77, 126)*

The climax of Jesus' preparation for the Church was the Last Supper. At this meal he took bread and wine and said: "Take and eat, this is my body: take and drink, this is my blood." With these words he actually gave himself to them. Receiving him in this way, the Twelve entered into a union of such total intimacy with him and with one another that nothing like it had ever before taken place. At that meal they became one body in Jesus. That the early Church understood the depth of this communion is shown in the earliest New Testament account of the Eucharist, the words of Saint Paul: "Because there is one bread, we who are many are one body, for we all partake of the one bread" (1 Corinthians 10:17). *(CCC 610, 1396)*

At the Supper, Jesus also spoke of the "new testament." God

was establishing a new relationship with humankind, a covenant sealed with the sacrificial blood of Christ himself. This new relationship was to be governed by a new law: the commandment of love. *(CCC 1339)*

The earliest account of the Eucharist, First Corinthians, reveals what the Last Supper meant for the future of the Church. Jesus is recorded as saying, "Do this in remembrance of me" (11:24). Jesus foresaw a long time in which his presence would not be visible to his followers. He intended that the Church repeat this Supper again and again during that time. In these memorials he would be intimately present, the risen Lord of history leading his people toward that future day when he will be "making all things new" (Revelation 21:5). *(CCC 1044, 1323, 1341–1344)*

The Last Supper was Jesus' final step before his death in preparing the Twelve. This celebration revealed how they, and their successors through the ages, were to carry out his mission of teaching, sanctifying, and governing.

According to the Gospels (Matthew 16:13–19; Luke 22:31 and following; John 21:15–17), the responsibility given to the apostles was given in a special way to Saint Peter. In Matthew, Jesus' words are: "And I tell you, you are Peter, and on this rock I will build my church, and the gates of Hades will not prevail against it" (16:18). Peter is to be the visible representative of Jesus, who is the foundation of the Church. Peter is to provide the Church with unshakable leadership against any forces that would destroy what Jesus brings to his people. *(CCC 552–553, 567)*

Jesus' founding of the Church was completed with the sending of the Holy Spirit. The actual birth of the Church took place on the day of Pentecost. This sending of the Spirit took place publicly, just as the crucifixion of Jesus took place in public view. Since that day, the Church has shown itself to be a divine-human reality—a combination of the Spirit working and the people striving, in their human way, to cooperate with the gift of his presence and Christ's Gospel. *(CCC 731–732, 763–768)*

THE CHURCH AS THE BODY OF CHRIST

The image of the Church as the Body of Christ is found in the New Testament writings of Saint Paul. In chapter 10 of 1 Corinthians, Paul says that our communion with Christ comes from "the cup of blessing," which unites us in his blood, and from "the bread that we break," which unites us to his body. Because the bread is one, all of us, though many, are one body. The eucharistic body of Christ and the Church are, together, the (Mystical) Body of Christ. *(CCC 787–796)*

In chapter 12 of both 1 Corinthians and Romans, Paul emphasizes the mutual dependence and concern we have as members of one another. In the Letters to the Ephesians and Colossians, the emphasis is on Christ as our head. God gave Christ to the Church as its head. Through Christ, God is unfolding his plan, "the mystery hidden for ages," to unite all things and to reconcile us to himself. Because this mystery is being unfolded in the Church, Ephesians calls the Church the mystery of Christ. *(CCC 669–776)*

THE CHURCH AS THE SACRAMENT OF CHRIST

In our own time Pope Paul VI has expressed the same truth with these words: "The Church is a mystery. It is a reality imbued with the hidden presence of God." *(CCC 751–757)*

When Saint Paul and Pope Paul call the Church a *mystery,* the word has the same meaning as the word *sacrament.* It means a visible sign of God's invisible presence. *(CCC 774)*

Just as Christ is the sacrament of God, the Church is your sacrament, your visible sign, of Christ. But the Church is not a sacrament "for members only." In its Dogmatic Constitution on the Church, the Second Vatican Council clearly says: "Since the

Church, in Christ, is in the nature of sacrament—a sign and instrument, that is, of communion with God and of unity among all men—she here purposes, for the benefit of the faithful and of the whole world, to set forth, as clearly as possible, and in the tradition laid down by earlier Councils, her own nature and universal mission" (§1). *(CCC 775, 1045)*

In the plan that God has for the human race, the Church is the sacrament, the primary visible instrument, through which the Spirit is bringing about the total oneness that lies in store for us all. *(CCC 776)*

This process of salvation, however, is a divine-human venture. We all have a part in it. Our cooperation with the Spirit consists of becoming a Church that sees Christ in others so that others see Christ in us. *(CCC 779–780)*

THE CATHOLIC PEOPLE OF GOD

In speaking of the Church, the Second Vatican Council emphasizes the image of the people of God more than any other one. *(CCC 781–804)*

Strictly speaking, all people are the people of God. In chapters 8 and 9 of Genesis, the Bible testifies that God has a covenant relationship with all of humankind. But the people-of-God image applies in a special way to Christ's New Testament followers and sheds light on important features of the Catholic community. *(CCC 762–766)*

One important fact about Catholics is this: we have a sense of being a people. Even though we are made up of the most varied ethnic and national groups, we have a sense of belonging to the same worldwide family. *(CCC 815)*

Another thing about the Catholic people is our sense of history. Our family line reaches back to earliest Christianity. Few of us know the whole panorama of our history as a Church. But most of us know stories of martyrs and saints. We know of groups, ancient and modern, who have endured persecution for the faith. And deep down we identify with these people and their history. All those generations who went before us are your people and mine. *(CCC 813–816, 834)*

Our sense of being a people goes very deep. There may be lapsed Catholics and nonpracticing Catholics. But good or bad, they are Catholics. When they want to come back, they know where home is. And when they do come home, they are welcomed. The Church has its imperfections. But at its heart is the endless stream of God's mercy and forgiveness. *(CCC 827)*

The Catholic community is not the whole of God's people. But it is that strong, identifiable core group who realize where we are all going. Like the Old Testament people trudging toward the Promised Land, we are keenly aware that "here we have no lasting city, but we are looking for the city that is to come" (Hebrews 13:14). Our faith instinct tells us that God is in our future and that we need one another to reach him. This is part of our strength, a facet of our mystery. *(CCC 2796)*

THE CATHOLIC CHURCH: A UNIQUE INSTITUTION

In the sixteenth century Cardinal Robert Bellarmine wrote: "The one and true Church is the community of men brought together by the profession of the same Christian faith and conjoined in the communion of the same sacraments, under the government of the legitimate pastors and especially the one vicar of Christ on earth, the Roman pontiff."

As a definition of the Church, the Bellarmine statement is incomplete; it speaks of the Church only as a visible institution. A more complete definition would note, as Pope Paul VI has done, that "the Church is a mystery...imbued with the hidden presence of God." But the Bellarmine definition lays stress on an important point: the Church is a visible social reality; it has an institutional side to its makeup. From the earliest years of its history, Christianity has had a visible structure: appointed leaders, prescribed forms of worship, and approved formulas of faith. Seen in terms of these elements, the Catholic Church is a visible society. Because it is also a mystery, however, the Church is unlike any other organized group. *(CCC 770–776)*

As a visible society, the Catholic Church is unique. Other Christian churches possess some of the same basic characteristics in common with it, such as the gifts of "one Lord, one faith, one baptism; one God and Father of all" (Ephesians 4:5–6). But as Vatican II points out, "Since these are gifts belonging to the Church of Christ, they are forces impelling towards Catholic unity" (Dogmatic Constitution on the Church, §8). *(CCC 819, 827)*

Furthermore—and this is a decisive point regarding the uniqueness of the Catholic Church—the Second Vatican Council states that "this Church, constituted and organized as a society in the present world, subsists in the Catholic Church…" (Dogmatic Constitution on the Church, §8). This key statement teaches that the basic fullness of the Church, the vital source of complete Christian unity in the future, is found uniquely in the visible Catholic Church. *(CCC 811–870)*

INFALLIBILITY IN THE CHURCH

Christ gave to the Church the task of proclaiming his Good News. (See Matthew 28:19–20.) He also promised us his Spirit, who guides us "into all the truth" (John 16:13). That mandate and that promise guarantee that we the Church will never fall away from Christ's teaching. This inability of the Church as a whole to stray into error regarding basic matters of Christ's teaching is called infallibility. *(CCC 2035)*

The pope's responsibility is to preserve and nourish the Church.

This means striving to realize Christ's Last Supper prayer to his Father, "That they may all be one. As you, Father, are in me and I am in you, may they also may be in us, so that the world may believe that you sent me" (John 17:21). *(CCC 820)*

Church teaching has a sacramental side to it; it is meant to be a sign and instrument of unity. Because the pope's responsibility is also to be a sacramental source of unity, he has a special role in regard to the Church's infallibility.

The Church's sacramental infallibility is preserved by its key instrument of infallibility, the pope. The infallibility which the whole Church has belongs to the pope in a special way. The Spirit of truth guarantees that when the pope declares that he is teaching infallibly as Christ's representative and visible head of the Church on basic matters of faith or morals, he cannot lead the Church into error. This gift from the Spirit is called papal infallibility. *(CCC 891)*

Speaking of the infallibility of the Church, the pope, and the bishops, Vatican II says: "This infallibility, however, with which the divine redeemer wished to endow his Church in defining doctrine pertaining to faith and morals, is co-extensive with the deposit of revelation, which must be religiously guarded and loyally and courageously expounded. The Roman Pontiff, head of the college of bishops, enjoys this infallibility in virtue of his office....The infallibility promised to the Church is also present in the body of bishops when, together with Peter's successor, they exercise the supreme teaching office" (Dogmatic Constitution on the Church, §25). *(CCC 877)*

9. Mary, Mother of Jesus and of the Church

In his book *Mary and Your Everyday Life*, theologian Bernard Häring remarks: "The Second Vatican Council has crowned the Dogmatic Constitution on the Church with a beautiful chapter on Mary, the prototype and model of the Church. The Church cannot come to a full understanding of union with Christ and service to his gospel without a profound love and knowledge of Mary, the Mother of our Lord and ourselves." With keen insight into the deeply personal nature of salvation, Vatican II focused on Mary's influence in our lives. *(CCC 963–972)*

Because she is the mother of Jesus, Mary is the mother of God. As Vatican II puts it: "The Virgin Mary, who at the message of the angel received the Word of God in her heart and in her body and gave Life to the world, is acknowledged and honored as being truly the Mother of God and of the redeemer" (Dogmatic Constitution on the Church, §53). *(CCC 484–507)*

As mother of the Lord, Mary is an entirely unique person. Like her Son, she was conceived as a human being (and lived her whole life) exempt from any trace of original sin. This is called her *Immaculate Conception. (CCC 490–493, 508)*

Before, during, and after the birth of her son, Mary remained physically a virgin. *(CCC 510–511)*

At the end of her life, Mary was assumed—that is, taken up—body and soul into heaven. This is called her *Assumption. (CCC 966)*

As mother of the Christ whose life we live, Mary is also the mother of the whole Church. She is a member of the Church, but an altogether unique member. Vatican II expresses her relationship to us as "pre-eminent and as a wholly unique member of the Church, and as its type and outstanding model in faith and charity....The Catholic Church taught by the Holy Spirit, honors her with filial affection and devotion as a most beloved mother" (Dogmatic Constitution on the Church, §53). *(CCC 971)*

Like a mother waiting up for her grown children to come home, Mary never stops influencing the course of our lives. Vatican II says: "She conceived, brought forth, and nourished Christ, she presented him to the Father in the temple, shared her Son's sufferings as he died on the cross....For this reason she is a mother to us in the order of grace.... By her maternal charity, she cares for the brethren of her Son, who still journey on earth surrounded by dangers and difficulties, until they are led into their blessed home" (Dogmatic Constitution on the Church, §§61–62). *(CCC 484–507, 2674)*

This mother, who saw her own flesh-and-blood son die for the rest of her children, is waiting and preparing your home for you. She is, in the words of Vatican II, your "sign of certain hope and comfort" (Dogmatic Constitution on the Church, §68).

The Church also honors the other saints who are already with the Lord in heaven. These are people who have served God and their neighbors in so outstanding a way that they have been canonized. That is, the Church has officially declared that they are in heaven, holds them up as heroic models, and encourages us to pray to them, asking their intercession with God for us all *(CCC 956–957, 962)*

10. The Scriptures and Tradition

The Second Vatican Council describes sacred tradition and Sacred Scripture as being "like a mirror, in which the Church, during its pilgrim journey here on earth, contemplates God" (Dogmatic Constitution on Divine Revelation, §7). *(CCC 80–83)*

God's Word of revelation comes to you through words spoken and written by human beings. "Sacred Scripture is the speech of God as it is put down in writing under the breath of the Holy Spirit" (Dogmatic Constitution on Divine Revelation, §9). Sacred tradition is the handing on of God's Word by the successors of the apostles. Together, tradition and Scripture "make up a single sacred deposit of the Word of God, which is entrusted to the Church" (Dogmatic Constitution on Divine Revelation, §10). *(CCC 95)*

THE BIBLE: ITS BOOKS AND ITS MESSAGE

Sacred Scripture, the Bible, is a collection of books. According to the canon of Scripture (the Catholic Church's list of books accepted as authentic), the Bible contains 73 books. The 46 books of the Old Testament were written approximately between 900 B.C. and 160 B.C.—that is, before the coming of Christ. The 27 books of the New Testament were written approximately between A.D. 50 and A.D. 140. *(CCC 120)*

The Old Testament collection is made up of historical books, didactic (teaching) books, and prophetic books (containing the inspired words of prophets, people who experienced God in special ways and were his authentic spokesmen). These books, with a few exceptions, were written originally in Hebrew. *(CCC 121–123)*

In brief, the Old Testament books are a record of the experience the Israelite people had of Yahweh, the God of their fathers. (Recall Exodus 3:13–15.) As a whole, these books reveal Israel's insight into the personal reality of the one God, Yahweh, who acts in human history guiding it with plan and purpose. Yahweh, the God of the Old Testament, is the same God whom Jesus, a Jew, called Father. *(CCC 128–130)*

The New Testament books, written originally in Greek, are made up of gospels (proclamations of the Good News) and epistles (letters). First, in the order in which they appear in the Bible, are the Gospels of Matthew, Mark, Luke, and John. The first three Gospels are called synoptic (from the Greek *synoptikos,* "seeing the whole together") because they tell much the same story in much the same way. The book called Acts of the Apostles, which follows the Gospel of John, is a sequel to the Gospel of Luke; written by Luke, Acts continues the narrative of his Gospel. The Gospel of John (also called the fourth gospel) fills out the view of Jesus found in the three synoptic Gospels. *(CCC 125–127)*

Next in sequence come the epistles of Saint Paul—the earliest New Testament documents—which were written in each case to meet particular needs of various local Christian communities.

After Paul's epistles come the Catholic epistles. These letters are called catholic, or universal, because they were not written to deal with particular needs of local churches but with matters important to all Christian communities.

The final book of the New Testament is the Book of Revelation, a message of hope for persecuted Christians, promising Christ's ultimate triumph in history.

The basic theme of the New Testament is Jesus Christ. Each book reveals a different side of his mystery. The four Gospels record the words and deeds of Jesus as they were remembered and handed down in the early generations of the Church. *(CCC 139)*

They tell the story of his Passion and death, and what that death means in the light of his Resurrection. In a sense the Gospels began with the Resurrection; Jesus' teachings and the events in his life made sense to the early Christians only after his Resurrection. The Gospels reflect the shared faith of the first Christians in the Lord who is risen and now dwells among us. *(CCC 638–658)*

The New Testament writings tell not who Jesus was but who he is. More than mere historical documents, these writings have the power to change your life. In the New Testament "mirror" you can find Jesus Christ. If you accept what you see in that mirror, the meaning Christ has for you in your life situation, you can also find yourself. *(CCC 101–104, 131–133)*

TRADITION, VATICAN II, AND PARENTS

Sacred tradition is the handing on of God's Word. This handing on is done officially by the successors of the apostles and unofficially by all who worship, teach, and live the faith as the Church understands it. *(CCC 173)*

Certain ideas and customs grow out of the tradition process and become instrumental to it, some even for a period of centuries. But a product of tradition is a basic element in it only if that product has served to hand on the faith in an unvarying form since the early centuries of the Church. Examples of basic elements are the Bible (as a tangible tool used in handing on the faith), the Apostles' Creed, and the basic forms of the Church's liturgy.

In a particular era a product of the tradition process can play a special role in handing on the Faith. The documents of ecumenical councils are prime examples. An ecumenical council is an official meeting, for the purpose of decision making, by the bishops of the world who are in union with the pope. The teachings of an ecumenical council—products of tradition in the strict sense—play a decisive role in the tradition process. The documents of the sixteenth-century Council of Trent have played such a role. So have the documents of Vatican I, which took place in the nineteenth century. *(CCC 9)*

In our time the documents of Vatican II are playing the same role in the handing-on process. As Pope Paul VI declared in a 1966 address: "We must give thanks to God and have confidence in the future of the Church when we think of the Council: it will be the great catechism of our times." *(CCC 10)*

Vatican II has done what the teaching Church has always done: it has spelled out the unchangeable content of revelation, translating it into thought-forms of people in today's culture. But this "translation of unchangeable content" is not just old news dressed up in new language. As Vatican II has stated: "The Tradition that comes from the apostles makes progress in the Church, with the help of the Holy Spirit. There is a growth in insight into the realities and words that are being passed on....As the centuries go by, the Church is always advancing towards the plenitude of divine truth, until eventually the words of God are fulfilled in her" (Dogmatic Constitution on Divine Revelation, §8). *(CCC 77–79, 2650–2651)*

Through Vatican II the Church has heeded the Spirit and engaged in its "responsibility of reading the signs of the time and of interpreting them in the light of the Gospel" (Pastoral Constitution on the Church in the Modern World, §4). Where the Spirit is leading us is not always clear. But the ground on which we, the Church, move forward in our pilgrimage is firm: the Gospel of Christ. At this stage in our history, one of our basic instruments of tradition—the handing on of the faith—is the documents of Vatican II. *(CCC 767–768)*

Tradition is an entirely personal process. The faith is handed on by people to people. Popes and bishops, priests and religious, theologians and teachers, pass on the faith. But the main people involved in the process are parents and their children. Children of Chinese parents seldom develop an Irish brogue. And children of nonreligious parents seldom develop a deep, living faith. So in regard to tradition, keep in mind the words of the noted English priest-educator, Canon Drinkwater: "You educate to some extent…by what you say, more by what you do, and still more by what you are; but most of all by the things you love." *(CCC 902, 1653–1658, 2204–2206)*

11. Sin: Original and Personal

THE ORIGINAL SIN AND ITS EFFECTS

In its Pastoral Constitution on the Church in the Modern World, Vatican II states: "Although set by God in a state of rectitude, man, enticed by the evil one, abused his freedom at the very start of history. He lifted himself up against God, and sought to attain his goal apart from him" (§13). *(CCC 396–409)*

In narrative form, chapters 1 through 11 of the Book of Genesis depict this somber fact about humankind. Chapters 1 and 2 of

Genesis tell the story of creation by God. God created all things, including man and woman, and saw that they were good. *(CCC 279–314, 355–379)*

But into this good world entered sin. In chapter 3 of Genesis, the man, Adam, rejects God and tries to become his equal. As a result of this original sin, the man feels alienated from God. He hides. When God confronts him, Adam blames the woman, Eve, for his sin, and she in turn blames the serpent. The point is simple and tragic: the man's guilt has distorted all his relationships. Sin has turned life into a harsh burden. *(CCC 397–401)*

Chapters 4 through 11 of Genesis depict the escalation of sin in the world, rippling out from Adam's original sin. Cain murders his brother, Abel. Sin reaches such proportions that God sends a great flood that covers the earth—a symbol of the chaos and destruction sin brought to creation. In chapter 11 human folly reaches its peak: man tries again to become God's equal by building a tower reaching to the heavens. This rejection of God spills over into man's rejection of his fellowman. There is now division and complete lack of communication among nations. *(CCC 56–60)*

According to Genesis, a world of beauty was deformed by sin. The ongoing result has been division, pain, bloodshed, loneliness, and death. This tragic narrative has a familiar feel to it. The reality it points to is a basic part of human experience. It is no surprise that this reality—the fact of original sin and its effects—is a teaching of the Church.

With the exception of Jesus Christ and his mother, Mary, every human being born into this world is affected by original sin. As Saint Paul declared in Romans 5:12, "Therefore, just as sin came into the world through one man, and death came through sin, and so death spread to all because all have sinned." *(CCC 402)*

While continuing to point out that there is evil in this world, the Church does not suggest that human nature is corrupt. Rather, humankind is capable of much good. While experiencing a "downward pull," we still maintain essential control over our decisions. Free will remains. *(CCC 386–390)*

And—most importantly—Christ, our Redeemer, has conquered sin and death by his death and Resurrection. This victory has swallowed up not only our personal sins but the original sin and its widespread effects. The doctrine of original sin, then, is best viewed as a dark backdrop against which can be contrasted the brilliant Redemption won for us by Christ our Lord. *(CCC 606–618)*

PERSONAL SIN

In addition to the effects of original sin, there is personal sin—sin committed by an individual. We sin personally whenever we knowingly and deliberately violate the moral law. By sinning, we fail to love God. We turn aside from—or even back away from—our lifetime goal of doing God's will. *(CCC 1849–1853)*

A mortal sin is a fundamental rejection of God's love. By it, God's grace-presence is driven from the sinner. *Mortal* means "death-dealing." This sin kills God's life and love in the person sinning. For a sin to be mortal, there must be (1) serious matter, (2) sufficient reflection, and (3) full consent of the will. *(CCC 1854–1861)*

A venial sin is a less serious rejection of God's love. *Venial* means "easily forgiven." A sin is venial if the offense is not serious. A sin can also be venial if the matter is serious and the person is not sufficiently aware of the evil involved or does not fully consent to the sin.

Venial sin is like a spiritual sickness that hurts but does not kill God's grace-presence within the person. There can be degrees of seriousness in sinning just as different sicknesses can be more or less serious. Even less serious sins, however, should not be taken lightly. People in love do not want to offend one another in any way, even the slightest. *(CCC 1862–1863)*

Sins, of whatever seriousness, do not have to be actions. A person can sin by thought or desire or by failing to do something that should be done. *(CCC 1849)*

God will forgive any sin—even the most serious—over and over if the person is truly sorry. *(CCC 1864)*

A person who judges himself or herself to be in mortal sin must be reconciled to Christ and the Church before he or she receives Holy Communion. See what Saint Paul says about worthiness to receive Holy Communion in 1 Corinthians 11:27–28. *(CCC 1385)*

A person in mortal sin can return to God's grace before confession by having perfect sorrow or contrition, but this perfect contrition must be accompanied by the intention to confess the sin and receive sacramental absolution. *(CCC 1452, 1455–1456)*

PERSONAL SIN AND SOCIAL EVIL

Patterns of evil can be institutionalized. Injustice, for example, can become part of a group's way of life, embedded in laws and social customs. Such patterns, in a ripple effect, contaminate the attitudes and actions of people in that environment. The influence of these patterns can be so subtle that people enmeshed in them may literally be unaware of the evil they promote. *(CCC 1865–1869)*

The mystery of original sin has a social dimension, and cooperation in evil patterns deepens the presence of evil in the world. It contributes to human suffering. Thus, Vatican II makes a point of focusing—especially during the penitential season of Lent—on "the social consequences of sin" (Constitution on the Sacred Liturgy, §109).

To go along with institutional evil makes a person "part of the problem"—an active descendant of the Old Man, Adam. To resist or confront social evil makes you "part of the answer"—a person alive with the life won for us by the New Man, Jesus Christ.

FORMATION OF A CORRECT CONSCIENCE

Speaking out for the dignity of human beings, Vatican II says: "Deep within his conscience man discovers a law which he has not laid upon himself but which he must obey. Its voice, ever calling him to love and to do what is good and to avoid evil, tells him inwardly at the right moment: do this, shun that. For man has in his heart a law inscribed by God. His dignity lies in observing this law, and by it he will be judged. His conscience is man's most secret core, and his sanctuary. There he is alone with God whose voice echoes in his depths" (Pastoral Constitution on the Church in the Modern World, §16). *(CCC 1776–1782)*

We are all morally bound to follow our conscience; following our conscience respects our human dignity. But this does not mean that what our conscience tells us is infallibly correct. Vatican II points out that conscience can go astray through ignorance—that is, from ignorance for which a person is not morally responsible. Seeking a correct conscience is part of our dignity and responsibility. *(CCC 1790–1794)*

Speaking of a correct conscience, Vatican II states: "Hence, the more a correct conscience prevails, the more do persons and groups turn aside from blind choice and try to be guided by the objective standards of moral conduct" (Pastoral Constitution on the Church in the Modern World, §16). *(CCC 1786–1789)*

Regarding the crucial matter of how to develop a right conscience, the Council says: "In forming their consciences the faithful must pay careful attention to the sacred and certain teaching of the Church. For the Catholic Church is by the will of Christ the teacher of truth. It is her duty to proclaim and teach with authority the truth which is Christ and, at the same time, to declare and confirm by her authority the principles of the moral order which spring from human nature itself" (Declaration on Religious Liberty, §14). In personal matters of conscience, "carefully attend to the sacred and certain teaching of the Church." Then, in the "most secret core and sanctuary" of your heart where you are "alone with God," seek his will. Seek and you will find. *(CCC 1783–1785, 2822–2823)*

12. The Sacraments of the Church

BAPTISM: NEW LIFE AND WAYS OF LIVING

Through symbolic immersion in the waters of baptism, you are "grafted into the paschal mystery of Christ." In a mysterious way, you "die with him, are buried with him, and rise with him" (Constitution on the Sacred Liturgy, §6). *(CCC 1086)*

As a baptized Christian, you are an adopted brother or sister of Christ, "hid with Christ in God," but a visible member of his Body. *(CCC 1266)*

Having died to sin (both original sin and personal sins are cleansed away in the waters of baptism), you have entered the community of the Church "as through a door." Your indelible baptism into Christ was the beginning of a unique lifelong vocation. *(CCC 1214–1216, 1263–1264, 1271)*

Many people exercise their baptismal calling through parish activities. Assisting their parish priests, they serve as distributors of Holy Communion, lectors, commentators, choir leaders, ushers, servers, members of the parish council, the Legion of Mary, the Society of St. Vincent de Paul, the Holy Name Society, and many other parish groups. *(CCC 911)*

Some serve the spiritual and community life of their parishes by teaching religion and taking part in adult-education programs, Scripture study, prayer groups, and family enrichment groups, such as Marriage Encounter. Many find their baptismal faith revitalized by praising God together as charismatic Catholics. These are only some of the ways in which baptized members of Christ's Body live out the mystery of their baptismal vocation. *(CCC 898–913)*

One way of living the life of baptism is called the religious life. Heeding a special grace from God, some people enter religious orders and congregations and become religious Brothers and Sisters. Some religious also become priests, blending their religious life with their special priestly ministry. *(CCC 914–933)*

As consecrated religious, these people dedicate themselves to God by vowing to live the evangelical counsels of poverty, chastity, and obedience. As Vatican II explains, their lives are devoted to God's service: "This constitutes a special consecration, which is deeply rooted in their baptismal consecration and is a fuller expression of it" (Decree on the Up-to-Date Renewal of Religious Life, §5). *(CCC 2102–2103)*

Through your baptism, you share with others "the sacramental bond of unity existing among all who through it are reborn" (Decree on Ecumenism, §22). Your baptism can never be repeated because it binds you to God forever. The bond is unbreakable. It is possible for you to lose grace and even faith, but you cannot lose your baptism. You are marked as one of God's own. That same bond links you to all other baptized persons in a sacramental way. You are one of us and we are all "sacrament persons." Together we are called to live until death the baptismal mystery into which we have been plunged. *(CCC 1271)*

CONFIRMATION: SEAL OF THE SPIRIT, GIFT OF THE FATHER

Confirmation is the sacrament by which those born anew in baptism receive the seal of the Holy Spirit, the Gift of the Father. Along with baptism and the Eucharist, confirmation is a sacrament of initiation—in this case, initiation into the life of adult Christian witness. The deepened presence of the Spirit, who comes to us in this sacrament, is meant to sustain us in a lifetime of witness to Christ and service to others. *(CCC 1285–1314)*

If you were being confirmed today, the celebrant would moisten his thumb with chrism, the specially blessed mixture of olive oil and balsam, and trace the sign of the cross on your forehead. This act is the laying on of hands, which is an actual part of the sacrament going back to the time of the apostles.

While anointing you, the celebrant would address you, using your new confirmation name, and say: "Be sealed with the Gift of the Holy Spirit." These words have rich connections with early Christianity. As Saint Paul wrote to the Christians in Ephesus, "In him you also…were marked with the seal of the promised holy Spirit, this is the pledge…" (Ephesians 1:13–14). *(CCC 1299–1300)*

The word *Gift*, used in confirmation, is spelled with a capital, because the Gift we receive in this sacrament is the Spirit himself. *(CCC 1293)*

PENANCE: RECONCILIATION

Penance is the sacrament by which we receive God's healing forgiveness for sins committed after baptism. The rite is called "reconciliation" because it reconciles us not only with God but with the Church community. Both these aspects of reconciliation are important. *(CCC 1468–1470)*

As members of Christ's Body, everything we do affects the whole Body. Sin wounds and weakens the Body of Christ; the healing we receive in penance restores health and strength to the Church, as well as to ourselves.

When a person turns aside or away from God's love, the harm is to the sinner. Venial sin strains one's relationship with God. Mortal sin ruptures the relationship. *(CCC 1854–1863)*

Sin is a tragic reality. But the sacrament of penance is a joyful reunion. Chapter 15 of Luke's Gospel expresses this joy poignantly:

the Pharisees accuse Jesus of being too merciful. In response, Jesus tells three parables. In the first, God is like a shepherd who leaves ninety-nine sheep to seek one who is lost. When he finds it, he is filled with joy. *(CCC 1443)*

In the second parable, a woman finds a valuable coin she had lost and throws a big party. Jesus comments: "Just so, I tell you, there is joy in the presence of the angels of God over one sinner who repents" (15:10). *(CCC 545–546)*

The third parable is the story of the wayward son. When the son returns home, his father receives him with a tender embrace. *(CCC 2839)*

When you confess your sins sincerely, with true sorrow and resolution not to sin again, God rejoices. The Pharisees depicted in Luke's Gospel were stern, rigid men—stricter judges than God. In contrast, the Father revealed by Jesus is almost too good to be true. And so is Jesus himself, whom you meet in this sacrament. Like Father, like Son. In penance, Jesus embraces and heals you. *(CCC 1441–1442)*

ANOINTING OF THE SICK

In serious illness you experience mortality. You realize that at some time you are going to die. If you are not seriously ill, but infirm or aged, you know this same experience. *(CCC 1499–1525)*

Because these circumstances lead you to face God in the light of your own death, there is something especially sacramental about the condition you are in. And so there is a formal sacrament for this sacramental situation: anointing of the sick. *(CCC 1522)*

Anointing does not hasten the act of death. In this sacrament, however, God does invite you to commune with him in the light of your final meeting with him. Through this sacrament, the entire Church asks God to lighten your sufferings, forgive your sins, and bring you to eternal salvation. *(CCC 1520)*

You need not be on the verge of dying to receive this sacrament. This is clear from the fact that the anointing and the prayers that accompany it have as a purpose the restoration of health. Therefore, if you are not in immediate danger of death, but are infirm or aged, you can and should ask for the sacrament. If you ever are in danger of death, either from sickness or old age, you should not delay receiving the sacrament. *(CCC 1514–1515)*

Anointing of the sick helps you to share more fully in the cross of Christ. By so sharing, you contribute to the spiritual good of the whole Church. By the fact that you share more fully in the cross of Christ through anointing, you are being prepared for a fuller share in Christ's Resurrection. *(CCC 1521)*

MATRIMONY: SACRAMENT OF LIFE-GIVING ONENESS

In all civilizations people have sensed a mysterious sacredness about the union of man and woman. There has always been a vague realization that the deep longing for oneness with "the other" is life-giving—and that it is a longing for oneness with the source of all life. This is why religious rituals and codes of behavior have always been connected with marriage. *(CCC 1601–1642)*

Jesus made marriage the sacrament of matrimony, giving matrimony a new dimension to the Christian vocation that begins in baptism.

In matrimony a husband and wife are called to love each other in a very practical way: by serving each other's most personal needs; by working seriously at communicating their personal thoughts and feelings to each other so their oneness is always alive and growing. This love is explicitly, beautifully sexual. As Vatican II points out, "Married love is uniquely expressed and perfected by the exercise of the acts proper to marriage" (Pastoral Constitution on the Church in the Modern World, §49). *(CCC 1643–1654)*

In matrimony a couple is also called to live their sacrament for others. By their obvious closeness, a couple affects the lives of others with "something special"—the love of Christ in our midst. They reveal Christ's love and make it contagious to their children and to all who come into contact with them. A major purpose and natural outcome of matrimony is the begetting of new life—children. But a couple's love also gives life—the life of Christ's Spirit—to other people. *(CCC 2366–2367)*

A couple does not live a life of love because they happen to be compatible. They do it consciously and deliberately because it is their vocation and because matrimony is called "a great mystery...applying it to Christ and the church" (Ephesians 5:32).

Matrimony is much more than a private arrangement between two people. It is a sacramental vocation in and for the Church. It is a medium through which Christ reveals and deepens the mystery of his oneness with us, his Body. Thus, husbands and wives live a truly sacramental life when they follow the advice given in Ephesians 5:21: "Be subject to one another out of reverence for Christ."

In the Catholic Church, a couple's sacramental union is exclusive (one man with one woman) and indissoluble (till death do us part). These are concrete ways in which the mysterious oneness between husband and wife, Christ and Church, becomes reality. *(CCC 2360–2379)*

The best thing parents can do for their children is to love each other. Similarly, one of the best things a couple can do for the Church and for the world is to strive for greater closeness. *(CCC 2201–2231)*

HOLY ORDERS: MINISTERIAL PRIESTHOOD

The Church is the Body of Christ. As such, the whole Church shares in the nature and tasks of Christ, our Head. This includes sharing in his priesthood. *(CCC 787–796, 1268, 1546)*

But beyond this "common priesthood of the faithful," there is the special or "ministerial priesthood" of Christ that certain members of the Church receive through the sacrament of holy orders. *(CCC 1536–1589)*

Each type of priesthood—common or ministerial—is a sharing in the priesthood of Christ. And both types are related to each other. But there is a basic difference between them. In the eucharistic sacrifice, for example, the ordained priest acts "in the person of Christ" and offers the sacrifice to God in the name of all, and the people join with the priest in that offering. The two roles—of priest and people—go together. *(CCC 901–903)*

Priests receive their priesthood from bishops, who possess the fullness of the sacrament of holy orders. When a bishop ordains priests, he gives them a sharing of his priesthood and mission. *(CCC 1562–1564)*

Priests share in Christ's ministry by preaching his Gospel, doing all in their power to bring their people to Christian maturity. They baptize, heal, forgive sin in the sacrament of penance, and act as the Church's witness in the sacraments of matrimony and anointing of the sick. Most importantly, priests celebrate the Eucharist, which is "the center of the assembly of the faithful over which the priest presides" (Decree on the Ministry and Life of Priests, §5). All priests are united in the single goal of building up Christ's Body. *(CCC 1565–1568)*

When priests are ordained, they "are signed with a special character," an interior capability that empowers them to "act in the person of Christ the head" (Decree on the Ministry and Life of Priests, §2). This special inner "character" unites priests in a sacramental bond with one another—a fact that, in a sense, sets them apart from other people. This "being set apart" is meant to help priests do God's work with total dedication. *(CCC 1581–1584)*

As Vatican II points out, priests "exercise other services for the benefit of men [and women]" just as Jesus did (Decree on the Ministry and Life of Priests, §2). One thing this means is that priests need their people just as their people need them. Laypeople who work closely with priests help them to be leaders in the community of God's people. *(CCC 910)*

In addition to bishops and priests, deacons also have a special sharing in the sacrament of holy orders. The diaconate, conferred by a bishop, is received as the first stage in ordination by those who go on to the priesthood. Since the Second Vatican Council, however, the ancient order of deacon has been restored in the Roman Catholic Church as an office in its own right. Many dioceses now have deacons who do not go on to become priests. They are known, therefore, as permanent deacons. Working under the authority of the local bishop, permanent deacons serve the people of God at the direction of priests in parishes. *(CCC 1569–1571)*

EUCHARIST: SACRIFICE AND SACRAMENT

In the Constitution on the Sacred Liturgy, Vatican II begins chapter 2, "The Most Sacred Mystery of the Eucharist," with these beautiful words:

> At the Last Supper, on the night he was betrayed, our Savior instituted the eucharistic sacrifice of his Body and Blood. This he did in order to perpetuate the sacrifice of the Cross throughout the ages until he should come again, and so to entrust to his beloved Spouse, the Church, a memorial of his death and resurrection: a sacrament of love, a sign of unity, a bond of charity, a paschal banquet in which Christ is consumed, the mind is filled with grace, and a pledge of future glory is given to us (§47). *(CCC 1322–1398)*

This mystery is the very center and culmination of Christian life. It is the "source and the summit of all preaching of the Gospel...the center of the assembly of the faithful" (Decree on the Life and Ministry of Priests, §5). *(CCC 1181, 1324–1327)*

In every Mass, Christ is present, both in the person of his priest and especially under the form of bread and wine. In every Mass, his death becomes a present reality, offered as our sacrifice to God in an unbloody and sacramental manner. As often as the sacrifice of the cross is celebrated on an altar, the work of our redemption is carried on. *(CCC 1333, 1350, 1372)*

At Mass we offer Christ, our passover sacrifice, to God, and we offer ourselves along with him. We then receive the risen Lord, our bread of life, in Holy Communion. In so doing, we enter into the very core of the paschal mystery of our salvation—the death and Resurrection of Christ. *(CCC 1330, 1356–1359)*

Eating the supper of the Lord, we span all time and "proclaim the Lord's death until he comes" (1 Corinthians 11:26). Sharing this banquet of love, we become totally one body in him. At that moment our future with God becomes a present reality. The oneness for which we are destined is both symbolized and made real in the meal we share. In the Mass, both past and future become really present in mystery. *(CCC 1382–1398, 1402–1405)*

If you prepare for it with care and enter into it with living faith, the Eucharist can draw you into the compelling love of Christ and set you afire. When you go out from the sacred mystery, you know you were caught up in it if you "grasp by deed what you hold by creed." And if you return to the place where the Blessed Sacrament is kept, Christ present in the tabernacle, you can regain your sense of the fathomless love of which his presence there silently speaks. *(CCC 1066–1073)*

13. Human Destiny

INDIVIDUAL DEATH AND JUDGMENT

The Church believes in two final destinies—one for individuals and one for humankind as a whole. *(CCC 678–679)*

What you can expect at death is expressed in the New Testament Letter to the Hebrews. It says, "It is appointed for mortals to die once, and after that the judgment..." (9:27). *(CCC 1013, 1021)*

Your life as an earthly pilgrim reaches its point of arrival at the moment of death. Having passed beyond the world of time and change, you can no longer choose a different reality as the ultimate love of your life. If your basic love-choice at the moment of death was the absolute Good whom we call God, God remains your eternal possession. This eternal possession of God is called heaven. *(CCC 1023–1029)*

If your ultimate love-choice at the moment of death was anything less than God, you experience the radical emptiness of not possessing the absolute Good. This eternal loss is called hell. *(CCC 1033–1037)*

The judgment at the instant of death consists in a crystal-clear revelation of your unchangeable, freely chosen condition—eternal union with God or eternal alienation. *(CCC 1021–1022)*

PURGATORY AND THE COMMUNION OF SAINTS

If you die in the love of God but possess any "stains of sin," such stains are cleansed away in a purifying process called purgatory. These stains of sin are primarily the temporal punishment due to venial or mortal sins already forgiven but for which sufficient penance was not done during your lifetime. This doctrine of purgatory, reflected in Scripture and developed in tradition, was clearly expressed in the Second Council of Lyons (A.D. 1274). *(CCC 1030–1032)*

Having passed through purgatory, you will be utterly unselfish, capable of perfect love. Your selfish ego—that part of you that restlessly sought self-satisfaction—will have died forever. The "new you" will be your same inner self, transformed and purified by the intensity of God's love for you.

Besides declaring the fact of purgatory, the Second Council of Lyons also affirmed that "the faithful on earth can be of great help" to persons undergoing purgatory by offering for them "the sacrifice of the Mass, prayers, almsgiving, and other religious deeds." *(CCC 958, 1032, 1055)*

Implied in this doctrine is the bond of oneness—called the communion of saints—that exists between the people of God on earth and those who have gone before us. Vatican II focuses on this bond of union by saying that it "accepts loyally the venerable faith of our ancestors in the living communion which exists between us and our brothers who are in the glory of heaven or who are yet being purified after their death" (Dogmatic Constitution on the Church, §51). *(CCC 828)*

The communion of saints is a two-way street. In the section quoted above, Vatican II points out that just as you on earth can help those who undergo purgatory, those in heaven can help you on your pilgrimage by interceding with God. *(CCC 946–959)*

HELL

God who is infinite love and mercy is also infinite justice. Because of God's justice, as well as his total respect for human freedom, hell is a real possibility as a person's eternal destiny. This side of God's mystery is difficult for us to grasp. But Christ himself taught it, and so does the Church. *(CCC 1033–1037, 1861)*

The teaching on hell is clearly in Scripture. In the Gospel of Matthew, Christ says to the just: "Come, you that are blessed by my Father, inherit the kingdom prepared for you from the foundation of the world." But to the unjust he says: "You that are accursed, depart from me into the eternal fire prepared for the devil and his angels" (25:34, 41). Elsewhere, Jesus is recorded as saying: "It is better for you to enter life maimed than to have two hands and to go to hell" (Mark 9:43).

One point that emerges quite clearly from this doctrine is the reality of human freedom. You are free to seek God and serve him. And you are free to do the opposite. In either case you are responsible for the consequences. Life is a serious matter. The way you live it makes a serious difference. You are free, radically free, to seek God. And you are free, radically free, to choose the inexpressible pain of his absence. *(CCC 1730–1742)*

HEAVEN

Grace, God's presence within you, is like a seed—a vital, growing seed that is destined one day to break forth full grown.

God has given himself to you, but in a hidden way. For the time being, you seek him even as you possess him. But the time will come when your seeking will be over. You will then see and possess God completely. This has been revealed. *(CCC 1024)*

In his First Letter, Saint John says: "Beloved, we are God's children now; what we will be has not yet been revealed. What we do know is this: when he is revealed, we will be like him, for we will see him as he is" (3:2). *(CCC 1720)*

And in his First Letter to the Corinthians, Saint Paul says: "For now we see in a mirror dimly, but then we will see face to face. Now I know only in part; then I will know fully, even as I have been fully known" (13:12). *(CCC 164)*

This is heaven: direct face-to-face vision of God as he is—Father, Son, and Spirit; total and perfect union with God, an ecstasy of fulfillment beyond human imagining; the "now" of eternity in which everything is ever new, fresh, and present to you; the warm flood of joy in the company of Jesus, his mother, and all those you have ever known and loved; a total absence of pain, regret, bad memories; the perfect enjoyment of all your powers of mind and (after the resurrection on Judgment Day) of body.

This is heaven. That is to say, this is a pale, human indication of what God has promised to those who love him, of what Christ has gained for us by his death and Resurrection. *(CCC 163, 1023–1029, 2519)*

A NEW EARTH AND A NEW HEAVEN

Belief in the Final Judgment on the last day is clearly expressed in the Creeds of the Church. On that day all the dead will be raised. Through divine power, we will all be present before God as bodily human beings. Then God—the absolute Lord of history—will conduct a panoramic judgment of all that humankind did and endured through the long centuries in which the Spirit struggled to bring us forth as one people. *(CCC 1038–1050)*

When will that day come? In a remarkable passage filled with hope for all things human, the Second Vatican Council addresses this question and expresses the Church's vision: "We know neither the moment of the consummation of the earth and of man nor the way the universe will be transformed. The form of this world, distorted by sin, is passing away and we are taught that God is preparing a new dwelling and a new earth in which righteousness dwells, whose happiness will fill and surpass all the desires of peace arising in the hearts of men" (Pastoral Constitution on the Church in the Modern World, §39). *(CCC 1001)*

Meanwhile, during the time that is left to us, "the body of a new human family grows, foreshadowing in some way the age which is to come" (Pastoral Constitution on the Church in the Modern World, §39). *(CCC 2820)*

After we have "spread on earth the fruits of our nature and our enterprise—human dignity, brotherly communion, and freedom—according to the command of the Lord and in his Spirit, we will find them once again, cleansed this time from the stain of sin, illuminated and transfigured....Here on earth the kingdom is mysteriously present; when the Lord comes it will enter into its perfection" (Pastoral Constitution on the Church in the Modern World, §39).

That kingdom is already present in mystery. The day has already begun when God "will wipe every tear from their eyes. Death will be no more; mourning and crying and pain will be no more." The day has already begun when he says to all living things: "See, I am making all things new....It is done! I am the Alpha and the Omega, the beginning and the end" (Revelation 21:4, 5, 6). *(CCC 1044, 1186)*

Meanwhile, we work and pray for the full flowering of that kingdom to come. With the early Christians, we cry out: *Marana tha!* Come, Lord Jesus! We seek you. *(CCC 1130, 1403, 2548–2550)*

SECTION TWO

Practices

1. God's Two Great Commandments

The basis of all law (your rule of life) rests on two commandments: "You shall love the Lord your God with all your heart, and with all your soul, and with all your mind....You shall love your neighbor as yourself" (Matthew 22:37, 39). *(CCC 2055, 2083)*

2. Commandments of God

These are an extension of the two great commandments. The first three tell you how to love your God; the rest show you how to love your neighbor. *(CCC 2084–2557)*

1. You shall honor no other god but me. *(CCC 2084–2132)*
2. You shall not misuse the name of the Lord your God. *(CCC 2142–2159)*
3. Remember to keep holy the Sabbath. *(CCC 2168–2188)*
4. Honor your father and your mother. *(CCC 2197–2246)*
5. You shall not kill. *(CCC 2258–2317)*
6. You shall not commit adultery. *(CCC 2331–2391)*
7. You shall not steal. *(CCC 2401–2449)*
8. You shall not bear false witness against your neighbor. *(CCC 2464–2503)*
9. You shall not covet your neighbor's wife. *(CCC 2514–2527)*
10. You shall not covet your neighbor's goods. *(CCC 2534–2550)*

3. Precepts of the Church

From time to time, the Church has listed certain specific duties of Catholics. Some duties expected of Catholic Christians today include the following. (Those duties traditionally mentioned as Precepts of the Church are marked with an asterisk.) *(CCC 2041–2043)*

1. To keep holy the day of the Lord's Resurrection: to worship God by participating in Mass every Sunday and every holy day of obligation; *to avoid those activities that would hinder renewal of soul and body, for example, needless work and business activities, unnecessary shopping, and so forth. *(CCC 1166–1167, 1389, 2174–2188)*

2. To lead a sacramental life: to receive Holy Communion frequently and the sacrament of penance regularly—minimally, to receive the sacrament of penance at least once a year (annual confession is obligatory only if serious sin is involved); *see explanation on pages 35 to 36 of this book. *(CCC 1389)* —minimally, to receive Holy Communion at least once a year, between the First Sunday of Lent and Trinity Sunday or, for a just cause, at another time during the year. *(CCC 1389, 2042)*

3. To study Catholic teaching in preparation for the sacrament of confirmation, to be confirmed, and then to continue to study and advance the cause of Christ. *(CCC 1309, 1319)*

4. To observe the marriage laws of the Church; *to give religious training (by example and word) to one's children; to use parish schools and religious-education programs. *(CCC 1601–1658)*

5. To strengthen and support the Church; *to strengthen and support one's own parish community and parish priests; to strengthen and support the worldwide Church and the Holy Father. *(CCC 1351)*

6. To do penance, including abstaining from meat and fasting from food on the appointed days. *(See pages 51 to 52 of this volume.) *(CCC 1438)*

7. To join in the missionary spirit and apostolate of the Church. *(CCC 2044–2046)*

4. Holy Days of Obligation

Holy days of obligation are special feasts on which Catholics who have reached the age of reason are seriously obliged, as on Sundays, to assist at Mass and to avoid unnecessary work. *(CCC 2043, 2180, 2698)* Serious reasons excuse us from these obligations.

In the United States these days are: Mary, Mother of God, January 1; Ascension Thursday, forty days after Easter; Mary's Assumption, August 15; All Saints' Day, November 1; Mary's Immaculate Conception, December 8; Christmas, December 25. (In Canada, Christmas and Mary, Mother of God are holy days. Others formerly specified have either been made nonobligatory or transferred to the following Sunday.)

5. Regulations for Fast and Abstinence

"All persons who have completed their fourteenth year are bound by the law of abstinence; all adults are bound by the law of fast up to the beginning of their sixtieth year." ("The completion of the fourteenth year means the day after one's fourteenth birthday. The beginning of the sixtieth year means the obligation ceases at midnight between the fifty-ninth birthday and the next day.") (See the Code of Canon Law, 1252.) The law of abstinence forbids the eating of meat. The law of fasting allows only one full meal and two lighter meals in the course of the day and prohibits eating between meals. *(CCC 1438, 2043)*

In the United States, Ash Wednesday and Good Friday are days of fast and abstinence; all other Fridays of Lent are days of abstinence only. Some form of penance is especially encouraged on all Fridays throughout the year. (Catholics living in Canada should consult their parish priests about Canadian regulations.)

Pregnant women and people who are sick are not obliged to

fast. Others who feel they are unable to observe the laws of fast and abstinence should consult a parish priest or confessor.

Fast and abstinence are recognized forms of penance. By doing these and other penances, we can realize that interior change of heart that is so necessary for all Christians. *(CCC 1434–1437)*

6. Confession of Sins

The precept to confess at least once a year is a reminder to receive the sacrament of penance (reconciliation) on a regular basis. If no grave sin has been committed in that time, confession is not necessary. However, frequent confession is of great value; it makes us more deeply conformed to Christ and most submissive to the voice of the Spirit. *(CCC 1423–1424)*

Reconciliation is a personal encounter with Jesus Christ represented by the priest in the confessional or reconciliation room. The penitent admits to God that he or she has sinned, makes an act of sorrow, accepts a penance (prayers, acts of self-denial, or works of service to others), and resolves to do better in the future. *(CCC 983, 1441–1442)*

After prayer and an examination of conscience to find out what sins you have committed, you enter the confessional. This new form which is described below, although preferable, is optional. *(CCC 1450–1460)*

Father greets you kindly.

You respond and then make and say the Sign of the Cross.

Father invites you to have confidence in God.

You answer, "Amen."

Father may read or recite some short selection from the Bible.

You introduce yourself (not by name) and tell how long it has been since your last confession. You then tell your sins. (Each mortal sin must be confessed as well as possible.) It is useful to mention your most frequent and most troublesome venial sins.

Father will give you any necessary advice and answer your questions. After he assigns a penance you make an Act of Contrition (see pages 64 to 65).

Father then places his hands on your head (or extends his right hand toward you) and prays these words of forgiveness: "God, the Father of mercies, through the death and resurrection of his Son has reconciled the world to himself and sent the Holy Spirit among us for the forgiveness of sins; through the ministry of the Church may God give you pardon and peace, and I absolve you from your sins in the name of the Father, and of the Son, and of the Holy Spirit."

You answer, "Amen."

Father then says, "Give thanks to the Lord, for he is good."

You answer, "His mercy endures for ever."

Father then dismisses you in these or similar words, "The Lord has freed you from your sins. Go in peace."

For further information on penance, read pages 35 to 36 of this volume.

7. Regulations for the Communion Fast

The conditions for receiving Holy Communion are the state of grace (freedom from mortal sin), the right intention (not out of routine or human respect, but for the purpose of pleasing God), and observance of the Communion fast. *(CCC 1387)*

This fast means that you must not eat anything or drink any liquid (other than water) one hour before the reception of Communion. However, the sick and aged, even those not confined to bed or a home (and those caring for them who wish to receive Communion but cannot fast for an hour without inconvenience), can receive Holy Communion *even if they have taken something during the previous hour.*

8. How to Receive Communion

Holy Communion may be received on the tongue or in the hand and may be given under the form of bread alone or under both species. *(CCC 1384–1390)*

When the minister of the Eucharist addresses the communicant with the words "The Body of Christ," "The Blood of Christ," the communicant responds "Amen" to each.

When the minister raises the eucharistic bread or wine, this is an invitation for the communicant to make an act of faith, to express his or her belief in the Eucharist, to manifest a need and desire for the Lord, to accept the good news of Jesus' paschal mystery.

A clear, meaningful, and purposeful "Amen" is your response to this invitation. In this way, you openly profess your belief in the presence of Christ in the eucharistic bread and wine, as well as in his Body, the Church.

9. Beatitudes

Positive Christianity involves more than obedience to laws. Those who follow Christ and live by his Spirit know that their salvation rests on struggle and pain. The beatitudes are a summary of the difficulties to be overcome by faithful Christians and the rewards that will be theirs if they are loyal followers of Christ (Matthew 5:3–10). *(CCC 1716–1717)*

1. Blessed are the poor in spirit, for theirs is the kingdom of heaven. *(CCC 544)*
2. Blessed are those who mourn, for they will be comforted.
3. Blessed are the meek, for they will inherit the earth.
4. Blessed are those who hunger and thirst for righteousness, for they will be filled.
5. Blessed are the merciful, for they will receive mercy.

6. Blessed are the pure in heart, for they will see God. *(CCC 1720, 2518)*

7. Blessed are the peacemakers, for they will be called children of God. *(CCC 2305–2306)*

8. Blessed are they who are persecuted for righteousness' sake, for theirs is the kingdom of heaven.

Here is a shorter version of the beatitudes.

1. Happy are those who need God.
2. Happy are those with self-control.
3. Happy are those who are sorry for sin.
4. Happy are those who hunger and thirst for holiness.
5. Happy are the merciful.
6. Happy are those who love with all their heart.
7. Happy are the peacemakers.
8. Happy are those who suffer for doing what is right.

10. Corporal (Material) Works of Mercy

Here are listed the corporal works of mercy—the actions by which we come to the material aide of our neighbors in Christ. *(CCC 2443–2447)*

1. To feed the hungry.
2. To give drink to the thirsty.
3. To clothe the naked.
4. To visit the imprisoned.
5. To shelter the homeless.
6. To visit the sick.
7. To bury the dead. *(CCC 1681–1690, 2300)*

11. Spiritual Works of Mercy

1. To admonish the sinner.
2. To instruct the ignorant.
3. To counsel the doubtful.
4. To comfort the sorrowful.
5. To bear wrongs patiently.
6. To forgive all injuries.
7. To pray for the living and the dead . *(CCC 958, 1032)*

Here is a restatement of the spiritual works of mercy.

1. Correct those who need it.
2. Teach the ignorant.
3. Give advice to those who need it.
4. Comfort those who suffer.
5. Be patient with others.
6. Forgive others who hurt you.
7. Pray for others.

12. How to Baptize in Case of an Emergency

Pour ordinary water on the forehead (not the hair) of the person to be baptized and say while pouring it: "I baptize you in the name of the Father, and of the Son, and of the Holy Spirit." (Note: Any person can and should baptize in case of necessity; the same person must say the words while pouring the water.) *(CCC 1240–1256)*

13. How to Prepare for a Sick Call: Reconciliation, Communion, Anointing

A sick-call visit made by a priest may include the administration of the sacraments of reconciliation, Communion, and anointing. Be sure to call the parish or a priest whenever a relative or friend has become seriously ill. The person does not have to be in danger of death for a sick call to be made. *(CCC 1517–1519)*

Cover a small table with a cloth. If possible, have the table near the bed or chair of the sick person. A crucifix and a vessel of holy water should be provided as well as candles.

Communion to the sick may be received at any hour. If the sick person cannot receive the Eucharist under the form of bread, it may be given under the form of wine alone. Those who care for the sick may also receive Communion.

When the priest (deacon, eucharistic minister) arrives, lead the minister to the sick person. Leave the room if the sick person wishes to receive the sacrament of penance. After reconciliation is finished, return and join in the prayers.

14. Liturgical Seasons of the Year

Through the liturgy, the work of our redemption is exercised. It is "through the liturgy, especially, that the faithful are enabled to express in their lives and manifest to others the mystery of Christ and the real nature of the true Church." It is "the summit toward which the activity of the Church is directed; it is also the fount from which all her power flows" (Constitution on the Sacred Liturgy, §§2,10). *(CCC 1163–1173)*

On appointed days in the course of the year, the Church celebrates the memory of our redemption by Christ. Throughout the year, the entire mystery of Christ is unfolded. The Church does this in sequence during the various seasons of the liturgical year. *(CCC 1166)*

Advent: This season begins four weeks (or slightly less) before Christmas. The Sunday which falls on or closest to November 30 is its starting point. *(CCC 524)*

Christmas Season: This season lasts from Christmas until the Baptism of the Lord, the Sunday after Epiphany. The period from the end of Christmas Season until the beginning of Lent belongs to Ordinary Time. *(CCC 1171)*

Lent: The penitential season of Lent lasts forty days, beginning on Ash Wednesday and ending with the Mass of the Lord's Supper on Holy Thursday. The final week is called Holy Week, and the last three days are called the Paschal Triduum. *(CCC 540, 1438)*

Easter Season: This season, whose theme is resurrection from sin to the life of grace, lasts fifty days, from Easter to Pentecost. *(CCC 1168–1169)*

Ordinary Time: This season comprises the thirty-three or thirty-four weeks in the course of the year that celebrate no particular aspect of the mystery of Christ. Instead, the mystery of Christ in all its fullness is celebrated. It includes not only the period between the end of the Christmas Season and the beginning of Lent but also all the Sundays after Pentecost to the last Sunday of the liturgical year (Christ the King). *(CCC 1166–1167, 2177)*

SECTION THREE

Prayers

1. What Is Prayer?

According to an ancient definition, prayer is "keeping company with God." Prayer is you relating to God in the deepest recesses of your personality. It is you seeking and communing with the living God—responding to him as he has made himself known to you through the teachings of the Church. *(CCC 2559–2565, 2697–2699)*

As personal as it is, prayer makes use of word formulas. Liturgical prayer—the official community prayer of the Church—uses approved formulas. So does unofficial group prayer. Even in private prayer, traditional formulas can be of great help.

At its most personal, private prayer is spontaneous or impromptu—and sometimes even wordless. Nonetheless, formulas are practical helps for breaking into prayer and expressing faith. For this reason some of the most loved, time-approved formulas of Catholic devotion are offered here—prayers that express the whole range of prayerful attitudes: adoration, thanksgiving, petition, and atonement. Also offered in this section is a suggested method of private meditative prayer. *(CCC 2700–2704)*

2. Sign of the Cross *(CCC 232–237)*

In the name of the Father, and of the Son, and of the Holy Spirit. Amen. *(Said at the beginning and end of prayers.)*

3. Our Father *(CCC 2759-2865)*

Our Father, who art in heaven, hallowed be thy name; thy kingdom come; thy will be done on earth as in heaven. Give us this day our daily bread; and forgive us our trespasses as we forgive those who trespass against us; and lead us not into temptation, but deliver us from evil. (For the kingdom, the power, and the glory are yours, now and for ever). Amen.

4. Hail Mary (CCC 2676–2677)

Hail Mary, full of grace. The Lord is with thee. Blessed art thou among women, and blessed is the fruit of thy womb, Jesus. Holy Mary, Mother of God, pray for us sinners, now and at the hour of our death. Amen.

5. Prayer of Praise (CCC 2639–2643)

Glory to the Father, and to the Son, and to the Holy Spirit; as it was in the beginning, is now, and will be for ever. Amen.

6. Apostles' Creed (CCC 198–1065)

I believe in God, the Father almighty, creator of heaven and earth. I believe in Jesus Christ, his only Son, our Lord. He was conceived by the power of the Holy Spirit and born of the Virgin Mary. He suffered under Pontius Pilate, was crucified, died, and was buried. He descended to the dead. On the third day he rose again. He ascended into heaven, and is seated at the right hand of the Father. He will come again to judge the living and the dead. I believe in the Holy Spirit, the holy catholic Church, the communion of saints, the forgiveness of sins, the resurrection of the body, and the life everlasting. Amen.

7. Morning Offering (CCC 2659–2660)

Most holy and adorable Trinity, one God in three Persons, I praise you and give you thanks for all the favors you have bestowed on me. Your goodness has preserved me until now. I offer you my whole being and in particular all my thoughts, words, and deeds, together with all the trials I may undergo this day. Give them your blessing. May your divine love animate them and may they serve your greater glory.

I make this morning offering in union with the divine intentions of Jesus Christ who offers himself daily in the holy sacrifice of the Mass, and in union with Mary, his Virgin Mother and our Mother, who was always the faithful handmaid of the Lord. Amen.

or

Almighty God, I thank you for your past blessings. Today I offer myself—whatever I do, say, or think—to your loving care. Continue to bless me, Lord. I make this morning offering in union with the divine intentions of Jesus Christ who offers himself daily in the holy sacrifice of the Mass, and in union with Mary, his Virgin Mother and our Mother, who was always the faithful handmaid of the Lord. Amen.

8. Evening Prayer

O my God, I thank you with all my heart for all the graces and blessings you have bestowed on me, especially for having called me to the true faith, for having given me Jesus Christ as my Savior, the Blessed Virgin Mary as my Mother, and for having preserved me this day.

O my God, I have repaid with ingratitude your many benefits. I detest my sins, because they displease you, who are deserving of all my love; I repent of them with my whole heart. Forgive me through the merits of Jesus Christ. Let me not die in my sins, as I deserve.

O my God, because you are infinite Goodness and worthy of infinite love, I love you with my whole heart, above all things. I love my neighbor as myself and forgive, for your sake, all who have injured me.

Bless, O Lord, all my relations, benefactors, friends, and enemies. Protect and bless our Holy Father, all the bishops and priests of your holy Church. Help the poor and all who are afflicted, prisoners and travelers, the sick and the dying.

O merciful God! Have pity also on the suffering souls in purgatory. Put an end to their sufferings and bring them to eternal rest.

O my God, I beseech you to preserve me this night from all evil. O Mary, my dear Mother, bless and protect me under your mantle. All my patron saints, intercede for me. Amen.

9. Act of Faith *(CCC 1814–1816, 2656)*

O my God, I firmly believe that you are one God in three divine Persons, Father, Son, and Holy Spirit; I believe that your divine Son became man and died for our sins, and that he will come to judge the living and the dead. I believe these and all the truths which the holy Catholic Church teaches, because you revealed them, who can neither deceive nor be deceived. Amen.

10. Act of Hope *(CCC 1817–1821, 2657)*

O my God, relying on your infinite goodness and promises, I hope to obtain pardon of my sins, the help of your grace, and life everlasting, through the merits of Jesus Christ, my Lord and Redeemer. Amen.

11. Act of Love *(CCC 1822–1829, 2658)*

O my God, I love you above all things, with my whole heart and soul, because you are all good and worthy of all my love. I love my neighbor as myself for the love of you. I forgive all who have injured me and I ask pardon of all whom I have injured. Amen.

12. Act of Contrition *(CCC 1450–1460)*

My God, I am sorry for my sins with all my heart. In choosing to do wrong and failing to do good, I have sinned against you whom I should love above all things. I firmly intend, with your help, to do penance, to sin no more, and to avoid whatever leads me to sin. Our Savior Jesus Christ suffered and died for us. In his name, my God, have mercy. Amen.

or

O my God, I am sorry for my sins because I have offended you. I know I should love you above all things. Help me to do penance, to do better, and to avoid anything that might lead me to sin. Amen.

or

Any spontaneous and heartfelt prayer that tells God that you are truly sorry for all your sins, that you will mend your ways, and that you firmly intend to avoid what leads to sin is a good Act of Contrition.

13. Come, Holy Spirit *(CCC 2670–2672)*

This is a prayer for guidance from the third Person of the Blessed Trinity.

Come, Holy Spirit.
Response: Fill the hearts of your faithful and make the fire of your love burn within them.

Send forth your spirit and there shall be another creation.
Response: And you shall renew the face of the earth.

Let us pray: O God, you have instructed the hearts of the faithful by the light of the Holy Spirit. Grant that through the same Holy Spirit we may always be truly wise and rejoice in his consolation. Through Christ our Lord. Amen.

14. Angelus *(CCC 973, 2617)*

The angel of the Lord declared unto Mary.
Response: And she conceived of the Holy Spirit. (Hail Mary)

Behold the handmaid of the Lord.

Response: May it be done unto me according to your word. (Hail Mary)

And the Word was made flesh.

Response: And dwelt among us. (Hail Mary)

Pray for us, O holy Mother of God.

Response: That we may be made worthy of the promises of Christ.

Let us pray: O Lord, it was through the message of an angel that we learned of the Incarnation of Christ, your Son. Pour your grace into our hearts, and by his Passion and cross bring us to the glory of his Resurrection. Through Christ, our Lord. Amen.

15. Queen of Heaven *(CCC 972, 2617–2619)*

This prayer is said at the Easter season instead of the Angelus.

Queen of Heaven, rejoice, alleluia.

Response: The Son whom you were privileged to bear, alleluia, has risen as he said, alleluia.

Pray to God for us, alleluia.

Rejoice and be glad, Virgin Mary, alleluia.

Response: For the Lord has truly risen, alleluia.

Let us pray: O God, it was by the Resurrection of your Son, our Lord Jesus Christ, that you brought joy to the world. Grant that through the intercession of the Virgin Mary, his Mother, we may attain the joy of eternal life. Through Christ, our Lord. Amen.

16. Grace Before and Thanksgiving After Meals *(CCC 2698)*

Bless us, O Lord, and these your gifts, which we are about to receive from your bounty, through Christ, our Lord. Amen.

We give thanks for all your benefits, almighty God, who lives and reigns forever. May the souls of the faithful departed, through the mercy of God, rest in peace. Amen. *(Spontaneous prayers may also be used at mealtime.)*

17. Memorare *(CCC 2673-2675, 2679)*

Remember, O most gracious Virgin Mary, that never was it known that anyone who fled to your protection, implored your help, or sought your intercession was left unaided. Inspired with this confidence, I fly to you, O virgin of virgins, my Mother. To you I come, before you I stand, sinful and sorrowful. O Mother of the Word Incarnate, despise not my petitions, but in your mercy, hear and answer me. Amen.

18. Prayer for Vocations *(CCC 914–933, 2004)*

Jesus, High Priest and Redeemer forever, we beg you to call young men and women to your service as priests and religious. May they be inspired by the lives of dedicated priests, Brothers, and Sisters. Give to parents the grace of generosity and trust toward you and their children so that their sons and daughters may be helped to choose their vocations in life with wisdom and freedom.

Lord, you told us that "the harvest indeed is great but the laborers are few. Pray, therefore, the Lord of the harvest, to send laborers into his harvest." We ask that we may know and follow the vocation to which you have called us. We pray particularly for those called to serve as priests, Brothers, and Sisters; those whom you have called, those you are calling now, and those you will call in the future. May they be open and responsive to the call of serving your people. We ask this through Christ, our Lord. Amen.

19. Prayer of Saint Francis of Assisi for Peace
(CCC 2302–2317)

Lord, make me an instrument of your peace! Where there is hatred, let me sow love; where there is injury, let me sow pardon; where there is doubt, faith; where there is despair, hope; where there is darkness, light; where there is sadness, joy. Amen.

20. Prayer of Saint Thomas More for a Happy Death
(CCC 2299)

Good Lord, give me the grace so to spend my life, that when the day of my death shall come, though I feel pain in my body, I may feel comfort in soul; and with faithful hope of your mercy, with due love toward you, and charity toward the world, I may, through your grace, depart into your glory. Amen.

21. Prayer on a Birthday (CCC 2626–2628)

God of all creation, you are the life of the faithful, the guardian and savior of those who fear you, and who has brought N., your servant through another year, enlarge your favor toward him/her; protect his/her life in your safekeeping; give him/her length of days; and by your grace lead him/her through a happy old age to the joys of your heavenly kingdom. Amen.

22. Prayer When Making an Important Decision
(CCC 2846)

Lord Jesus Christ, open the eyes and ears of my heart, so that I may hear and understand your word and do your will, for in this world, Lord, I am a stranger and an exile. Hide not your commandments from me. Draw the veil from my eyes, and let me ponder the wonderful workings of your law. Make known to me the obscure and hidden ways of your wisdom and of my own heart. For in you, God, is my hope; enlighten my thoughts and my understanding. Amen.

23. Prayer to Jesus Christ Crucified *(CCC 618)*

Behold, my beloved and good Jesus. I cast myself upon my knees in your sight, and with the most fervent desire of my soul I pray and beseech you to impress upon my heart lively sentiments of faith, hope, and charity, with true repentance for my sins and a most firm desire of amendment; while with deep affection and grief of soul I consider within myself and mentally contemplate your five most precious wounds, having before my eyes that which David the prophet long ago spoke about you, my Jesus: "They have pierced my hands and my feet; / I can count all my bones" (Psalm 22:17–18, *New American Bible*).

24. Mary's Rosary *(CCC 971, 1674, 2678, 2708)*

The complete rosary is composed of fifteen decades, divided into three distinct parts, each containing five decades. The first part consists of five joyful events in the life of Jesus and Mary, the second part recalls five sorrowful events, and the third part considers five glorious events.

We begin by making the Sign of the Cross.

Then we say the Apostles' Creed, one Our Father, three Hail Marys, and one Glory to the Father (Prayer of Praise) on the small chain. Then recall the first mystery, say one Our Father, ten Hail Marys, and one Glory to the Father. This completes one decade. All the other decades are said in the same manner with a different mystery meditated upon during each decade. At the end of the rosary, the prayer Hail, Holy Queen may be recited.

The mysteries of the rosary are scenes from the life of Jesus and

Mary. By meditating on these sublime truths, we come to a better understanding of our faith: the Incarnation of the Lord, the Redemption, and the Christian life—present and future.

In the following outline the words in parentheses indicate practical applications to our daily lives.

The Joyful Mysteries

1. The messenger of God announces to Mary that she is to be the Mother of God. (Humility)
2. Mary visits and helps her cousin Elizabeth. (Love of Neighbor)
3. Mary gives birth to Jesus in a stable in Bethlehem. (Spirit of Poverty)
4. Jesus is presented in the Temple. (Obedience to God's Will)
5. Jesus is found in the Temple. (Fidelity to Vocation)

The Sorrowful Mysteries

1. Jesus undergoes his agony in the Garden of Gethsemane. (Spirit of Prayer)
2. Jesus is scourged at the pillar. (Modesty and Purity)
3. Jesus is crowned with thorns. (Courage)
4. Jesus carries the cross to Calvary. (Patience in Suffering)
5. Jesus dies on the cross for our sins. (Self-denial)

The Glorious Mysteries

1. Jesus rises from the dead. (Faith)
2. Jesus ascends into heaven. (Hope)
3. The Holy Spirit comes to the apostles and the Blessed Mother. (Wisdom, Love, Zeal, Fortitude)
4. The Mother of Jesus is taken into heaven. (Eternal Happiness)

5. Mary is crowned queen of heaven and earth. (Devotion to Mary and Final Perseverance)

25. Hail, Holy Queen *(CCC 963–972, 2617–2622)*

Hail, holy queen, mother of mercy, our life, our sweetness, and our hope. To you we cry, poor banished children of Eve; to you we send up our sighs, mourning and weeping in this valley of tears. Turn then, O most gracious advocate, your eyes of mercy toward us, and after this our exile, show unto us the blessed fruit of your womb, Jesus. O clement, O loving, O sweet virgin Mary.

Pray for us, O holy Mother of God.
Response: That we may be made worthy of the promises of Christ.

Let us pray: O God, whose only begotten Son, by his life, death, and Resurrection, has purchased for us the rewards of eternal life, grant, we beseech you, that meditating upon these mysteries of the most holy rosary of the Blessed Virgin Mary, we may imitate what they contain and obtain what they promise. Through the same Christ our Lord. Amen.

26. Prayer to Our Redeemer

Soul of Christ, sanctify me; body of Christ, save me.

Blood of Christ, inebriate me;

Water from the side of Christ, wash me.

Passion of Christ, strengthen me. O good Jesus, hear me. Within your wounds hide me. Never permit me to be separated from you. From the evil one protect me, at the hour of death call me, and bid me come to you that with your saints I may praise you forever. Amen.

27. Stations of the Cross *(CCC 617, 1674)*

Meditations on the Suffering and Death of Jesus

Introductory Prayer

1. Jesus is condemned to death on the cross.
2. Jesus accepts his cross.
3. Jesus falls the first time.
4. Jesus meets his sorrowful mother.
5. Simon of Cyrene helps Jesus carry his cross.
6. Veronica wipes the face of Jesus.
7. Jesus falls the second time.
8. Jesus meets and speaks to the women of Jerusalem.
9. Jesus falls the third time.
10. Jesus is stripped of his garments.
11. Jesus is nailed to the cross.
12. Jesus dies on the cross.
13. Jesus is taken down from the cross.
14. Jesus is placed in the tomb.

Closing Prayer (recalling the Resurrection):

(At each station, contemplate the scene and pray a brief, heartfelt prayer.)

28. Prayer to Our Lady of Perpetual Help *(CCC 972)*

O Mother of Perpetual Help, behold at your feet a wretched sinner who turns to you and puts all trust in you. Mother of mercy, have pity on me! I hear those who call you the refuge and hope of sinners: be then my refuge and my hope. Help me for the love of Jesus Christ; hold out your hand to fallen sinners who commend and dedicate themselves forever to your service. Praise and thanks be to God, who in his great mercy has given me this trust in you, sure pledge of my eternal salvation.

Alas, it is but too true that in the past I have fallen miserably, because I did not turn to you. I know that with your help I shall conquer; I know that you will help me, if I commend myself to you; but I fear that in the occasions of sin I may forget to call upon you and so be lost. This, then, is the grace I ask; for this I implore you with all my heart and soul: that in the assaults of hell I may ever run to your protection and say to you: Help me, Mary; Mother of Perpetual Help, let me not lose my God. Amen.

29. Prayer of Saint Bernard to the Sacred Heart of Jesus *(CCC 771)*

How good and sweet it is, Jesus, to dwell in your heart! All my thoughts and affections will I sink in the Heart of Jesus, my Lord. I have found the Heart of my king, my brother, my friend, the Heart of my beloved Jesus. And now that I have found your Heart, which is also mine, dear Jesus, I will pray to you. Grant that my prayer may reach you, may find entrance to your Heart. Draw me to yourself. O Jesus, who is infinitely above all beauty and every charm, wash me clean from my defilement; wipe out even the smallest trace of sin. If you, who is all-pure, will purify me, I will be able to make my way into your Heart and dwell there all my life long. There I will learn to know your will, and find the grace to fulfill it. Amen.

30. Prayer to One's Guardian Angel *(CCC 335–336)*

Angel of God, my guardian dear, to whom his love commits me here, ever this day (night) be at my side, to light and guard, to rule and guide. Amen.

31. Prayer for the Faithful Departed *(CCC 958, 1032)*

Eternal rest grant unto them, O Lord.
Response: And let perpetual light shine upon them.

May their souls and the souls of all the faithful departed, through
the mercy of God, rest in peace.
Response: Amen.

32. Liturgical Prayers of the Mass
(CCC 1145–1162, 1345–1390)

The celebration of every Mass is an action not only of Christ but of
the Church. As the central act of worship on the part of Catholics,
it calls for total and meaningful community participation. God
speaks to you through his Revelation; you speak to him through
your prayers, your songs, your heartfelt responses. You offer your-
selves and your gifts to him; he offers himself (through his priest)
in an unbloody sacrifice. And, because the Mass is also a sacred
banquet, you receive him as nourishment for the spirit.

To help you better understand the Mass and participate more
fully, study the following order (or arrangement) of the Mass.

33. Order of the Mass (Community Prayer)
(CCC 1345–1355)

Introductory Rites

Entrance Song
Greeting
Penitential Rite
Gloria
Opening Prayer

Liturgy of the Word

(We hear and respond to the Word of God.)
First Reading
Responsorial Psalm
Second Reading
Alleluia or Gospel Acclamation
Gospel
Homily
Profession of Faith (Creed)
General Intercessions (Prayer of the Faithful)

Liturgy of the Eucharist

(We offer Jesus to the Father.)
Preparation and Offering of Gifts
Prayer Over the Gifts
Eucharistic Prayer

(Our gifts of bread and wine become the body and blood of Christ.)
Memorial Acclamation
Lord's Prayer
Sign of Peace
Breaking of the Bread
Reception of Communion
Prayer After Communion
Concluding Rites
Blessing
Dismissal

34. A Method of Meditation (Private Prayer)
(CCC 2705–2708)

I. Preparation

As a remote preparation try to remain conscious of God as you go about your daily schedule. Frequently remind yourself of this truth: God is everywhere and is very interested in your welfare and the world around you.

At the beginning of the meditation, make a deliberate act of faith regarding God's presence. Ask him for pardon of any faults. Ask for help to make a good meditation. Add a prayer to our Blessed Mother and other favorite saints for assistance.

II. Consideration

Quietly and reflectively read for a few minutes from the Bible or other spiritual book. Ask yourself: What have I read? What does it teach me? How have I acted in regard to this until now? What shall I do about it in the future?

Since the advantage of meditation is not so much in the thinking as in the praying that it leads to, it is important to devote the greater part of meditation to affections (short prayers from the heart), petitions (requests for help from God), and resolutions (practical plans for changing your life, with God's help).

Affections: "Lord, I am sorry for having offended you." "Thank you for the blessings you have given me." "I want to love you above all things." "I praise you, Lord!" "Your will be done!" "I place my trust in you."

Petitions: Ask for whatever you need: for example, forgiveness of sins, greater confidence and deeper faith, help in a stressful situation, specific graces to forgive someone, to be more patient, to die a good death.

Resolutions: Make them short and specific, for example, to stop gossiping with…, to be kind to…, not to lose patience with…, to be faithful to times of prayer.

III. Conclusion

1. Thank the Lord for the many insights and graces gained during this meditation.
2. Repeat your resolutions.
3. Ask for help to keep your resolutions.
4. Choose some special thought or short prayer to carry with you during the day.

Further Suggestions for Meditative Prayer

1. Do not do all the talking yourself. Stop now and then to listen to the Lord. The inspirations he gives on occasion are wordless insights or sentiments that you "hear" in your heart.
2. Do not try to feel the acts of love and other affections you express. They are acts of your will and usually do not spill over into felt emotions. If you experience dissatisfaction because your mind keeps wandering, have patience with yourself. Enduring this inability to pray is a valuable part of your prayer.
3. If you are drawn to thinking about or looking silently at God—or you become vaguely aware of his presence—stay with that. But if your mind wanders, return to expressing affections such as love, praise, sorrow. Some people maintain this simple focus on God by slowly repeating a phrase like "Lord Jesus Christ, have mercy on me"—or a single word such as "God" or "Jesus."

35. Benediction of the Most Blessed
Sacrament *(CCC 1330)*

PRAYER TO CHRIST IN THE EUCHARIST

As Catholics, it is our privilege to participate in offering the eucharistic sacrifice and in receiving Holy Communion. But there are many additional acts of devotion that help extend Christ's real presence among us. Such a devotion is Benediction of the Most Blessed Sacrament.

Christ's promise is to be with us always (Matthew 28:20). The practice of reservation of the Blessed Sacrament arose early in the history of the Church. (This was for the convenience of the sick—that Communion might be taken to them.) People then began spontaneously to gather in the churches to pray and worship in the very presence of Christ. Later, because Christ's presence meant so much to them, they asked that the host be exhibited to them on a throne in a monstrance (an ornamental receptacle). Still later, prayers and songs were added, and the priest would bless the people with the host enthroned in the monstrance.

Benediction is an amazingly simple and beautifully proportioned act of worship. We begin by contemplating God's presence in our midst. (Most of the time we are so busy talking or doing things or going places that Christ hardly gets a chance to say anything to us. Contemplation means that we let God "soak into us.") Then follows the actual sacramental blessing: the priest makes the Sign of the Cross over us with the host enshrined in the monstrance. Finally, we make our spontaneous response in words of praise and thanksgiving.

While the congregation sings an opening song (any eucharistic hymn), the celebrant removes the host from the tabernacle, places it in a monstrance, and enthrones it on the altar. After he incenses the host (a symbolic action indicating our prayerful worship), a period of silent contemplation or public prayer ensues. Then, after the homily (if there is one), a hymn such as "Down in Adoration Falling" is sung.

The celebrant then says or sings a prayer such as the following:

Celebrant: Lord Jesus Christ, you gave us the Eucharist as the memorial of your suffering and death. May our worship of this sacrament of your body and blood help us to experience the salvation you won for us and the peace of the kingdom where you live with the Father and the Holy Spirit, one God, for ever and ever.

People: Amen.

The celebrant blesses the people with the host and then returns the Eucharist to the tabernacle. Afterward the people themselves may say or sing an acclamation such as the Divine Praises.

Blessed be God.
Blessed be his holy name.
Blessed be Jesus Christ, true God and true man.
Blessed be the name of Jesus.
Blessed be his most Sacred Heart.
Blessed be his most Precious Blood.
Blessed be Jesus in the most Holy Sacrament
    of the Altar.
Blessed be the Holy Spirit, the Paraclete.
Blessed be the great Mother of God,
    Mary most holy.
Blessed be her holy and Immaculate Conception.
Blessed be her glorious Assumption.
Blessed be the name of Mary, Virgin and Mother.
Blessed be Saint Joseph, her most chaste spouse.
Blessed be God in his angels and in his saints.

Living the Faith in the Spirit of Vatican II

1. Daily Life of Faith

Our Catholic faith calls us to a way of life in imitation of Jesus and in accordance with tradition and Church teachings. We assent by belief to truths our minds accept and fulfill certain commandments, but living the faith means more than that. This section contains practical ways Catholics carry out in daily life whatever vocation the Church has called them to undertake.

2. We Meet God in the Sacred Words of Scripture

Vatican II, stressing the importance of both the Old and New Testaments as God's revelation, encouraged Catholics to make the Bible an important part of their faith and spirituality. *(CCC 103–114)*

The Bible is more "user-friendly" for Catholics today for a variety of reasons. It's available in readable versions and convenient formats. Biblical scholarship has shed light on obscure passages, making the Bible more understandable. The discovery of ancient manuscripts has led to a greater knowledge of the culture, customs, geography, and peoples of biblical lands.

The liturgy provides a greater variety of Scripture readings in the language of the people. Religious education is now focusing on a "lectionary-based catechesis," instruction based on the liturgical readings. The increase in the number of study groups and adult-education programs in parishes throughout the country demonstrate the interest of today's Catholics in the Bible.

THE NATURE OF THE BIBLE

Although the Bible comes to us in the guise of a printed book, more accurately it is the record of God's relationship with his people and their responses. This living experience is seen through the eyes of certain individuals who recorded the events under the inspiration of the Holy Spirit. The Bible deals with what any relationship demands: discoveries, difficulties, conversion, change, and love. *(CCC 101–112)*

In the Bible we meet people like ourselves who love, hate, backslide, sin, dream, and despair. They are prototypes of how God loves humans through any situation and of how humans relate to God in a variety of ways. Though time and culture differ, we can get caught up in the biblical drama and identify with the persons we meet within the sacred pages.

The Bible is not a frozen collection of tales of the past; rather, it is the Lord speaking to us today. The Bible is a useful avenue to strengthen our love-relationship with the Lord.

Catholics believe the Bible is the inspired Word of God written in the words of human authors who, under the inspiration of the Holy Spirit, selected a literary form, style, and genre that effectively conveyed the experience of the Lord. These ancient writers were more concerned with the meanings of events than with exact details: the why rather than the what.

THE CHALLENGE OF FUNDAMENTALISM

Although Catholics consider the Bible part of the living tradition, some Christians consider the Bible to be the only source of faith. For them, all the fundamental truths are contained within the Scriptures, hence the label fundamentalist. Fundamentalists often challenge, and in their zeal attempt to change, the faith of those whose beliefs differ from theirs. *(CCC 115–119)*

Fundamentalists believe that the exact words of the Bible have been dictated by God, that the Bible is the only way God has revealed himself, and that all doctrine is found in Scripture and can be proven there. Without considering the literary forms used by the authors of the Scriptures, fundamentalists take the Bible literally and refuse to consider the human role in the compiling of Scripture.

How can you deal with overzealous fundamentalists?

First, be confident and familiar with your own faith so you will not feel threatened by other interpretations. Second, listen courteously to what fundamentalists say without becoming defensive. Finally, ask them about their own faith commitment. In this way, you redirect their attention and focus them on their faith rather than on yours.

A response such as "I understand what you are saying, but I don't see it that way" is amicably assertive, yet preserves your right to your own viewpoint. If the person persists in his or her opinion, be friendly yet firm. Don't attempt to counter the fundamentalist's Bible quotes with your own. Catholics can well imitate and admire the zeal of fundamentalist friends but not their methods or opinions.

THE BIBLE AS IDEAL SPIRITUAL ENRICHMENT

Reading the Bible is a powerful way to experience the presence of the Lord in your life. The Bible is the Living Word, and God continues to reveal himself today through the Scriptures. The following guidelines can aid Catholics in utilizing the Scriptures in a more meaningful way. *(CCC 131–133)*

- Make a conscious effort to listen actively and attentively to the Scripture readings during the Liturgy of the Word. This not only enhances your appreciation of the Scriptures but also contributes toward a deeper spirituality and a more meaningful liturgy.
- Set aside some time each day for reflective reading of the Bible. Consider it as necessary spiritual nourishment and enrichment. Use a Bible you are comfortable marking up and underlining. Begin and end your Scripture reading with a prayer. In order to understand obscure passages better, take time to read the intro-

duction to the biblical book from which you are reading. Who wrote it? Why was it written? What were the cultural and religious customs of the time in which the book was written?

- Select passages you can relate to and listen to what God tells you. Imagine the scene, the setting, and the people involved. Use all your senses: seeing, feeling, hearing, touch, and smell. Put yourself in the picture. Ask yourself these questions: What does this passage mean for me now in my situation? What does this passage teach me to believe? What is it helping me to become? How is it improving my relationship with God and with others? Either converse familiarly with the Lord or just listen and relax in his caring presence. Perhaps just one sentence "jumps out" at you. If so, stay with that inspiration; it will be enough.
- Share the Scriptures with others. Join a Bible-study group led by someone with a Scripture background and the expertise to explain unclear passages. Be aware that the Bible says different things to different people and that practical applications vary.

The Bible is dynamic. On every page God breaks into our lives in mysterious ways. To ensure this communication give-and-take, here are two prayers: one to say before reading the Bible, and one to say after you have finished.

PRAYER BEFORE READING THE BIBLE

Our Father, who art in heaven, sacred is your Word. Your kingdom come, your words be heard on earth as they are in heaven. Give us today your sacred Word. Forgive our neglect of it in the past as we forgive those who neglect us. Lead us toward an encounter with you each time we delve into the Scriptures. For your presence, your power, and your glory are ever present among us now and forever. Amen.

PRAYER AFTER READING THE BIBLE

Lord, I thank you for your special presence to me during this time. I thank you for the opportunity to know you and your ways better. Open my heart that I put into practice that which you have revealed to me. Thank you, Lord, for the gift and love of your sacred Word. Amen.

3. We Worship the Lord in Liturgy

The liturgical community gathering known as the Mass is the soul of Catholic worship. We consider here the external changes, attitudes, and practical ways for making Mass a meaningful celebration. *(CCC 1136–1209)*

Our coming together in worship as a people and a community is called *Mass* because we are sent out in "mission" to spread the Good News. The Mass is also referred to as *liturgy, the worship of the people,* or *Eucharist*, which means "thanksgiving." Throughout the ages, the Mass changed from a simple community gathering to a ritualized formal worship service conducted solely by the priest. To bridge the gap between priest and people and to promote greater laity participation, Vatican II initiated changes, variety, and options in the eucharistic worship. *(CCC 1328–1333)*

The altar of sacrifice, the focal point of worship, is placed so the priest faces the people. The language of the people replaces Latin. The laity serve in various liturgical capacities: lectors read the Scriptures, commentators make announcements and offer petitions, Eucharistic ministers distribute Communion, cantors lead the congregation in song. Others bring the gifts in procession. The congregation also joins in with responses and song. Although the presider and the assisting ministers set the tone, all who take part are responsible for fitting worship. The following observations can contribute toward making the liturgy a rich faith experience on both the personal and communal level.

PRACTICAL GUIDELINES FOR PARTICIPATION AT LITURGY

The Mass is an opportunity to worship and honor God. Along with the priest, we are offering the most precious gift we can, the Lord himself. While waiting for the Mass to begin, we can offer to the Lord the concerns of all who worship with us. In this way, we make the Mass a true community celebration. We pray and sing together, and we observe silence in common. (Private devotions, as their name indicates, are out of place in the public ceremony called the Mass.) *(CCC 1345–1355)*

We should listen to the Scriptures attentively; the Lord is speaking to us. We recite the Creed as a renewal of our baptism commitment. We offer ourselves and our gifts to the Lord and join in acclaiming the sacramental presence of Christ and the Father. We should extend ourselves in true reconciliation to those around us at the sign of peace. We believe with all our hearts that the Lord truly heals: "Only say the word, and I shall be healed." As we receive Communion, our wholehearted "Amen" says, "Yes, Lord, I believe in you; make me a better person." The liturgy brings the sacramental presence of Christ into our midst. The final blessing, "Go in peace, to love and serve the Lord," sends us forth to continue the mission of Christ.

The more active and attentive we are at Mass, the greater will be the intensity of Christ's presence in the world. No matter how solemn or simple, the Eucharistic Liturgy is God's perfect gift to us. It is our frail imperfect human attempt to "Do this in remembrance..." and to celebrate in ritual and symbol the divine mystery of Christ's sacramental presence.

4. We Worship the Lord in the Sacraments

In the seven sacraments, we celebrate through ritual and symbol the Lord's special presence in individual lives. The sacramental life of the Church is an integral part of our Catholic faith. *(CCC 1076, 1113–1131, 1210–1666)*

The sacraments are moments of God touching our lives in a special way and opportunities for growth in our relationship with God. The sacraments of initiation—baptism, confirmation, and Eucharist—are moments of new beginnings, recommitment, and continued spiritual strength. Moments of healing are experienced in reconciliation, or the sacrament of penance, and anointing of the sick. Vocational commitments are sacramentally celebrated through matrimony and holy orders. *(CCC 1533–1535)*

The sacramental life calls us to continual conversion. We are always on the way toward greater union with God. Through the sacraments, we respond to the Lord's desire to be with us always and especially at significant moments of our journey of faith.

Sacraments are neither isolated actions nor magical moments. They are the continuing presence of Christ in the world. The more intense our sacramental life, the greater is our Christian witness. Liturgy and life are closely bonded.

Over the years the true nature of some of the sacraments became clouded by undue emphasis on supplementary rituals or unbalanced theology. The Second Vatican Council called for revision of the sacramental rites so their original purpose, meaning, and essence would be more obvious.

Sacraments of Initiation. In the early Church, baptism, confirmation, and Eucharist were considered as one ritual when new members came into the Church. When infant baptism became common in the Western Church, the sacraments of initiation became three separate rites, but remained as one ceremony in the Eastern rites. Vatican II revised the Rite of the Sacraments of Initiation so the baptism-confirmation-Eucharist link is reestablished. This change is most evident when adults who have gone through the RCIA become Catholics and receive the sacraments of initiation at the Easter Vigil. *(CCC 1247–1252)*

Baptism. Although the Church has practiced infant baptism for centuries, Vatican II shifted the theological stance of the sacrament. The Rite of Baptism for Children now being used emphasizes the role of the parents. When a child is baptized, the parents hand on a tradition and legacy they value. Before an infant is brought to baptism, the Church requires that the parents be suitably catechized, be active Catholics, and be instructed in the meaning of baptism and their responsibility as their child's primary religious educators. *(CCC 2226, 2250–2253)*

Confirmation. After confirmation became a separate rite, it was customary to consider it a sacrament of maturity. It began to be received later, usually in the early teens. Currently, practices vary, especially regarding the age when confirmation is given, since confirmation is governed by diocesan norms. *(CCC 1307–1308, 1318)*

Penance (Reconciliation). The new Rite of Reconciliation stresses the healing presence of Christ. No longer is it merely the telling of specific sins, but a compassionate forgiveness of one's sinfulness in an attitude of sorrow. Penitents can opt to receive the sacrament either anonymously in the confessional or face to face in a reconciliation room. *(CCC 1441–1442)*

Anointing of the Sick. Anointing of the sick gives spiritual strength and healing to those who are aged or ill. It is no longer "extreme unction," given only to those in danger of death. It can be received any time during illness. Parishes conduct communal anointings to show a compassionate solidarity with the sick and to experience and celebrate corporately the healing presence of Christ. *(CCC 1499–1532)*

Holy Orders. The Decree on the Ministry and Life of Priests recognizes that "the pastoral and human circumstances of the priest have been thoroughly changed." As leader of the community of faith, the priest is responsible for implementing the reforms of Vatican II at the local level. This demands modifying styles of leadership, working in collaboration with laity, updating and adjusting to newer modes. The priest does the work of Christ and in his ministry mirrors Christ's compassionate and healing qualities. *(CCC 1562–1566)*

5. We Serve the Lord in Ministry

The Catholic faith lives on today because in every age persons faithful to their baptismal commitment heeded the call, "Like good stewards of the manifold grace of God, serve one another with whatever gift each of you has received" (1 Peter 4:10). Christ's ministry was carried forward; the Church grew. *(CCC 897–913)*

The Second Vatican Council provided direction and opened new channels for Catholics to serve in a variety of ministries in the Church.

When we think of ministry, we usually think of what we do and how we serve. But unlike other works or jobs, "ministry in service to the Church" is a response to a special call. There is present a deeper reality, a sacred dimension that is Trinitarian: creative, redemptive, and sanctifying.

Creative. God the Father in creation extended himself most generously, diffusing his presence with his infinite love. He thereby gifted all creation with his infinite goodness. We are called to share our giftedness, extending ourselves in love to others, rechanneling the talents we've been given and using them for the benefit of others and the growth of the kingdom of God. *(CCC 279–324)*

Redemptive. Jesus as God and man perfectly fused the dichotomies of divine and human in his person. He responded to all human needs and ultimately to the need for redemption. He modeled his ministry on the team approach, depending on and working with others. Redemptive ministry responds to the needs of all. It is men and women, clergy and laity, old and young, rich and poor, working, praying, and celebrating together, sharing a common goal: building up the Body of Christ. *(CCC 456–460, 535–560)*

Sanctifying. The Holy Spirit vitalizes and energizes the Church, providing spiritual impetus and growth. Through the Spirit's abiding presence, ministries are endowed with a deeper reality, an attitude that enlivens. The role of the Spirit is vital because the elements of a caring presence and compassion are essential for any ministry. *(CCC 683–688)*

What follows are some practical ways these spiritual qualities can be applied on the parish level toward more effective ministry.

Before Vatican II, priests were solely responsible for the parish. Today the viability of the Church is also the responsibility of the people. Needs vary from place to place and from parish to parish. The degree of lay involvement also fluctuates, depending on the availability of priests, their willingness to allow the laity to participate more fully, and the initiative and cooperation of the people. Parish councils, mandatory in some dioceses, advise the pastor in the administration of the parish. *(CCC 911)*

Lay leadership is to be encouraged and supported. It is the task of every parish to assess its needs and organize meaningful ministries accordingly. The variety of ministries is as varied as are human needs. Wherever there are cries for support and compassion, wherever there are hurts in need of healing, there is ministry. Parish ministries are generally grouped under the following areas: sacramental, educational, administrative, pastoral ministry, and outreach. *(CCC 898–913)*

Although the purpose of ministry never changes, the ways Christ's mission is fulfilled changes with the times. New techniques, attitudes, tools, and skills are necessary for productive and effective ministry in the Church today.

PERMANENT DIACONATE

One of the significant ways Catholic men can participate more directly in ministry is through the diaconate. Deacons played an important role in the early Church. As time passed, however, the need for them diminished, and the diaconate was inactive for many centuries. Vatican II, seeing its value for today's Church, reactivated the permanent diaconate. *(CCC 1569–1571)*

After a period of formation, married or celibate men can be ordained deacons and receive holy orders. However, the permanent diaconate is a ministry in its own right and is not the preparatory step to priesthood, as is the transitional diaconate. A permanent deacon is assigned by the bishop to liturgical and service roles in parishes or diocesan institutions. He can assist at liturgies, baptize, give homilies, and preside at other services, either full time or along with his regular occupation. He is also a valuable asset in marriage preparation and counseling.

Through their service in administrative, liturgical, educational, and pastoral roles, deacons provide a vital ministry, especially in areas where there is a shortage of priests and a need for lay leadership. The role of the deacon is expected to become more prominent and prevalent in the Church of the future.

ROLE OF WOMEN

Throughout the history of the Church, women have always served and ministered. The Gospels and the Acts of the Apostles record specific instances of women's influence and presence. Prior to Vatican II, women, mainly religious, were directly involved in ministry in schools, hospitals, parishes, orphanages, and other Church-sponsored institutions. *(CCC 369–373, 1934–1938)*

Women's role in the Church was specifically addressed in the Vatican II Decree on the Apostolate of Lay People: "Since in our days women are taking an increasingly active share in the whole life of society, it is very important that their participation in the various sectors of the Church's apostolate should likewise develop" (§9).

Although women's participation in some areas needs fuller recognition, in the past twenty-five years women have become more actively involved in ministry and pastoral service. Women are becoming increasingly visible in liturgical celebrations as readers, Eucharistic ministers, and leaders of music.

Women have always been in the forefront of education in the Church. As more women enroll in advanced degree programs in theology and pastoral ministry, they can expect to move into leadership roles in greater numbers. More laywomen serve in academic positions in colleges and seminaries, as directors of religious education (DREs), and catechists. They serve as directors of diocesan offices, vicars for religious, bishops' assistants, canon lawyers, tribunal members, and in other diocesan administrative positions.

In areas where there are few priests or where priests are available only for periodic liturgies, women are administering parishes so that a stable presence of Church is available.

Women serve as pastoral ministers, counselors, hospital chaplains, spiritual directors, and in other ministries not generally open to the laity before Vatican II.

As ministry needs expand and women become more aware of the many and varied opportunities that exist to share their gifts, we can expect to see women's leadership roles in Church ministry increase even more in the future.

6. We Live Our Faith Through Life Commitments

Catholicism is lived in its fullness when the faith we profess in worship is carried into daily life and activities. Our lives, our families, our faith through baptism, are among God's gifts to us. In addition, God gives us a free will, so we can make our own choices and decisions. *(CCC 1730–1748, 1877)*

LIFE COMMITMENTS AND VOCATIONS

One of the most responsible choices we have is the state of life we will follow. Our life commitment mirrors our covenant relationship with God, for through our individual lives and vocations, we serve the Lord. Saint Paul exhorts: "Lead a life worthy of the calling to which you have been called, with all humility and gentleness..." (Ephesians 4:1).

Our decision to live in a specific state of life does not lessen our responsibility to live a faith-filled life. It merely channels our actions into areas where we can use our gifts and the opportunities that come our way. Regardless of the life commitment we have chosen, we are responsible for contributing to the good of the world. Vatican II reminds us of our common call to holiness: "All Christians in any state or walk of life are called to the fullness of Christian life and to the perfection of love, and by this holiness a more human manner of life is fostered also in earthly society" (Dogmatic Constitution on the Church, §40). *(CCC 828, 2004, 2013)*

We are all called by virtue of our baptismal vows to live life faithfully and to let our light shine before all. We have the light; what are we doing with it? *(CCC 1267–1270)*

ROLE OF THE LAITY IN THE WORKPLACE

The call to holiness extends beyond our private life commitment and Church allegiance into all spheres of daily activity. Religion fully lived is an around-the-clock endeavor, an in-the-workplace task. *(CCC 897–913, 1878–1885)*

In the aftermath of their increased participation in ministry, the basic role of the laity cannot be overlooked: "They [the laity] live in the world, that is, they are engaged in each and every work and business of the earth and in the ordinary circumstances of social and family life, which, as it were, constitute their very existence. There they are called by God that, being led by the spirit of the Gospel, they may contribute to the sanctification of the world…" (Dogmatic Constitution on the Church, §31). Therefore, the laity's task is to inspire a basic goodness, flavoring the world with the salt of Christian values and the leaven of holiness. *(CCC 1905–1912)*

We Catholics gather at Sunday worship to revitalize and energize our faith, and we scatter on Monday to our workplaces. It is in this "animating the temporal affairs from within" that the liturgy is brought to its fruitful completion. *(CCC 1166–1167)*

Gospel values can be instilled into the sin-scarred, evil-infested world by those who work in its midst. The kingdom of God is brought to earth in homes, offices, schools, stores, businesses, and hospitals. Everywhere there are people, there is work. And where there is work, there is the Church. Catholics need to take along into the workplace a priority of values, coloring every activity in the world of daily work with inspiring goodness and truth.

MARRIED STATE

Throughout the ages, the love between man and woman has been extolled as sacred and celebrated in solemn rituals. Those entering marriage make a commitment not only to each other but also to God, so the Church raised marriage to the dignity of a sacrament. Through lives of mutual love, the married attain holiness and witness to Christ's love for the Church. *(CCC 1601–1666)*

One of the main responsibilities of married couples is to provide an atmosphere of goodness in the home. They are also bound to raise their children with Christian values. Formerly, parents relied almost solely on professional religious for their children's religious formation. Today the parents are the prime religious educators and play an active role in their children's sacramental preparation. *(CCC 902, 2204–2206)*

It has been proven that no matter how much outside instruction children receive, it will avail nothing if values are not carried out in the home. The nurturing of the children in the faith is one of the most serious responsibilities parents have. Parents are to live their commitment responsibly, that is, according to a formed and informed conscience. *(CCC 2221–2231)*

The number of children a married couple decides upon is a personal decision. However, their method of family planning must be in accord with Church teachings. The Church stands firm in its upholding of the sacredness of life at all stages. *(CCC 2259–2283)*

In the past the ministry of the Church has been oriented toward the traditional family of mother, father, and children. Today, we must recognize and embrace other, nontraditional situations. The Church needs to extend pastoral care toward those couples who, for whatever reason, remain childless. Many single parents are trying to raise their children alone. Sensitive pastoral concern must be extended when the "ideal" family is often extolled and the childless couple or single parent may feel uneasy. No matter what their circumstances, those in the married state and the parental role live out their commitment insofar as they attempt to make a Christ-centered, value-oriented home. *(CCC 2201-2206)*

The marriage commitment has undergone many challenges in recent years. In an attempt to alleviate the failure of marriages because of incompatibility or immaturity, Vatican II has authorized the establishment of comprehensive marriage-preparation programs.

SEPARATED AND DIVORCED

After a couple separates, a civil divorce is often required for legal purposes. This civil divorce in itself does not constitute an impediment to the sacraments for the Catholic party. One cannot receive the sacraments if one enters another marriage while the previous bond still exists. *(CCC 1650, 2382–2386)*

If, after much investigation and discussion, it is proven that the parties were not maturely or morally responsible and a true marriage bond never existed, an annulment is granted. An annulment is not a divorce.

Many factors contribute to the increased divorce rate: our mobile society, loosened family ties, the pressures of modern living. The Church realizes that divorce affects many Catholics and has increased its concern for ministry to the divorced and separated. A recent survey shows that most dioceses have established pastoral care and ministry for the separated and divorced.

Although society's attitude toward divorce has changed, the trauma of divorce is a major stressor. It is a deeply rooted personal crisis that affects those who experience it at the depths of their being. The Church is called upon to be caring and concerned about these people. The greatest empowerment and most effective healing happens when the divorced minister to others who are divorced. Those who have walked in the same moccasins are able to empathize more. In many areas, there are support groups of divorced persons ministering to one another.

The Church needs to extend pastoral care to the divorced and to accept them into the faith community. By their trauma and pain, the divorced and separated remain a potent sign that the suffering Church needs to experience Christ's compassion, healing, and understanding.

SINGLE STATE

Although most people marry, many live their commitment as single persons by choice or by circumstance. Though the Catholic Church is becoming more aware of its responsibility to minister to singles, there is still much that can be done toward making the singles feel fully accepted. The Church needs to recognize more clearly the validity of the single life in the world as a call no less sacred than the call to be married, to be ordained, or to be a religious. The Church also needs to be sensitive in its overall planning of programs and parish celebrations. They should be all-inclusive so members of the faith community, no matter what their state of life, can take part without embarrassment or without feeling out of place. *(CCC 2004, 2348–2349)*

WIDOWED STATE

One of the first ministries of the early Christians was the care of the widowed. The need today is no less real. In fact, because of increased longevity and other social conditions, there is an increase in the number of widows and widowers. *(CCC 2349)*

Each parish and neighborhood has its share of those who have lost their mates. The Church needs to be aware of their presence and provide ways for them to attain meaning in their lives. The parish may have a formal program, but caring compassion and a human presence to walk with the widowed in their grief is an even more effective way to carry out the Church's call to care for all its members. *(CCC 2443)*

7. We Respond in Faith to Social Needs

Our responsibility in life is not just to become better persons. As John Donne wrote, "No man is an island." Because the kingdom of God is a kingdom of justice, love, and peace, the Church's mission includes responsibility for the humanization of the world in the fullest sense. As Catholics, we need to be concerned about actively striving to bring into the world Christ's justice and peace. Our Christian commitment calls us to "Christify" the world, to make the love of Christ more visible and more fully experienced. To be true to our moral responsibility, we are called to develop a sincere social consciousness. Morality consists in more than mere avoidance of acts that are "sins." We must strive to squelch the sinfulness in ourselves and in the world around us. *(CCC 1877–1879, 1928–1942)*

A mere awareness of the presence of evils in our midst is insufficient. Saint James warns: "If a brother or sister is naked and lacks daily food, and one of you says to them, 'Go in peace; keep warm and eat your fill,' and yet you do not supply their bodily needs, what is the good of that? So faith by itself, if it has no works, is dead" (2:15–17). A living faith requires active concern for the oppressed, the homeless, and the downtrodden. *(CCC 2443–2448)*

Social concerns must embrace our untiring efforts to eliminate hunger, disease, discrimination, poverty, and war on all levels. We are called to become actively involved and to strive toward solidarity with those who suffer, those who need healing, those with whom we can share our abundance. We must link ourselves directly with the poor. *(CCC 1913–1917)*

The activities of everyday life mirror the creative work of God and share in the redemptive act of saving the world. The corporal works of mercy are not merely charitable deeds under the auspices of pious organizations. Rather, the corporal works are carried out in the daily grind of our lives. Farmers, butchers, and grocers feed the hungry; water purification crews and waiters give drink to the thirsty; morticians and coroners bury the dead; parole officers, guards, counselors, and fellow inmates tend the imprisoned; construction workers, carpenters, plumbers, and electricians do their part in sheltering the homeless; garment workers, tailors, and shopkeepers clothe the naked. But we are challenged to do more; we are challenged to extend ourselves beyond our own concerns.

All of us are called to permeate the structures of society with so much goodness that it oozes out and counters evil. If a bad apple affects the good ones, cannot we as Christians and Catholics reverse the procedure and be the good that affects the bad?

The responsibility for infusing values into secular society resides primarily with the laity, who can influence laws, social structures, and the civic community with a Christian sense of life. It is a challenging task in a world where materialism and standards of success run counter to basic Christian values.

The challenge of the Christian is to be countercultural, to go against the false promises of the world and to fight evil and sinfulness with saintliness and goodness. Without this renewal and perfecting of the social order, the building up of the Body of Christ cannot be effected, for it occurs in the world by a serious concern for the common good. *(CCC 1905–1917)*

Today we face social concerns previously unheard of. Modern medicine can do marvels, but we take a stand about genetic tampering, the right to life, and life-support systems that interfere with natural laws. *(CCC 2292–2295)*

The abortion issue touches every aspect of life. Its profound moral implications plague the nation's lawmakers, the medical profession, the educational system, and the very foundation of society, the family. The Church continues to affirm and uphold the sacredness of life at every stage of development. Catholics must not only abide by natural and God-given laws but also take an active stance in moral issues revolving around the sacredness of all life. *(CCC 2258–2283, 2319, 2322)*

Our social consciousness must also extend toward preserving the earth. "Increase and multiply and preserve the earth" is the Genesis mandate. In our day this includes working toward a healthier, safer environment by avoiding pollution and littering, recycling, and using wisely our natural resources without wastefulness. Environmental concerns are an essential part of a Christian's social justice agenda. *(CCC 2402, 2415, 2456)*

Concern for goodness reaches beyond our own nation into the global community to espouse justice and lasting peace for all peoples. Our concern for justice cannot be displayed in violent ways. True to the beatitudes, we must hunger and thirst for justice, yet in a nonviolent way, which in essence is the way of Christ. Our social structures and lifestyles must be vitalized by the spirit of nonviolence.

Nonviolence creates an atmosphere of true liberty, where everyone can live peaceably and partake of the goods of the earth. To assist our sisters and brothers to reach their full potential as God intended, and to do so in a Christian manner, involves striving for peace within ourselves and within our relationships. Peace and justice in the world will come about only if we ease suffering, not inflict it. A deep Christian concern encourages those systems of justice that aim to save humanity from its own selfishness. *(CCC 2302–2317)*

A fully formed social conscience likewise does all in its power to support those organizations that work toward the betterment of the human condition. It is informed and actively involved in social and political issues that affect the common good on local, national, and global levels.

In *Building the Earth*, Teilhard de Chardin challenges: "What we need is a passionate love of growth and of being. Life is moving toward unification. Our hope will become a reality only if it's expressed in greater cohesion and human solidarity. The future is in our hands. How shall we decide?"

In his closing address at the Second Vatican Council, Pope Paul VI noted that "the story of the Good Samaritan is the model of the spirituality of the Church today." Renewal makes no sense unless the Church aims at serving wounded humanity and healing life's hurts. The ultimate norm of an authentic Catholic lies in the response to the query "How caring and compassionate am I?" *(CCC 2083, 2443, 2822)*

8. We Share and Spread the Good News Through Evangelization

There are many different ways to spread the Gospel. The practice of evangelization and the proper use of the RCIA are two examples. *(CCC 904–913)*

Our basic baptismal commitment calls us to make the kingdom of God more visible on earth. Evangelization calls us to continue Christ's mission: "Go therefore and make disciples of all nations, baptizing them..." (Matthew 28:19). *(CCC 849, 1257)*

Although evangelization is a recurrent theme in the Gospels, the word has now taken on nuances comparatively new to Catholic thinking. To avoid confusion it may be helpful to begin by pointing out what evangelization is not. It does not mean using outright conversion tactics such as foisting beliefs on new members. It does not mean trying to persuade persons who already have a religious commitment to accept the Catholic faith. The vision of evangelization is broader than merely the effort to draw others into the faith. *(CCC 850–851)*

In his encyclical on evangelization, Pope Paul VI notes: "The

Church evangelizes when, in seeking to convert, she relies solely on the power of the message she proclaims." To evangelize, in essence, is to proclaim the Good News and to be a more visible sign of God's presence in the world. At the heart of evangelization is an inner change, which affects all life's values. External works flow from the inner attitudes. *(CCC 2044–2047)*

The tasks of evangelization are sharing the Good News with those who have never heard it, the spiritual renewal of the baptized, and the promotion of unity among Christians. *(CCC 821)*

The baptized are called to evangelize as well as to be evangelized by actively proclaiming the Good News and living it faithfully and fully in their daily lives.

How do Catholics evangelize? They do it by living in such a way that no matter what they do, where they are, or whom they reach, they diffuse goodness into the world. Each time Catholics witness to God's love and better the human condition, they are evangelizing. Catholics embody the message of Christ and proclaim the Good News with their lives. Evangelization is not limited to the formal ministries of catechizing, teaching, and serving in the Church. *(CCC 5–7)*

You can be an effective evangelizer without even realizing it simply by example and presence. This is true of the sick and infirm who witness to the suffering Christ by nobly accepting their plight. Evangelization succeeds primarily by example and motivation rather than direct confrontation. Others find the Catholic way of life attractive and are drawn to inquire about it.

It is appropriate at times to evangelize actively by taking the initiative. Reach out to inactive Catholics, inviting them to return. Share your faith with those you sense are searching and questioning. *(CCC 4–10)*

In order to do this, you need to feel comfortable with your own beliefs and to be conversant about your faith. Most Catholics today are aware that a religious education that ended with grade school or high school is insufficient in postconciliar times. Through continuing education programs and Catholic reading, you can keep informed of the ways Catholics can understand and proclaim the Good News more effectively.

Evangelization is "building up the Body of Christ" by positive means; it is inviting others to follow Christ by an innate magnetic attractiveness and witness to the Gospels. *(CCC 2472)*

9. We Share the Spread of the Good News Through RCIA

One of the most significant ways Catholics today can be evangelizers is to become involved in the Rite of Christian Initiation of Adults (RCIA). Since 1988 the RCIA has been mandated as the ordinary way adults are brought into full communion with the Catholic faith, whether from another Christian denomination or through baptism. The RCIA is designed to be a progressive journey of faith and a recurrent experience of conversion not only for the searcher but also for the whole Catholic community of faith. *(CCC 1232–1233, 1247–1249, 1285)*

The formation of new members is a communal responsibility. It encompasses each phase of parish life: witnessing, praying together, studying Scripture, sharing liturgy, and fellowship. The RCIA is not a parish program nor something to study about. The RCIA is a parish's call to conversion; it is evangelization in action at the local level.

Although the primary aim of the RCIA is the formation of new Catholics, a parish in which the RCIA flourishes experiences additional benefits. These include improved liturgies, greater community spirit and parish pride, and more active involvement and participation in parish activities and celebrations. There also will be an increased interest in adult education and formation.

Catholics within the parish become involved in the RCIA by

being sponsors, working on the RCIA team, sharing personal faith stories, and actively searching out those who have no faith community or identity.

The RCIA is a gradual process that embodies the elements of a growing relationship. Through four specific phases, the inquirers move from casual acquaintance to full commitment. *(CCC 1229–1232)*

Period of Evangelization and Precatechumenate. This is the time of getting acquainted. Those contemplating the Catholic faith—called inquirers—join with Catholics in informal discussions, ask questions, get rid of stereotyped ideas, undo fears or anxieties, and share their personal faith stories.

Period of Catechumenate. After the inquirers have decided to become Catholic, the Rite of Acceptance Into the Order of Catechumens is celebrated. During this time, the catechumens enter more deeply into the formation in faith. This period may last from several months to several years. Catechumens attend the Liturgy of the Word and participate more fully in the Church's liturgical life. They receive a sponsor who walks the journey of faith with them in a one-on-one relationship in which they feel free to ask questions and share their faith journey.

Period of Purification and Enlightenment. This stage of deeper commitment ordinarily begins on the First Sunday of Lent and is celebrated in a solemn rite at the cathedral of the diocese. The catechumens write their names in the book of the elect. The Lenten liturgies center on forgiveness, and the elect express their readiness through the scrutinies. The catechumens' example serves as a reminder of our constant need for purification and spiritual renewal. *(CCC 1438)*

The climax of the catechumenate, the most solemn celebration of the Church year, takes place at the Easter Vigil on Holy Saturday evening. The sacraments of initiation—baptism, confirmation, Eucharist—are bestowed, and the new, full-fledged Catholics are now called neophytes. *(CCC 1212, 1233)*

Period of Mystagogy. A post-Easter period of continued instruction and formation integrates the neophyte more fully into the community of faith. Mystagogia is from a Greek word meaning "being initiated into mystery." The new Catholics are introduced into a greater explanation of the faith and of the various ministries in the parish. *(CCC 1075, 1233)*

The new Catholics' energy and enthusiasm for the faith can be a catalyst for lifelong Catholics to become more involved. In its gradual unfolding, the RCIA process calls to mind the challenge and responsibility of every Catholic. The spiritual growth and maturity of a parish community can be measured in part by its understanding of the basic RCIA rationale. *(CCC 1886–1896)*

The RCIA brings to parishioners a deeper sense of what conversion means and emphasizes the Church's identity as a community of faith and the people of God. When carried out ideally as intended, the RCIA becomes a most powerful sign of a Church alive and of a community of faith that understands its mission to bring the reign of Christ more intensely into the world. The RCIA, then, can be the most effective avenue for evangelization on the local level.

10. We Respect Other Religions

In our age of increased global awareness, cultural mingling, and media coverage, religious pluralism is an obvious fact. Vatican II recognized the vast array of religious expressions in the world and addressed the issue in its Declaration on the Relation of the Church to Non-Christian Religions: "Men look to their different religions for an answer to the unsolved riddles of human existence....The Catholic Church rejects nothing of what is true and holy in these religions" (§§1–2). *(CCC 816, 830, 842–843)*

Catholics are to respect, preserve, and promote the spiritual and moral good found in all religions as well as the values in their society and culture. *(CCC 2104)*

Special mention is made of our indebtedness to the Jewish faith. The Old Testament is the basis and root of Christianity. Jesus was a practicing Jew, and many Christian rituals stem from Jewish customs and traditions. *(CCC 574–594)*

Although other religions have risen out of the human quest for God, Christianity is God becoming human. The Council presented a dynamic concept of "Church" as a divine mystery, but it upheld the conviction that the full revelation of God through Jesus is embodied in the teachings and traditions of the Catholic Church under the direction of the pope. It recognizes, too, that other Christian bodies, as the "Church of Christ," contain certain aspects of the faith: "Many elements of sanctification and of truth are found outside its visible confines [of the Catholic Church]" (Dogmatic Constitution on the Church, §8). *(CCC 819, 855–856)*

11. Practical Guidelines Toward Interfaith Understanding

The Decree on Ecumenism of Vatican II further bridged the gap between religions and set forth useful guidelines for fruitful dialogue. *(CCC 821, 855–856)*

• Have a clear understanding of and be conversant with your own faith. Those who worship differently are sincere in their attempt to communicate with the Divine in ways they perceive and believe. *(CCC 847, 2106)*

- Be willing to interpret another's faith in its best light, giving it the benefit of a good interpretation. Keep an openness and suspend judgment about the motives of other belief systems. Try to see the value in others' beliefs, focusing on what is held in common rather than what divides. *(CCC 1636)*
- Develop a deep respect for the variety of ways in which others experience the Divine in their lives, realizing that people's basic religious view results from culture and heritage. *(CCC 855–856)*

Catholics today have many opportunities for interfaith understanding and dialogue. The climate of openness allows greater freedom than formerly for Catholics to discuss their religious beliefs with others and learn how others approach God.

It is useful to heed the advice of Mahatma Gandhi: "I open my doors and windows allowing all cultures and religions to blow about freely, but I refuse to be swept off my feet by any."

The call to religious openness is basic if we are to live peaceably and in harmony with all peoples. Father Avery Dulles, S.J., summed up the ecumenical spirit in an address on Church unity: "To be truly Catholic, in the literal sense of the word, is to be universal and open to all truth and goodness from whatever source it may come."

12. A Guide to Action for Today's Catholic

Today's Catholic, in keeping with the spirit of Vatican II,

- realizes that Jesus is the key and focal point of human destiny and that our call is to continue his mission
- strives to become a fully integrated human being by working for moral goodness in his or her personal and work life and in relationship to God and to others

- is faithful to his or her baptismal commitment by being active in a community of faith, participating regularly in the sacraments, and acknowledging the tenets of faith expressed in the Creed
- develops an intense personal relationship with God through Jesus by a deep life of prayer and love of the Bible
- recognizes the presence of Jesus as personified in the pope, bishops, pastors, and people of God
- lives fully in the spirit of "How much good can I do?" not minimally in a "What must I do?" attitude
- contributes to the betterment of the world by living according to his or her state of life and with a deep concern for the needs of all
- brings the message of the Good News by a faith-filled, love-filled life and willingly shares gifts and talents for the good of the kingdom of God
- possesses an open, loving spirit toward all persons of all religions who strive to live a spiritual life
- attempts to bring peace to all by working for justice and love in all life's situations

SECTION FIVE

A Summary of the
Documents of Vatican II

The Constitution on the Sacred Liturgy
(Sacrosanctum concilium)

Issued on December 4, 1963, this is the first major document of the Second Vatican Council. It sets the stage for the work of the Council that followed. It emphasizes liturgy as the focus of community worship and piety, as well as liturgical renewal and more active participation of the liturgy.

Decree on the Means of Social Communication
(Inter mirifica)

Issued on December 4, 1963, this decree focuses on the responsibility of the media in supporting the moral order of world communications. Further, it challenges the media to promote faith and values, and urges the faithful to promote good films, radio, and television.

Dogmatic Constitution on the Church
(Lumen Gentium)

This document contains eight chapters covering the following topics: the mystery of the Church, the Church as the people of God; the hierarchical structure of the Church, the laity, the universal call to holiness in the Church, religious communities in the Church, the nature of the pilgrim Church, and the Blessed Virgin Mary as she pertains to the mystery of Christ and of the Church. This Vatican II document was issued on November 21, 1964.

Decree on the Catholic Eastern Churches
(Orientalium Ecclesiarum)

This document, released on November 21, 1964, is addressed to Uniate Churches of Eastern rites; it recognizes diversity in rites and encourages retaining traditions.

Decree on Ecumenism (*Unitatis redintegratio*)

This decree encourages Christian unity, affirms respect for the beliefs of others, and sets forth guidelines for interfaith endeavors. It was promulgated on November 21, 1964.

Decree on the Pastoral Office of Bishops in the Church (*Christus Dominus*)

This decree, issued on October 28, 1965, is organized into three chapters that treat various aspects of the office of bishops. The first chapter deals with the bishops' collegial responsibility for the universal Church and their relationship to the pope. The second chapter outlines the bishops' responsibilities in terms of the local diocese, especially the role of teacher. The third chapter focuses on the cooperation of the bishops' responsible for the Church in a particular region and calls for the use of synods and councils.

Decree on the Up-to-Date Renewal of Religious Life (*Perfectae caritatis*)

This document calls on congregations and orders to renew their relevance and challenges them to live in conformity to gospel values. It was issued on October 28, 1965.

Decree on the Training of Priests (*Optatam totius*)

This document contains directions for the formation of candidates for the priesthood, and was promulgated on October 28, 1965. Among other topics it treats the need for fostering priestly vocations, the incorporation of pastoral concerns into all aspects of priestly training, and the continuing education of priests beyond the seminary.

Declaration on Christian Education
(Gravissimum educationis)

This document focuses on the education of the young in the home, the school, and the Church. It insists on the need for education to values and the fact that parents have the prime responsibility for the moral training of their children. This document was issued on October 28, 1965.

Declaration on the Relation of the Church to Non-Christian Religions (Nostra aetate)

This document, issued on October 28, 1965, praises the sacredness in non-Christian religions and sees them as valid approaches to the Divine. It especially emphasizes respect for Judaism, especially as the root of Christianity, and it forcefully condemns anti-Semitism.

Dogmatic Constitution on Divine Revelation
(Dei verbum)

This document characterizes Scripture and tradition as the main sources of divine revelation and upholds the primacy of the Word of God in both the Old and New Testaments. This Vatican II document was issued on November 18, 1965.

Decree on the Apostolate of Lay People
(Apostolicam actuositatem)

This decree, issued on November 18, 1965, stresses the fact that the laity have their own role to play in the mission of the Church and that holiness is a call for everyone. The laity are involved in the Church either as individuals or as members of organizations and associations.

Declaration on Religious Liberty *(Dignitatis humanae)*

Issued on December 7, 1965, this document declares conscience as a basic norm of morality, and asserts the dignity and rights of the human person. It condemns all types of discrimination.

Decree on the Church's Missionary Activity *(Ad gentes divinitus)*

This document declares that all share in the missionary work of the Church, and that evangelization is more effective by example than by direct tactics. It was officially published on December 7, 1965.

Decree on the Ministry and Life of Priests *(Presbyterorum ordinis)*

This document calls on priests to integrate their lives with work and spirituality. The pastoral dimension of the priestly life is stressed. This document was issued on December 7, 1965.

Pastoral Constitution on the Church in the Modern World *(Gaudium et spes)*

In this document, issued on December 7, 1965, the bishops reflect on the nature and mission of the Church in the modern world. It sees the Church and world as mutually related; it avows the dignity of all persons; it reconfirms the nobility of marriage and family; and it addresses issues of culture, society, economics, politics, and peace.

Dictionary of
Essential Catholic Terms

A

abba An Aramaic word for *father*. This familiar form of address was often used by children. Jesus used the intimate address *abba* when he invoked his Father in the greatest crisis of his life (Mark 14:30). Two other New Testament occurrences of *abba* also are used in the context of prayer. See Romans 8:15 and Galatians 4:6. *(CCC 2605)*

abbess; abbot An abbess is the superior of a monastic community of nuns (for example, Benedictines). An abbot is the superior of a monastic community of monks (for example, Trappists). Both are elected by the community and have general authority and ordinary jurisdiction over it.

abbey See **monastery.**

ablution A washing or cleansing. In the Latin Rite, the baptismal bath and the rite of sprinkling holy water on the congregation at the beginning of the liturgy are associated with cleansing from sin. In liturgy, ablution refers principally to the washing of the hands at Mass by the presider, the purification of the fingers that have touched the sacred species, and the ritual purification with water of the sacred vessels. Ordinarily this is done by pouring wine and/or water over the index fingers and thumbs of the presider into the chalice.

abortion Deliberate, intentional destruction of the human fetus at any stage after conception or the expulsion of it from the womb when it is not viable.

Morally, from the viewpoint of natural law ethics and from divine revelation, abortion is a fundamental evil. The right to life is the most basic of all human rights; the right to life of the innocent is inviolable. The destruction of innocent human life is contrary to the law of God and is, in the words of the U.S. Catholic Bishops, "an unspeakable crime, a crime which subordinates weaker members of the human community to the interest of the stronger" (To Live in Christ Jesus: A Pastoral Reflection on the Moral Life, §64).

Legally, the right to life of the unborn has traditionally been fully protected by law. In 1973, however, the Supreme Court of the United States rendered a decision legalizing abortion, thus denying legal protection to the unborn. It is the conviction of many U.S. citizens, including the majority of Catholics, that the Supreme Court's decision was morally and legally wrong and should be reversed.

Socially, this decision has brought about the formation of pro-life groups whose main purpose is to educate U.S. citizens on the basic issues at stake, to bring about a reversal of the Supreme Court decision and so to insure legal protection for the unborn, and to address the specific needs of women with problems related to pregnancy so that they will have alternatives to abortion.

According to canon law, a Catholic who actually procures an abortion incurs automatic excommunication (Canon 1398); accomplices (that is, those without whose assistance the abortion would not have been committed) also incur excommunication. *(CCC 2269–2274, 2322)* See **excommunication.**

Abraham An extraordinary person whose story is told especially in the Book of Genesis, chapters 12 to 25. Born in the nineteenth century before Christ, he was originally named Abram. When he was ninety-nine years old, the Lord appeared to him and said: "And I will make my covenant between me and you, and will make you exceedingly numerous....No longer shall your name be Abram, but your name shall be Abraham; for I have made you the ancestor of a multitude of nations" (Genesis 17:2–5). Because of his special calling, he is known as the father of the Jewish people and by extension, the spiritual father of all believers. (The first Eucharistic Prayer refers to him as "our father in faith.") Faith, especially in the sense of absolute trust in God and fidelity to his will, was Abraham's outstanding characteristic. *(CCC 145–146, 705–706, 2570–2572)*

absolution In the sacrament of penance, absolution is the form (words) spoken by an authorized priest for the forgiveness of sins. The Church teaches that "[t]hrough the sign of absolution God grants pardon to sinners who in sacramental confession manifest their change of heart to the Church's minister; this completes the sacrament of penance" (Rite of Penance, 6d). *(CCC 1449)* See **penance, sacrament of.**

abstinence In Catholic teaching, abstinence is a penitential practice of doing without (abstaining from) meat or another food or drink. According to the Code of Canon Law, "Abstinence from eating meat or another food according to the prescription of the conference of bishops is to be observed on Fridays throughout the year unless they are solemnities" and also on Ash Wednesday and Good Friday (Canon 1251). The National Conference of Catholic Bishops is also empowered "to determine more precisely the observance of fast and abstinence and to substitute in whole or in part for fast and abstinence other forms of penance, especially works of charity and exercises of piety" (Canon 1253). The Catholic bishops of the United States have determined that abstinence from meat is specifically required only on Fridays of Lent (as well as on Ash Wednesday), but that some penance should be performed on each Friday of the year. *(CCC 1434, 2043)* See **fasting.**

acculturation   The process of socialization which happens when members of diverse cultures come into continuous firsthand contact with the consequence that each culture influences the other and cultural changes take place. Acculturation is one of the ways in which worship is adapted through accommodation, that is, by making adjustments in the liturgy without necessarily referring to the culture of a people. Acculturation is also an introductory process in which worship is adapted to a specific culture in an external or a partial way while respecting the singular character of the Roman liturgy. The term also refers to the efforts by missionaries to learn the language and to adapt the customs of a society in order to be more effective in the communication of the faith.

acedia   Spiritual sloth, which is characterized by laziness or indifference in religious matters. *(CCC 1866)*   See **capital sins.**

acolyte   This word denotes the office, ministry, or order of clerics who assist at the altar and at other liturgical functions. Since Vatican II it designates the ministry into which men are instituted on a permanent or transitory manner to assist the celebrant at Mass and to distribute Holy Communion when necessity dictates. The term is also commonly used to designate any layman who serves Mass or who assists at other Church services. In this latter capacity, the acolyte's role consists of lighting and carrying candles in the procession and in ministering wine and water at Mass. *(CCC 903)*   See **servers, altar.**

acts, human   Saint Thomas Aquinas says "Those acts are called human of which a [person] is master, and he is master of his actions in virtue of his reason and his will" (Saint Thomas I–II, I,1). Actions of human beings are human acts when the person does them deliberately, that is, when the agent is master. An act may be performed less voluntarily when ignorance, passionate desire, or fear are present. *(CCC 1732)*

Acts of the Apostles   Book of the New Testament, written by the evangelist Luke about A.D. 70 to 75. It describes the faith and way of life of the early Christians and the origin and spread of Christian communities in New Testament times. It is a kind of history of the early Church (from about A.D. 30 to A.D. 67), but the author is not as much concerned with historical details as he is with the action of

God in history, especially through the preaching of the apostles. He is also concerned with the Church as a human organism compelled to adapt itself to actual circumstances in order to carry out its mission to other places and cultures.

actual grace   See grace.

actual sin   See sin.

A.D.   This designation for the Christian era is derived from the Latin words *anno Domini*, meaning "in the year of the Lord." Time is measured on the calendar before and after the year Jesus Christ was born. A date followed by the abbreviation A.D. means so many years after the birth of Jesus Christ. In consideration to those of other faiths many now favor B.C.E. and C.E.

Adam and Eve   According to the Book of Genesis, Adam and Eve are the first human beings created by God (Genesis 1 and 2). They were expelled from the Garden of Eden because they disobeyed God's command not to eat of a certain tree. The Christian doctrine of original sin is traced back to Adam and Eve; through them the entire human race fell away from God's plan. In the New Testament, Jesus is described as the new or second Adam, bringing salvation to the human race. *(CCC 399)*   See **original sin.**

ad limina visit   Every five years all ordinaries of dioceses are required to make a visit to Rome and the Apostolic See. This is a time of spiritual renewal for the bishop as he prays at the tombs of Saints Peter and Paul in Rome, as well as an opportunity for him to visit the pope and other curial officials and make a detailed report on the state of his diocese.

Adonai   Several centuries before the Christian era Jews, out of reverence for the name for God, stopped pronouncing the name of Yahweh and substituted the Old Testament Hebrew term for God, meaning "Lord" or "my Lord" in its place. *(CCC 209)*

adoration   A conscious act of an intelligent creature by which God alone—infinitely perfect and having supreme domination over nature—is recognized as worthy of supreme worship. Adoration is essentially an act of the mind and will, but is commonly expressed in external acts of sacrifice, prayer, and reverence. Adoration in the strict sense is due to God alone. *(CCC 2096–2097)*

adultery   A voluntary act of sexual intercourse between a married person and another who is not that person's wife or husband. It is forbidden by the sixth commandment of the Decalogue ("You shall not commit adultery") and condemned as immoral in the New Testament (see Matthew 5:27 and Mark 10:19). Under the concept of adultery, Jesus also included lustful desires. *(CCC 2380–2381)*

Advent   The season that opens the liturgical year of the Church. It begins on the fourth Sunday before Christmas and ends before the Evening Prayer of Christmas. The liturgical readings and prayers place emphasis on the coming (advent, arrival) of Jesus Christ. The first part of Advent highlights his Second Coming at the end of time, and the second part (notably December 17–24) his coming into human history at the time of his birth in Bethlehem. This liturgical season features joy, hope, repentance, expectation, and preparation for the coming of Christ. *(CCC 524)*

Advent wreath   A wreath of laurel, spruce, holly, or similar foliage with four candles that are lighted successively in the weeks of Advent to symbolize the coming of Christ, the Light of the World. The lighting of the candles is usually accompanied by an appropriate hymn, a reading from Scripture, and/or prayers. Of German origin, the Advent wreath is now popular in North American churches, schools, and homes.

advocate   A clerical or lay lawyer appointed by a bishop who pleads causes before the canonical courts to safeguard the rights of a party. There are also several specialized meanings to this word: in Scripture it is a name used for Christ (1 John 2:1) or the Holy Spirit (John 14:16).

affective prayer   This form of prayer uses the emotions or feelings in a positive way to lift up the heart to God in words and silent expressions of loving devotion. It is often called prayer of the heart. Many mystics experienced God in profoundly affective ways; and the Psalms and the Song of Songs are examples of affective prayer. Some types of affective prayer are the loving repetition of the words in the Jesus Prayer or the rosary, praying in tongues as in charismatic prayer or a simple quiet opening of the heart to God's loving presence.

agape   This Greek term occurs in the synoptic Gospels only twice (Matthew 24:12; Luke 11:42). It is used several times in the Gospel of John and in the letters of John and Paul to refer to love, specifically the love of God for us and our love for God and one another. It is the most singularly Christian form of love. Christ used it to describe the love among the persons of the Trinity, and it is the love he instructed his followers to have for one another (John 13:34–35). Agape is totally selfless love, which seeks not one's own interest but only the concern for the well-being of another. Among the earliest followers of Jesus, the agape was a holy meal celebrated as a memorial of the Last Supper (1 Corinthians 11:20–22, 33–34). The custom of sharing agape-style meals in Christian settings is often linked to the festive spirit of the seder or Passover meal.

age of reason   The time of life at which a person is believed to be morally responsible and able to distinguish between right and wrong, normally at about seven years of age. *(CCC 1244)*

aggiornamento   This Italian word for updating was used by Pope John XXIII when summoning the Vatican Council II. Pope John called it "the opening of the window of the Church to let fresh air enter." Aggiornamento has become synonymous with Church renewal and calls for a new openness on the part of the Church toward the world and other religions and to the internal reform and renewal in its liturgical life.

agnosticism   The view that we cannot know anything with certainty about God, the other world, and the afterlife. Agnosticism denies the possibility of knowing God through reason. The term covers various forms of religious skepticism. *(CCC 2127–2128)*

Agnus Dei   This prayer is said three times at Mass during the breaking of the bread and the commingling. *Agnus Dei* is translated "Lamb of God."

Agnus Dei refers also to a sacramental that consists of a small disc of wax with an imprinted figure of a lamb representing Christ on one side and the coat of arms of the pope on the reverse side. These discs are solemnly blessed by the pope on the Wednesday of Holy Week during the first and seventh year of his pontificate and are worn by the recipients as a protection against Satan, temptations, sickness, fires, tempests, and sudden death, and for pregnant women to have safe deliveries.

AIDS   This is the abbreviation for acquired immune deficiency syndrome, the name of the disease from HIV, an accompanying virus which attacks the human immune system and leaves the person susceptible to infectious diseases. AIDS is spread through the exchange of bodily fluids and is sometimes passed from an infected mother to her unborn child.

aisle   This is the walkway along the inside of a church on either side of the nave between the exterior wall and the pillars. An aisle may also run alongside a choir or transept. See **nave**.

alb   See **vestments.**

alcoholism, morality of   This addiction has genetic, biological, and social dimensions. The habitual excessive consumption of alcoholic beverages is characterized by preoccupation with alcohol, an abnormal and chronic desire to drink, drinking to excess and over a longer period, often giving up important activities to drink and drinking even though it causes problems. The habit is often enabled by a system of denial and role playing maintained by family and friends. In time chronic alcoholism produces psychological and physical changes. One of its most serious effects is the lessening of willpower that is needed to stop the addiction. In time all the higher faculties are damaged and occasionally insanity results.

aliturgical days   These are the days on which it is not permitted to celebrate Mass. In the Roman Rite, this occurs only during the Triduum on Good Friday when Communion is distributed after a service consisting of the Liturgy of the Word and the Adoration of the Cross. In a sense Holy Saturday is also aliturgical since the one Mass permitted, in the evening, is that of Easter day.

alleluia   A word of Hebrew origin meaning "praise Yahweh," it is used frequently in the liturgy, especially during the Easter season and at the "alleluia verse" that precedes the reading of the Gospel at the Eucharistic Liturgy.   See **Yahweh.**

All Saints, feast of   A liturgical solemnity celebrated on November 1. This feast commemorates all the blessed in heaven, but is especially designed to honor the blessed who have not been canonized and who have no special feast day. All Saints is a holy day of obligation on which Catholics are bound to participate in the Mass. *(CCC 1173)*   See **holy days of obligation.**

All Souls, feast of   A feast commemorating all the faithful departed, observed each year on November 2 (or, if November 2 is a Sunday, on November 3). Special prayers for the dead are offered, a tradition that has come down from the earliest days of the Church. Pope Benedict XV granted each priest the privilege of celebrating three Masses on this day. A plenary indulgence for the souls in purgatory may be obtained on this feast day. *(CCC 1032)*   See **indulgence; purgatory.**

almsgiving; alms   This act of freely giving material or financial assistance to a needy person must be motivated by Christian charity. Almsgiving is recognized in the Christian tradition as a corporal work of mercy and is one of the principal forms of penance, especially during Lent. *(CCC 1434)* See **mercy, corporal and spiritual works of.**

Alpha and Omega When the first and last letters of the Greek alphabet are combined they are a symbol of the divinity of Christ, who is the beginning and the end. These words were spoken by Jesus of himself in the Scriptures (Revelations 1:8). (See also Revelations 21:6 and 22:13.) The symbols frequently occur in church art and architecture. During the Easter Vigil the presider cuts the letter *Alpha* above the cross and *Omega* below the cross on the paschal candle.

Alphonsus Liguori, Saint Born near Naples, 1696, he was trained in law and practiced at the bar for eight years. Ordained a diocesan priest in 1726, he had great pastoral concern for the unevangelized poor in the country places outside the city. Founded the Congregation of the Most Holy Redeemer (Redemptorists) in 1732 especially to preach the Gospel to these poor people. He wrote over one hundred books on the Christian life; he is perhaps best known for his monumental four-volume work on moral theology for the guidance of confessors. His writings were instrumental in opposing the heresy of Jansenism. He was ordained a bishop in 1762 and served the diocese of Saint Agatha of the Goths until 1775. He died in 1787, was canonized in 1839, declared a Doctor of the Church in 1871, and named the patron of confessors and moralists in 1950. See **Jansenism.**

altar A table on which the Eucharistic sacrifice is celebrated. According to the Code of Canon Law, an altar may be fixed or movable; it is "*fixed* if it is so constructed that it is joined to the floor and therefore cannot be moved; it is *movable* if it can be transferred" (Canon 1235, §1). According to Catholic custom the table of a fixed altar is to be of stone; nevertheless, even another material, worthy and solid, in the judgment of the conference of bishops also can be used. A movable altar can be constructed from any solid material appropriate for liturgical use. Moreover, "the ancient tradition of keeping the relics of martyrs and other saints under a fixed altar is to be preserved according to the norms given in the liturgical books" (Canon 1237, §2). *(CCC 1181–1182)*

altar bread The round, flat wafers used in the Eucharistic Liturgy. The unleavened bread is made of pure wheat flour mixed with water and baked between iron molds.

altar cloth The fabric, usually of white linen or other suitable material, that covers the entire altar during the celebration of the Eucharist. The current legislation requires only one cloth.

altar society   A group of the faithful who take it upon themselves to care for the altar and its accessories in the parish church.

altar stone   The phrase can mean two things. First, it is the large permanent table of the altar consisting of one slab of stone or marble into which are set the relics of two martyrs and is consecrated as one with the rest of the altar. Second, it may consist of the small square flat stone, consecrated by a bishop, that contains the relics of canonized martyrs or saints that is usually inserted in the center of an altar that is blessed.

altar wine   The wine used for the Eucharistic Liturgy must be made from grapes, natural and unadulterated, that is, not mixed with any additives. A small quantity of water is mixed with the wine by the deacon or priest at Mass. Symbolic meanings associated with this action are the union of Christ with the people of God and the union of the human and divine in Jesus.

amen   Hebrew word meaning "truly" or "so be it." It was used in the Jewish synagogue as a personal agreement with a prayer offered in the name of the community. In apostolic times it was taken over by the Christian community for scriptural and liturgical use. It is commonly used by Roman Catholics at the end of liturgical prayers and as an affirmation of faith in receiving the Eucharist. *(CCC 451)*

amice   See **vestments**.

analogy   A comparison between two things or beings that implies likenesses but also dissimilarities. All language about God is based on analogy because we humans can only speak of God from our own limited perspective. *(CCC 1099)*

anamnesis   The Greek word means *remembrance, commemoration, memorial*. It refers specifically to the first prayer following the consecration of the Mass that recalls the Passion, Resurrection, and Ascension of Jesus. *(CCC 1353–1354)*

anathema   This solemn formula of excommunication or exclusion from the ecclesial community is used by the Church to assert that some position or teaching contradicts Catholic faith and doctrine. Saint Paul used this expression against anyone who preached a false gospel (Galatians 1:8–9 and 1 Corinthians 5:4–5) or rejected the love of Christ (1 Corinthians 16:22). Anathema was abolished by Vatican II.

anchor-cross   This symbol combines the anchor, a sign of safety, with the cross, a sign of salvation, to symbolize the Christian hope in eternal salvation. The early Christians used this figure in the catacombs as a symbol of hope. The theological virtue of hope is said to be the anchor of the soul (Hebrews 6:19–20). The anchor-cross is often associated with Saint Nicholas, the patron saint of sailors.

anchoress; anchorite   An anchoress or anchorite is a woman or man who lives in almost total seclusion in order to follow a life of contemplation and sacrifice.

angels   From the Greek word for messenger, angels are often spoken of in the Bible. There are many Old Testament references to them (see, for example, Genesis 32:1; Isaiah 6; Tobit 5). Of special note is the teaching of Jesus that angels are spiritual beings (Matthew 22:30), who always enjoy the vision of God in heaven (Matthew 18:10) and who will accompany him at his Second Coming (Matthew 16:27). In the course of centuries, theologians have described angels as created spirits without bodies, endowed with intellect and free will, inferior to God but superior to human beings. The Catholic Church professes that angels exist, but does not define any details about them. *(CCC 328–336)*

Angelus   The prayer, formulated in honor of the Incarnation, commemorates the angel Gabriel's announcement to Mary that Jesus was to be born of her. The prayer is recited three times a day at approximately 6 A.M., noon, and 6 P.M. when the Angelus bell is rung. Where its practice exists the ringing of the bells follows a certain pattern: there are three strikes at each invocation, each followed by a pause, and then nine strikes in succession during the recitation of the final prayer. The Angelus is replaced by the Marian antiphon Regina Coeli at Eastertime.

anger; wrath   A capital or deadly sin, anger is a feeling of displeasure, usually accompanied by antagonism, aroused by real or imaginary injury; it is sinful when accompanied by a deliberate desire for unjust retaliation. *(CCC 1765, 2262)*   See **capital sins.**

Anglicans   A word describing the churches united in faith and ecclesial organization to the English See of Canterbury. Anglicanism originated in 1534 with Henry VIII's Act of Supremacy, which declared that the king should be the supreme head of the Church of England. (Note that, in the United States, Anglicans have been called Episcopalians since the Revolutionary War.) The absolute break with the Catholic Church occurred in 1563, when Parliament made the so-called Thirty-Nine Articles of religion mandatory for all citizens. Among the articles: the Bible contains all that is necessary for salvation; ecumenical councils are not infallible; transubstantiation is not acceptable (though today some Anglicans hold views on the Eucharist similar to those of the Roman Catholic Church); the civil ruler has authority over the church. The *Book of Common Prayer* is perhaps the most important bond of unity among Anglican churches.

animals   God entrusted animals to the care of humans, and thus the Church legitimatizes their use for food, clothing, domestic uses, and medical experimentation within limits. *(CCC 2515)*

animism   In the past this expression was applied to the belief of less developed peoples that certain plants and material objects have a spirit or soul of their own.

Anima Christi   Saint Ignatius of Loyola is often credited with this prayer to Christ in his passion. The prayer was traditionally used as a private act of thanksgiving after Holy Communion. The prayer is also known as "Prayer to the Most Holy Redeemer." There are translations in all the modern languages. Authorship and exact date of this prayer are unknown.

anno Domini   See A.D.

anointing   Holy oil is placed or poured on persons, places, or things in a religious ceremony in order to make the "anointed" sacred and consecrated to God. Anointing is used in the sacraments of baptism, confirmation, anointing of the sick, and orders. Churches and altars are anointed when they are consecrated. Oil is used in the blessing of bells and sacred vessels. Bishops are anointed during the rites of their episcopal consecration. The epistle of James (5:14–15) notes that anointing the sick and infirm with oil, in the name of the risen Jesus, will help strengthen them and heal them. In the New Testament anointing alludes to messianic joy, honor, healing of the sick and the forgiveness of sin. *(CCC 1293)*   See **anointing of the sick; baptism; confirmation; ordination.**

anointing of the sick   One of the seven sacraments of the Church, described thus in the Code of Canon Law: "The anointing of the sick by which the Church commends to the suffering and glorified Lord the faithful who are dangerously sick so that He can relieve and save them, is conferred by anointing them with oil and using the words prescribed in the liturgical books" (Canon 998). This sacrament can be administered only by a bishop or priest. It is properly "administered to a member of the faithful who, after having reached the use of reason, begins to be in danger due to sickness or old age" (Canon 1004, §1). *(CCC 1511–1513)*

annulment   A term for what is known in the Code of Canon Law as a decree of nullity—namely, a declaration by a competent authority of the Church that a marriage was invalid from the beginning because of the presence of a diriment (invalidating) impediment, a basic defect in consent to marriage, or an inability to fulfill the responsibilities of marriage, or a condition placed by one or both of the partners on the very nature of marriage as understood by the Church. The annulment procedure may be started at the parish level; the investigation of the facts is usually carried out by a marriage tribunal under the leadership of a bishop. *(CCC 1628–1629)*   See **impediments to marriage; marriage, Christian; marriage tribunals.**

Annunciation   A liturgical solemnity, celebrated on March 25, that commemorates the angel Gabriel's announcement of the Incarnation of the Son of God to the Virgin Mary. (See Luke 1:26–38.) The origin of this feast goes back to at least the fifth century. *(CCC 484)*

anthropomorphism   The attributing to God of human traits and characteristics, both physical such as face, mouth, heart, and hands, and emotional qualities such as love, compassion, kindness, sorrow, joy, and anger. To counter the error that can come from a literal understanding of this metaphorical way of portraying God, the Church teaches that God is a pure spirit without physical or spatial dimensions.

antichrist   A term used to describe the chief of Christ's enemies. The term is used in the New Testament only, in 1 John 2:18, 24; 4:3; and 2 John 7. Historically, the antichrist has been identified with individual persons (for example, Caligula and Hitler) or with social institutions. Some non-Catholics preach that the Catholic Church is the antichrist. We have no definite identification of the antichrist from the Bible or from the Church. *(CCC 675)*

anticlericalism   This demeanor and behavior reflects a negative attitude toward the clergy. It denies the right and duty of Church leaders to speak out on political issues of public morality and to have any real part in a country's political and sociocultural life. Anticlericalism usually arises from secular or prejudicial sources and it can exist among Catholics. The effect of anticlericalism ranges from mere dislike to the persecution of the Church and clergy.

antiphon   A brief refrain, usually from the Bible, that is sung or said at the beginning and end of psalms or canticles and between each verse. The antiphons of Our Lady are associated with the four seasons: "Loving Mother of the Redeemer" (Advent); "Hail Queen of

Heaven" (Lent); "Heavenly Queen" (Paschal season); and "Hail Holy Queen" for the remainder of the year. Though the antiphons of Our Lady were first sung in association with the psalms, they are now most often heard as independent hymns.

antipope   A claimant to the papacy in opposition to a validly elected pope. Some thirty or more of these have existed in the history of the Church.

anti-Semitism   Hostile and discriminatory behavior toward Jews based on religious, racial, and political grounds. In the Declaration on the Relation of the Church to Non-Christian Religions, the Second Vatican Council rejected the charge against the Jews of guilt in the death of Jesus. Anti-Semitism is completely incompatible with Christian charity since Christians are bound to see all human beings as their kin, and all forms of racism and persecution of Jews are expressly condemned.

anxiety   In theological terms, fear and apprehension that engender unnecessary doubts about one's faith. *(CCC 2088)*

Apocalypse   The name often given to the last book of the New Testament written by Saint John the Apostle. Today the book is known to many as the book of Revelation. *Apocalypse* means an *uncovering* or *revealing*. The Apocalypse focuses on the visions of events to come and included fearful warnings about crisis-times faced by the earliest Christians. *(CCC 2642)*

Apocrypha   Some Old Testament books written in Greek are often printed in Catholic Bibles and are often omitted in Protestant Bibles. These books include such works as Tobit, Judith, Sirach, Wisdom, and I and II Maccabees.

apologetics   A branch of theology concerned with the skillful presentation of the reasonableness, truth, and ultimate value of Christian beliefs about God, Christ, the Church, and our common human destiny.

apostasy; apostate   The act of total rejection by a baptized person of the true Christian faith and defection from the believing community is called apostasy. One who totally and deliberately defects from the Christian faith that he or she once professed is an apostate. *(CCC 2089)*

apostles   From the Greek meaning *one who is sent*, this term is used often in the New Testament. It is specifically used to describe the Twelve whom Jesus gathered around him for special instruction and the eleven of them chosen as prime witnesses of the Resurrection and for leadership roles in the Christian community. According to Catholic teaching, Christ ordained them priests at the Last Supper and commissioned them to preach the Gospel to all humankind (see Matthew 28:19–20). *(CCC 75–76)*

Apostles' Creed A summary of Christian faith expressed in twelve articles. Its name came from a popular belief that it was actually written by the twelve apostles; its substance clearly stems from the New Testament. Historians, however, date the actual text anywhere from A.D. 150 to A.D. 400. It is clear that at a very early date the Western Church required catechumens (new members) to learn the Apostles' Creed before baptism. It is still considered an excellent summary of the Christian faith. The "Profession of Faith" in the *Catechism of the Catholic Church* follows the Apostles' Creed. *(CCC 194, 196)*

Apostleship of Prayer This organization, founded in France in 1844, is associated with the League of the Sacred Heart. The members recite the Daily Offering to sanctify their prayers, works, and sufferings of the day by uniting them with the Holy Sacrifice of the Mass throughout the world, and pray for the monthly general and mission intentions recommended by the Holy Father. The association is under Jesuit direction, has centers all over the world, and publishes its magazine the *Messenger of the Sacred Heart* in many different languages.

apostolate The work or office of an apostle is the ministry of the Word of God, setting up the Church, spreading the faith, and bringing others to Christ. The apostolate refers to labors done in the name of Christ and for laypersons includes the responsibility to preach Christ in their homes and workplaces and to bring others to him. Participation in the apostolate is an obligation for all the baptized and confirmed. *(CCC 8653–864)*

apostolic delegate This cleric or layperson is an official representative of the Holy See who deals with the hierarchy of a country. The apostolic delegate in the United States lives in Washington. His home and office are called the apostolic delegation.   See **nuncio.**

Apostolic See The diocese of Rome is the supreme seat of authority for the whole Church.   See **Holy See.**

apostolic succession A term that affirms the uninterrupted handing on of episcopal power and authority from the apostles to contemporary bishops. This successive transfer is effected whenever a validly ordained bishop ordains a successor by the laying on of hands.

Those ordained as bishops have continued to fulfill the roles of the apostles, and have been continually in communion with the Apostolic See, that is, with the Bishop of Rome. *(CCC 77–79)*

apparitions of the Blessed Virgin Mary   An apparition is an extraordinary, visible appearance seen by one or more persons. This manifestation may occur in the form of a supernatural vision or private revelation. The authenticity of apparitions is a matter for inquiry and evaluation by the Church or a skilled spiritual companion.

Recently some Church-accepted apparition sites have become places to which Christian pilgrims and spiritual seekers frequently journey. The places and dates of the apparitions include: Guadalupe (Mexico), 1531; Rue de Bac (France), 1830; La Salette (France), 1846; Lourdes (France), 1858; Fátima (Portugal), 1917; Beauraing (Belgium), 1933; and Banneau (Belgium), 1933. Although the Church community has officially approved a number of apparitions and shrines, it does not view the messages communicated to persons in supernatural appearances as part of official Catholic doctrine.

apse   The semicircular end of the sanctuary in romanesque and gothic churches terminates the chancel, aisles, or transepts. The altar is often located in the center of the apse.   See **basilica.**

archangels   See **choirs of angels.**

archbishop   The bishop of an archdiocese has limited authority over the bishops of the several dioceses in his territory. The bishops are suffragan bishops and the archbishop is their metropolitan and occupies the metropolitan see. The title of titular archbishop is given to a prelate who does not have the special duties of an archbishop or who has no bishops under him. The appropriate form of address for an archbishop is "Your Excellency."

archdiocese   The ecclesiastical territory governed by an archbishop. The archdiocese is the principal diocese within an ecclesiastical province.

aridity   The absence of consolation, emotional warmth or affection in prayer is often called aridity or dryness during which a person often loses enthusiasm for prayer and meditation. Aridity ranges from the lack of sensible affection to complete desolation. Aridity may come from the good spirit, from one's bodily condition, or from carelessness in one's spiritual life. Spiritual writers advocate patience and faithfulness to prayer even though the feelings of joy or other fruits of prayer are temporarily absent.   See **prayer.**

ark of the covenant   The people of Israel carried a small box of precious wood in their wanderings which they placed in the Temple at Jerusalem. The two tablets of the law, which were given to Moses by God, on which were written the Ten Commandments, a golden dish of Manna, and the rod of Aaron, which blossomed, were enclosed in this sacred chest made of acacia wood. The ark came to be regarded as the sign of God's abiding presence and protection. One of the images in the litany of Loreto addresses Mary as the ark of the covenant, that is, of the new covenant between God and humanity.

Armageddon   The mountain of Megiddo borders the plain of Esdraelon in present-day Israel. This mountain was the great battlefield of ancient Palestine where the fortunes of kings and nations were decided. In the New Testament, Armageddon is a symbol of the struggle between good and evil that goes on in the world and in every person (Revelation 16:16). It has come to be synonymous with the place of the final cosmic battle between God and Satan, where good prevails over evil.

armed forces   Citizens of a legitimate public authority have an obligation to participate in the national defense either as a sworn member of the armed forces or in some other way that does not involve the bearing of arms. *(CCC 2310)*

arms, production and sale of   These undertakings may be regulated by public authorities in order to protect the common good and to ensure that these acts do not promote violence and armed conflict. *(CCC 2376)*

art   See **liturgical art.**

artificial insemination   In this process the male spermatozoa and the female ovum are brought together in a woman apart from the act of natural intercourse.   See **marriage, Christian.**

Ascension, feast of   The rising of Christ to heaven after his Resurrection, witnessed by the apostles and referred to frequently in the New Testament (see, for example, Mark 16:19; Luke 24:51; Acts 1:9). His return marked the exaltation of Christ to the right hand of God, where Jesus' supremacy over all creation was revealed. (See, for example, John 14:2 and Philippians 3:21.) Ascension Thursday (kept on the sixth Thursday after Easter) is one of the principal feast days of the Christian year and is for Catholics a holy day of obligation. *(CCC 660–667)*

ascesis; asceticism   Christians under the action of the Spirit have adopted means of self-discipline in order to have greater union with God. True ascesis brings a growth in contemplation and love of God that fosters personal maturity and social responsibility. Asceticism can be exercised internally as discipline applied to the mind, heart, and will, or externally through renunciations signified by the voluntary vows of poverty, chastity, and obedience or by various forms of fasting, bodily mortification, and austerity. Newer types of asceticism include confrontation of addictions to alcohol, drugs, food, tobacco, television, work, and whatever else holds the heart captive. *(CCC 1734)*

ashes   These symbols of penance and reconciliation are made by burning the palms blessed on the previous Passion Sunday. These ashes are blessed and then the sacramental is used to mark the foreheads of people on Ash Wednesday.

Ash Wednesday   The first day of Lent. On this day, ashes from the burning of palms from the previous year's Passion Sunday are blessed and placed on the foreheads of the faithful as a sign of penance. In the early Church, public penance was performed by people wearing sackcloth, who were then sprinkled with ashes. As public penance gradually died out, about the eleventh century, the custom of receiving ashes at the beginning of Lent gradually came into being.

asperges   In a ceremony, the altar, priest, and people are sprinkled with blessed water. The rite dates at least to the ninth century and is a reminder of baptism. Today the ceremony is the Rite of Sprinkling and an optional replacement for the Penitential Rite.

aspergillum   Holy water is sprinkled on persons or things to be blessed with a liturgical instrument consisting of a short handle with a bunch of bristles or a perforated metal bulb at the end. Sometimes the handle is hollow in order to hold more water. A small branch or twig of box, laurel, or other shrub is occasionally used.   See **holy water.**

aspersion   The sprinkling with holy water in blessings. Aspersion is also a form of baptism in which the candidate is sprinkled with water.

aspiration   See **ejaculation.**

associate pastor   This term from the 1917 Code of Canon Law for a priest assigned to a parish to assist the pastor in parish ministry is replaced in the 1984 code by *parochial vicar.*

Assumption of the Blessed Virgin Mary   A truth of faith, proclaimed as a dogma by Pope Pius XII on November 1, 1950, which holds that "the Immaculate Mother of God, Mary ever Virgin Mary, when the course of her earthly life was finished, was taken up body and soul into the glory of heaven." This belief was evident from the very early days of the Church. The feast of Mary's Assumption, celebrated on August 15, is one of the principal Marian feasts of the Church year and is for Roman Catholics a holy day of obligation. *(CCC 966)*

astrology   The practice is a form of divination based on the speculation that the planets and stars influence human activities. It is condemned by the Church because it shows a lack of trust in God's providence and instead places trust in the works of God's creation.   See **divination**.

atheism   Denial of the existence of God. A distinction is often made between intellectual atheism (that is, a system of thought which asserts that the existence of God is contrary to fact or reason) and practical atheism (that is, that human acts have no relationship to God). There are innumerable variations of atheism, a number of which are described in Vatican II's Pastoral Constitution on the Church in the Modern World (§§19–21). *(CCC 2123–2128)*

atonement   The word means "at one." It is an act of reconciliation in which humanity is made one with God through the mediation of Jesus by his Incarnation, life, suffering, and death for the Redemption of all (Romans 5:10). *(CCC 616)*

attrition   Sorrow for sins because they are hateful in themselves or because the person is shamed or fears God's punishment is sometimes referred to as imperfect contrition or attrition. Imperfect contrition is sufficient for the reception of the sacrament of reconciliation. *(CCC 1453)*

audience, papal   A person or a number of persons may have a formal visit with the pope. Public audiences in which a number of persons visit the pope in a group are more common than private audiences in which a single person or a small group is allowed to pay respects to the Holy Father. The appropriate form of address for the pope is "Your Holiness."

Augustine of Hippo, Saint   Born in Tagaste, North Africa, in A.D. 354, of a pagan father and a Christian mother (Saint Monica), Augustine was educated somewhat in the Christian faith, but soon lost it as he became involved in many of the philosophical currents of his time.

After a number of years spent searching for the meaning of life and living in a pagan way, he was converted and baptized in 387. He later became the bishop of Hippo and is considered one of the most influential Fathers of the Church because of his penetrating explanations of Christian truth. He wrote many books on Christian faith and life, including the well-known *Confessions* and the *City of God*. He died in A.D. 430.   See **Fathers of the Church.**

aumbry   This small boxlike recess, set into the wall of the sanctuary, is used for the reservation of the holy oils.

aureole   The gold band, the rays of gold leaf, gilt paint or metal surrounding the figures of the Blessed Trinity and the Blessed Virgin Mary in sacred art, particularly in icons, signifies the sanctity attached to those persons. In early Byzantine art the aureole appeared as an oval shape behind the person depicted. The Italians gave the name *mandorla* to this contour because of its almond shape. An aureole is distinct from the nimbus or halo.   See **halo.**

authority   The person who is in command or who has jurisdiction is the one in authority. The word can also be applied to persons to whom acquiescence is given because of their expertise. Religious authority is the ability to inspire belief or behavior without force or threat of injury.

autopsy   Dissection of the bodies of the dead can be morally permitted for scientific or for legal reasons as long as due respect is observed. *(CCC 2301)*

auxiliary bishop   A bishop acts as an aid to the diocesan bishop who may need assistance because of the amount of work, illness, or age. The auxiliary bishop is appointed by the Holy See and is a titular bishop of an ancient see which has ceased and no longer endures except in records. He does not have ordinary jurisdiction in a diocese, nor does he have the right to succession. Canon law recommends that he also be appointed an episcopal vicar or a vicar general.

avarice; covetousness   A capital or deadly sin, avarice is an excessive love for material things to the neglect of spiritual goods and one's obligations of justice and charity. *(CCC 2536)*   See **capital sins.**

Ave Maria   See **Hail Mary.**

aversion   One of the passions which compels a person to turn away from an object. Aversion is the opposite of attachment, and can be either put into the service of spiritual growth or allowed to become destructive.

B

baldachino This umbrellalike structure provides a covering or canopy over the altar. It is composed of metal, stone, or wood and is generally dome-shaped and supported by chains or columns. Its original purpose was to protect the Sacred Species from dust. The baldachino is absent from many modern churches.

Baltimore Catechism This book containing the basic doctrines and practices of the Catholic faith in a question-and-answer format was used in the United States for simple religious instructions for young persons and adults. Commissioned in 1884 by the American bishops at the Third Plenary Council of Baltimore, this catechism underwent numerous text revisions. The Baltimore Catechism was the official religion text in Catholic schools and religious-education programs until after Vatican II. Since 1992 this manual has been replaced by the contemporary catechism for the worldwide Christian community—the *Catechism of the Catholic Church*.   See *Catechism of the Catholic Church*

banns of marriage A public announcement of the promise of marriage. Publication is usually accomplished either through an announcement at Sunday Masses or written in the parish bulletin. The purpose of the announcement is to discover if any impediments to a marriage exist or if there is any reason why a marriage should be prohibited or postponed. Canon 1067 leaves the bishops' conferences of each country "to issue norms concerning...the marriage banns or other appropriate means for carrying out the necessary inquiries which are to precede marriage."

baptism The first of the seven sacraments, described by the Code of Canon Law in this way: "Baptism, the gate to the sacraments, necessary for salvation in fact or at least in intention, by which men and women are freed from their sins, are reborn as children of God and, configured to Christ by an indelible character, are incorporated in the Church, is validly conferred only by washing with true water together with the form of words" (Canon 849).

The following points of canon law should be noted: (a) baptism may be conferred either by immersion or by pouring; (b) the water used in baptism should be blessed, but in case of necessity unblessed water is licit; (c) the required form of words is "I baptize you in the name of the Father, and of the Son, and of the Holy Spirit"; (d) it is recommended that baptism be celebrated on a Sunday or if possible at the Easter Vigil; (e) the proper place for baptism is a church or oratory, but in case of necessity it may be conferred in a private home or in a hospital; (f) the ordinary minister of baptism is a bishop, priest, or deacon, but others may be deputed for this function (as often happens in mission territories) and in case of necessity any person can and should confer baptism. *(CCC 1213, 1226–1228, 1239–1240)*

baptism of blood   Also called baptism of martyrdom, this term refers to the case of a person who freely and patiently suffered death for the Christian faith before he or she could actually receive the sacrament of baptism—not an uncommon occurrence in the first three centuries of Christianity and in other times of persecution. *(CCC 1258)*

baptism of desire   This term refers to the state of those who, in the words of Vatican II, "through no fault of their own, do not know the gospel of Christ or His Church, yet sincerely seek God and, moved by grace, strive by their deeds to do His will as it is known to them through the dictates of conscience..." (Dogmatic Constitution on the Church, §16). *(CCC 1258)*

baptism of infants   The teaching of the Catholic Church on the baptism of infants is this: "From the earliest times, the Church, to which the mission of preaching the Gospel and of baptizing was entrusted, has baptized not only adults but children as well. Our Lord said: 'Unless a man is reborn in water and the Holy Spirit, he cannot enter the kingdom of God.' The Church has always understood these words to mean that children should not be deprived of baptism, because they are baptized in the faith of the Church, a faith proclaimed for them by their parents and godparents, who represent both the local Church and the whole society of saints and believers....To fulfill the true meaning of the sacrament, children must later be formed in the faith in which they have been baptized...so that they may ultimately accept for themselves the faith in which they have been baptized" (Rite of Baptism for Children, §§2–3).

Present Church law obliges parents to "see to it that infants are baptized within the first weeks after birth"; in danger of death, an infant is to be baptized "without any delay" (Canon 867, §§1–2). *(CCC 1252)*

baptismal candle   In the Catholic Rite of Baptism there is a section called the "Presentation of a Lighted Candle." A smaller candle is lit from the Easter candle, symbol of Christ as Light of the World, and presented to an adult being baptized or, in the case of an infant, to someone from the infant's family (in the absence of a family member, the sponsor), with the admonition to "walk always as a child of the light" and keep the flame of faith alive in your heart. *(CCC 1243)*

baptismal font   See font, baptismal.

baptismal name   The name given to the person at baptism; according to a long Christian tradition, this name should be that of a saint, so that the baptized will have a special heavenly patron and will be encouraged to imitate the life and holiness of that saint. The present law of the Church expresses this tradition in a negative way: "Parents, sponsors and the pastor are to see that a name foreign to a Christian mentality is not given" (Canon 855).

baptismal preparation   A period of preparation before baptism. An adult who wishes to be baptized must first "be sufficiently instructed in the truths of faith and in Christian obligations and be tested in the Christian life by means of the catechumenate" (Canon 865, §1). Before the baptism of an infant, the parents (or at least one parent) must give consent to the baptism and must give assurance that the infant will be brought up in the Catholic religion. If such assurance is lacking, the baptism is to be delayed with the hope that the parents will become more aware of their religious responsibilities. *(CCC 1229–1233)*   See **catechumenate.**

baptismal register   A record of a baptism to be completed by the priest or deacon who administers the sacrament; it is kept in the archives of the parish. A copy of this record is usually given to the baptized at the time of the baptism and is available on request.

baptismal robe   In the Catholic Rite of Baptism there is a section called the "Clothing With a Baptismal Garment"; at this time the person being baptized is symbolically covered with a white garment and exhorted to "bring it unstained to the judgment seat of our Lord Jesus Christ so that you may have everlasting life." *(CCC 1243)*

baptismal sponsors   Popularly known as godparents, sponsors play an important part in baptism. Canons 872–874 give the following norms in reference to baptismal sponsors or godparents: (a) "Insofar as possible one to be baptized is to be given a sponsor who is to assist an adult in Christian initiation, or, together with the parents, to present an infant at the baptism, and who will help the baptized to lead a Christian life in harmony with baptism, and to fulfill faithfully the obligations connected with it"; (b) "Only one male or one female sponsor or one of each sex is to be employed"; (c) "To be admitted to the role of sponsor, a person must: 1° be designated by the one to be baptized, by the parents or the one who takes their place or, in their absence, by the pastor or minister and is to have the qualifications and intention of performing this role; 2° have completed the sixteenth year, unless a different age has been established by the diocesan bishop or it seems to the pastor or minister that an exception is to be made for a just cause; 3° be a Catholic who has been confirmed and has already received the sacrament of the Most Holy Eucharist and leads a life in harmony with the faith and the role to be undertaken; 4° not be bound by any canonical penalty legitimately imposed or declared; 5° not be the father or mother of the one to be baptized." Finally, it should be noted that a non-Catholic may not be a baptismal sponsor for a Catholic, but may serve as a witness to the baptism together with a Catholic sponsor. *(CCC 1255)*

baptismal vows or promises   The renunciation of Satan and all his works and the profession of faith by the one to be baptized or, in the case of an infant, by the parents and sponsor. The solemn renewal of these vows is part of the Easter Vigil. The private renewal of these vows is a commendable act of piety. *(CCC 1237)*

baptismal water   During the Easter Vigil water is specially blessed for use in baptism. At other times water may be blessed at each baptism by the one who administers the sacrament. The Roman ritual provides three ritual blessings, two of which involve the symbolic touching of the water by the presider and an interchange of responses by the people.

   In case of necessity, ordinary natural water—fresh, salt, warm, cold clean, dirty—may be used for baptism.

baptistry   A section of a church, or even a separate room or building, that contains the baptismal font and that is set aside for the celebration of the Rite of Baptism. Commonly found near the main entrance of the church, it is considered a structure of great importance in a church building.

Baptists   The largest Protestant denomination in the world, it originated in Europe in the seventeenth century, with strong roots in Calvinism. Roger Williams founded the first Baptist church in the United States in Rhode Island. A wide variety of theological views is found among Baptists, and there are a large number of separate groups bearing the name. In a most general way, however, it can be said that Baptists agree that the Bible is the sole rule of faith, that the adult believer should be baptized by total immersion, that infants should not be baptized, that all the faithful share in the priesthood, that the local church should be independent, and church and state should be separated. The Baptists in the United States have a strong commitment to evangelization and to overseas missions.

base communities Small groups of the faithful led by laity gather to participate more effectively in liturgy and sacraments, pastoral ministry, apostolic ministry, and personal and social development. Some groups gather for Scripture and Communion services in the absence of a priest; the participants consider the relationship of the Scripture to their daily lives and often make social decisions resulting from these reflections. The concept of base communities originated in Latin America. Where they exist, they contribute to the vigor of parish and diocesan life. They are truly small churches in action and are supported by Pope Paul VI in his letter *Evangelii nuntiandi*. The apostolic exhortation "On the Mission of the Lay Faithful in the Church and in the World" signed by Pope John Paul II in January 1989 provides clear support for building these communities throughout the Catholic world (n. 26) and are a great help in the formation of lay leadership (n. 61).

Basil, Saint Born in A.D. 329, he dedicated himself to the monastic life for many years. In 370 he became the bishop of Caesarea and strongly defended the teaching of the Church against the heresy of Arianism, which denied the divinity of Christ; between 358 and 364 he produced a monastic rule which is still in use. Today he is known as "the father of Eastern monasticism." He died in 379.

basilica A name given primarily to certain ancient churches of Rome, Bethlehem, and elsewhere which were built in the rectangular style of Roman public buildings. Now the term applies to churches of particular religious or historical significance.

Basilicas are classified as major, or patriarchal, such as the great Roman churches of St. Peter's and the Lateran, and as minor. Minor basilicas are other important churches in Rome and abroad which the Holy Father has honored with this designation. Their distinctive emblem is an umbrella in yellow and red to stand for the papal and Roman senatorial colors. Minor basilicas usually also have special privileges, such as certain indulgences. There are more than 30 minor basilicas in the United States.

B.C./B.C.E. B.C. is the abbreviation for "before Christ." A date followed by these initials means so many years before the birth of Jesus. This is sometimes called "Before the Christian Era" and is abbreviated B.C.E.

beatification   A declaration by the pope that a deceased person lived a holy life and is now in heaven and is worthy of public veneration on a limited (not universal) basis in the Church. This act usually follows upon a process by which the life, virtue, reputation for holiness, ministry, and writings of the person are intensely scrutinized by the Congregation for the Causes of Saints in Rome. Those who are beatified are called "Blessed."   See **canonization**.

Beatific Vision   In Catholic theology, this term refers to the essential happiness of heaven, namely, that the redeemed will see the very essence of God—unsurpassably beautiful and good; and in this marvelous vision they will enjoy the love of God forever. *(CCC 163)*

beatitude   The blessed who see God in the Beatific Vision enjoy perfect happiness in heaven. Beatitude is the ultimate goal of human life, and persons can experience this gift of God to some degree already in this life.

beatitudes   The promises of Christ concerning happiness or blessedness as proclaimed in the Sermon on the Mount. In the Gospel of Matthew (5:3–12) eight are listed; in the Gospel of Luke (6:20–23) four are stated. They are considered basic qualities of Christian holiness that will be generously rewarded by God. *(CCC 1716–1719)*

Beguines; Begherds   Associations of laity living in community and practicing charitable and apostolic activities. The female groups were called Beguines and the male, Beghards. Their residences were called Beguinages. These groups developed chiefly in Flanders and the Low Countries during the Middle Ages. The Beguines were nearly suppressed as a result of being confused with similar heretical groups. Several Belgian Beguinages witness to this form of spirituality today.

Benedict, Saint   Born about A.D. 480 he became a hermit around the age of twenty and lived this way of life for some years. He founded a series of monasteries, beginning at Subiaco, Italy; around 525 he founded the monastery at Monte Cassino and there developed his highly acclaimed monastic rule; he is known as "the father of Western monasticism"; his rule is still used not only by his own religious (men and women known as Benedictines) but also by some other religious orders. Benedictine monasteries (with the famous motto *Ora et Labora*, that is, "Pray and Work") exist in almost every nation of the world. Saint Benedict's sister was Saint Scholastica. Benedict died circa 546.

Benedictine spirituality   The practice of prayer and life developed by the followers of the Rule of Saint Benedict places great weight on the essential attitudes and methods found in that document. Those who embrace a Benedictine spirituality choose life in community in which each member supports with the greatest patience the weakness of body and behavior of another, own all goods in common, pray the Liturgy of the Hours in community, prayerfully reflect on the Scriptures and related spiritual reading through *lectio divina* and prefer nothing other than Christ. Wherever members exist they try to live Benedict's well-known exhortation "That in all things God may be glorified."

Benediction of the Blessed Sacrament   A devotion centering on the Eucharist and approved by the Church for certain occasions and under certain conditions. It consists in the benediction (blessing) of the people with the sacred host (usually contained in a monstrance); the blessing is to be preceded by readings from the word of God, hymns, prayers, and a suitable time for silent adoration. Its purpose is to highlight the marvelous presence of Christ in the Eucharist. *(CCC 2548–2550)*

Benedictus   The words proclaimed by Zechariah, the father of John the Baptist, as soon as his lips were loosened at the time of the circumcision of his son (Luke 1:68–79). The canticle begins with the words "Blessed be the Lord God of Israel," and has served traditionally as part of the Morning Prayer in the Liturgy of the Hours.

benefice   This permanent, ecclesiastical foundation consists of a sacred office and the right of the occupant to the annual revenue derived from the endowment. Clergy who hold a benefice have free use of their income, using what they need and spending what is extra for the poor or in good works. Benefices are rare today. In fact, the Second Vatican Council and the 1983 Code of Canon Law recommended their suppression.

benevolence   A disinterested generosity that is a hallmark of true charity. *(CCC 1829)*

Bible   Also called Sacred Scripture or the Scriptures, the Bible is a collection of books accepted by the Church as the inspired, authentic account of God's revelation and plan of salvation for the human race. The Bible is divided into the Old Testament and the New Testament. The Old Testament contains 46 books, written principally in Hebrew between the years 900 B.C. and 160 B.C. Included are books with distinct purposes: historical, moral, prophetic. These books are a record of God's dealing with the Israelites, "the Chosen People," and how they came to know the one true God and how they awaited the arrival of the Messiah and savior promised by God. The New Testament contains 27 books, written in Greek between the years A.D. 50 and A.D. 140. Included are the four Gospels of Matthew, Mark, Luke, and John, the Acts of the Apostles, the Epistles (Letters) of Saint Paul, other Epistles, and the Book of Revelation. The major theme of the New Testament is Jesus Christ: his person, his preaching, his saving death and Resurrection, and his relationship to us as Lord and Savior. *(CCC 120–127)*   See **Gospel.**

Bible, books of the   The Bible is the collection of books written by human authors under divine inspiration which, along with tradition, is the source of revelation given by God for the salvation of humankind. The Bible contains seventy-three books grouped into two testaments: forty-six in the Hebrew Scriptures and twenty-seven in the Christian Scriptures. The decision about which books should be included in the official Catholic canon of the Bible was made during the Council of Trent. The following books are those included in the Old and New Testaments.

Hebrew Scriptures

The Pentateuch

Genesis	Leviticus	Deuteronomy
Exodus	Numbers	

Historical Books

Joshua	1 Chronicles	Tobit
Judges	2 Chronicles	Judith
1 Samuel	Ruth	Esther
2 Samuel	Ezra	1 Maccabees
1 Kings	Nehemiah	2 Maccabees
2 Kings		

The Prophets

Isaiah	Hosea	Nahum
Jeremiah	Joel	Habakkuk
Ezechiel	Amos	Zephaniah
Lamentations	Obadiah	Haggai
Baruch	Jonah	Zechariah
Daniel	Micah	Malachi

Wisdom Books

Job	Ecclesiastes	Wisdom
Psalms	Song of Songs	Sirach
Proverbs		

Christian Scriptures

Matthew	Ephesians	Hebrews
Mark	Philippians	James
Luke	Colossians	1 Peter
John	1 Thessalonians	2 Peter
Acts of the Apostles	2 Thessalonians	1 John
Romans	1 Timothy	2 John
1 Corinthians	2 Timothy	3 John
2 Corinthians	Titus	Jude
Galatians	Philemon	Revelation

Bible service   In this paraliturgical service, public readings from the Scriptures are combined with periods of prayer, singing, and silence. Often a homily or reflection on the themes of the readings is included. The Constitution on the Sacred Liturgy of Vatican II recommended Bible services on the vigils of feasts, Sundays, and holidays and on some Advent and Lenten weekdays.

bilocation   This personal presence of an individual in more than one place at the same time has been recorded of some of the saints.

bioethics   Moral questions arising from the progress made in biological sciences may be of two kinds. First, settling problems such as genetic engineering and artificial insemination created by the rapid technology of the life sciences. Second, studying the possibilities of new developments in ethical procedures compatible with Christian principles of morality, such as natural family planning and organ transplantation.

biretta   The clergy occasionally wear a stiff square cap with three upright ridges on top and sometimes a tuft in the middle. The priest's biretta is black, a bishop's is purple, a cardinal's is scarlet without a tuft, a Cistercian abbot's is white. The biretta is worn on entering the church for service and on leaving the church and at certain times during the services. Since the Second Vatican Council, the biretta is no longer commonly worn by priests in the United States, but is still required of all the clerics of the patriarchal basilicas in Rome.

birthday of the Church   The birth of the Church is envisioned in the institution of the Eucharist and fulfilled on the cross. The Dogmatic Constitution on the Church states "The origin and growth of the Church are symbolized by the blood and water which flowed from the open side of the crucified Jesus…" (§3). See also John 19:34. This is reiterated in The Constitution on the Sacred Liturgy: "For it was from the side of Christ as he slept the sleep of death upon the cross that there came forth 'the wondrous sacrament of the whole Church'" (§5). *(CCC 765, 767)*

birth control   A popular, less technical term for contraception.   See **contraception; natural family planning**.

bishops; episcopate   According to the Code of Canon Law, "Through the Holy Spirit who has been given to them, bishops are the successors of the apostles by divine institution; they are constituted pastors within the Church so that they are teachers of doctrine, priests of sacred worship and ministers of governance. By the fact of their episcopal consecration bishops receive along with the function of sanctifying also the functions of teaching and of ruling, which by their very nature, however, can be exercised only when they are in hierarchical communion with the head of the college and its members" (Canon 375, §1 and 2). Bishops are empowered to ordain priests and deacons and other bishops. *(CCC 886)*

bishops, college of   The assembly of bishops is headed by the pope and carries on the teaching authority and pastoral guidance in the Church. A person becomes a member of this college upon ordination as bishop. The college exerts absolute authority in the Church when it functions in an ecumenical council or by the collegial action of the bishops around the world in one with the pope. *(CCC 885)*

black fast   Only one meal in the evening is allowed on these days of penance. In addition, meat, eggs, dairy products, and alcohol are forbidden. Only bread, water, and vegetables form the diet of such a fast. The black fast no longer exists except in specific religious houses or as a practice of individual devotion.   See **abstinence; fasting**.

Blaise, Saint, blessing of   The prayerful placing of two crossed candles on the throats of the faithful on February 3, the feast day of Saint Blaise. After his martyrdom, Saint Blaise was invoked as one of the Fourteen Holy Helpers on behalf of those suffering from throat ailments. This devotional practice arose because Blaise saved the life of a boy who was choking on a fishbone.

blasphemy   Speaking or acting against God (or persons or objects consecrated to God) in a contemptuous or irreverent way; a serious violation of the reverence and love due to God. *(CCC 2148)*

Blessed Sacrament   The sacrament of the Eucharist is called "blessed" because all blessings and graces spring from it. The bread and wine after their consecration in the Mass are often called the Blessed Sacrament. The Blessed Sacrament in the form of consecrated bread is reserved in Catholic churches in a prominent place or in a special chapel of adoration and is marked by a burning sanctuary lamp. See **Eucharist; consecration; transubstantiation.**

blessing Placing a person or object under the care of God or dedicating a person or thing to the service of God. A simple blessing is usually made with the sign of the cross, sometimes accompanied by sprinkling holy water. The Church also has a large number of specific blessings for various times and occasions. *(CCC 1671–1672)* See **sacramentals; sign of the cross.**

blood of Christ Jesus shed his blood on the cross in atonement for the sins of humankind. We share in the life of Christ through the blood of Christ received sacramentally in Holy Communion (1 Corinthians 10:16). *(CCC 517)*

blue army An institute whose full title is the Blue Army of Our Lady of Fátima. Founded in 1946, its purpose is to pray for the conversion of Russia and for world peace as requested by Our Lady of Fátima. The society has worldwide membership, engages in charitable and educational works, and is headquartered in Washington, New Jersey.

boasting Prideful bragging which is an offense against truth. *(CCC 2481)*

boat, incense Before incense is burned it is kept in a boat-shaped liturgical vessel.

body An essential part of the human person, the body is a fundamentally good creation of God; according to Catholic teaching, the body is a temple of God and therefore deserving of respect by oneself and others. *(CCC 364–365)*

Body of Christ This term refers to the ways that Christ is present to humankind and to the world. It has many meanings that stem from the human body of the historical Jesus. This biblical image and its extension to other images is well developed in the Dogmatic Constitution on the Church (§7).

body of the Church The visible organized community of the faithful consists of its human members on earth.

body, resurrection of According to Scripture and the formal teaching of the Church, the body will be resurrected and reunited to the soul after death. Christ taught the resurrection of the body (see Matthew 22:29–32; Luke 14:14; John 5:29). The doctrine was preached as a fundamental mystery of Christian faith (1 Corinthians 15:20; Revelation 20:12) and was included in all the early creeds. *(CCC 998–1001)*

Book of Blessings   The portion of the Roman Ritual which contains the blessings of persons, places, and things was published by the Holy See in 1984 as the *Book of Blessings* and reflects the liturgical principles declared by Vatican II. There are six parts to the *Book of Blessings*. Part I includes blessings directly pertaining to people. The blessings in Part II are related to buildings and different forms of human activity. Parts III and IV present blessings for items used in public and private prayer. Parts V and VI provide a rich collection of blessings that can be used on the parish level.

Book of Hours   This prayer book, used in monasteries during medieval times, contained prescribed prayers for the canonical hours of the day, the Little Office of Our Lady and the Office of the Dead. These books were commonly commissioned by wealthy people and were usually works of fine calligraphy, lavish artistic illumination and viewed as works of art.

bowing   This liturgical gesture involves either a simple inclination of the head, a medium bend of the upper part of the body, or a profound bend from the waist. Bowing is the normal method of communicating devotion and respect. The gesture is used in the liturgy in reverence to the Blessed Sacrament, the altar, the cross, or some person. Head bows are made during ceremonies to inform the ministers when they are to perform an action. Bowing is a lesser form of reverence than genuflecting.

bread, breaking of   In the Mass the breaking of the bread takes place before the *Lamb of God*. The priest breaks the host into two pieces, one of which he places on the paten. He breaks a small segment from the other half and drops it into the chalice containing the blood of Christ.

The expression is also used to signify the Eucharistic celebration during which, at the Lord's command, bread is taken, blessed, broken, and shared (Acts 2:42).

bread, Eucharistic   The altar bread used in the liturgy is an unleavened, round wafer made of wheaten flour. It is consecrated during the Eucharistic Prayer and distributed during the Communion rite at Mass.

breviary   A book or books containing the official and public prayer of the Church known as the Liturgy of the Hours (also called Divine Office): that is, a set form of prayers, hymns, and readings designed to sanctify the various hours of the day; at present, the breviary contains the Office of Readings, Morning Prayer, Daytime Prayer, Evening

Prayer, and Night Prayer. Men in holy orders and men and women in solemn vows are required by Church law to pray the Liturgy of the Hours; all other members of the Church are strongly encouraged to do so. *(CCC 1174–1178)* See **Book of Hours.**

broadstole   This is not a stole, but the name given to the chasuble worn by the deacon. The broad strip of fabric, either purple or black, is worn over the left shoulder and under the right arm by deacons.

brothers, religious   This collective title is used for laymen or for members of religious orders who do not become priests. The title *brother* is sometimes used to designate those who are in various stages of formation within a religious community.

Buddhism   The religious thought and practice of Siddhartha, a Gautama, born in 563 B.C., known as the Buddha or Enlightened One, who in meditation was enlightened as to the passing nature of the visible world and concluded that suffering comes from desire, and therefore the extinction or suppression of desire will cause suffering to cease. The Buddhist Way of Perfection teaches how desire can be suppressed by following an eightfold path: right understanding, right purpose, right speech, right conduct, right work, right effort, right mindfulness, right contemplation. Buddhism (including the more modern versions) is still one of the largest religions of the world, especially in the Orient. Buddha died around 483 B.C. *(CCC 842–843)*

bull, papal   The most important document issued by the pope is sealed with a disk of lead called a *bulla* from which it gains its name. Each bishop is appointed by a papal bull.

burial, Christian   The interment of a deceased person in consecrated ground after the funeral rites in which "the Church asks spiritual assistance for the departed, honors their bodies, and at the same time brings the solace of hope to the living" (Canon 1176, §2); Canon 1184 forbids ecclesiastical burial for certain persons, such as notorious apostates or public sinners, who have not given some signs of repentance. *(CCC 2300–2301)* See **cremation.**

burse   The corporal was carried to and from the altar in a small square pocket about twelve inches square covered with the same fabric and color as the vestments. This small square, known as a burse, is not often used today. The corporal is a square piece of linen on which the bread and wine are placed.

Byzantine rite   Official ritual practice of the Church of Constantinople (formerly Byzantium) which also has its own general law; after the Roman rite, it is the most widely used of the rites, practiced both by many Eastern Orthodox Christians and also by Catholics of the Byzantine rite (that is, those who are in union with the pope of Rome). See **Eastern Churches, Catholic; Eastern Churches, separated.**

C

calumny (slander) Also referred to as slander, calumny is the injuring or ruining the reputation of another by lies, and is a violation of charity, justice, and truth. *(CCC 2477, 2479)* See **detraction.**

Calvary Place where Jesus was crucified, Calvary is a Latin translation of the word *Golgotha* meaning "place of the skull." Calvary was the place then outside the city of Jerusalem where criminals were usually executed.

candle A sacramental symbolizing divine life and purity. Lighted candles are carried in procession, held by the faithful when renewing their baptismal vows, and placed on the altar to indicate Christ's presence.

canon law The official body of laws for Catholics of the Roman, or Latin, rite contained in a work called the Code of Canon Law. (Note that Eastern rite Christians in union with Rome have their own laws.) The first Code of Canon Law for the Roman Church, containing 2,414 canons (laws) on all aspects of the Church's life, was promulgated in 1917; the revised Code, containing 1,752 canons, was promulgated in 1983. It contains laws that apply to all members of the Church, others that define and govern the hierarchy of the Church and members of religious communities; there are norms governing the teaching office and the sanctifying office of the Church, including a long section on the sacraments. The Code of Canon Law, in the words of Pope John Paul II, "is in no way intended as a substitute for faith, grace, charisms, and especially charity in the life of the Church and the faithful. On the contrary, its purpose is rather to create such an order in the ecclesial society that, while assigning the primacy to love, grace and charisms, it at the same time renders their organic development easier in the life of both the ecclesial society and the individual persons who belong to it." See **law.**

Canon of the Mass A term referring to the Eucharistic Prayer of the Mass and containing the solemn and essential act of consecration in which the species of bread and wine are changed into the Body and Blood of Jesus Christ and the sacrifice of Christ on the cross is perpetuated over the centuries. The prayers of the Canon recall the great mysteries of the Christian faith and include prayers for the Church, for the living and the dead, and remembrance of the saints and martyrs. At present the Church has approved four Eucharistic Prayers for general use, three for Masses with children and two for Masses of reconciliation. *(CCC 1353)* See **Mass.**

canon of the Scripture The list or collection of books of the Bible officially recognized and accepted by the Church as the inspired word of God and therefore to be taken as the rule or norm of faith. *(CCC 120)*

canonization The declaration by the pope that a person is a saint, is now in heaven, and is worthy of veneration by all the faithful. This declaration is usually preceded by the process of beatification and by a detailed examination of the person's life and writings; two miracles ascribed to his or her intercession must ordinarily be authenticated by the Church before the declaration is made. *(CCC 828)* See **beatification.**

canticle A sacred song, not including the psalms, taken from the Bible and used in liturgical services. Two well-known canticles are the *Magnificat* of the Blessed Virgin and the *Benedictus* of Zechariah.

capital punishment A form of punishment whereby the state takes the life of the person proven guilty of serious crimes. The morality of the death penalty has been debated for centuries. In general, Catholic teaching has accepted in principle that the state has the right to take the life of a person proven guilty of serious crimes. But there continues to be a serious debate about whether capital punishment is justified in practice, that is, in the concrete circumstances of modern life. In recent years Pope John Paul II and the U.S. Catholic bishops have strongly opposed the actual use of capital punishment and have called for its practical abolition. *(CCC 2266)*

capital sins Popularly referred to as "the deadly sins," they are the chief sinful tendencies of fallen human nature, the main sources from which other particular sins arise; traditionally, they are pride, avarice, lust, envy, gluttony, anger, and sloth. *(CCC 1866)*

capitalism An economic system marked by private ownership of the means of production and a for-profit free market for goods and services. The Church does not see the capitalist system as unlawful, but it condemns its abuses, such as unbridled materialism and the absolute control of the marketplace over human labor. *(CCC 2425)*

cardinal virtues   Prudence, justice, fortitude, and temperance are called the cardinal (from the Latin word *cardo* meaning "hinge") virtues because all the other virtues hinge on or are related to them. *(CCC 1833–1834)*

catacombs   The below-ground burial places used by the early Christians of Rome and where the Eucharist was celebrated, often for reasons of safety.

catechesis   Instruction and formation in the Catholic faith, both for those who are preparing to be baptized and for those who are already baptized but in need of continuing instruction and formation according to their age and their level of maturity in the Christian life. *(CCC 4–10)*

catechism   A summary or manual containing the basics of Christian doctrine.

Catechism of the Catholic Church   A universal text summarizing the doctrines of the Catholic Church which was first published in French in October 1992. It was prepared by a Vatican commission and is intended to help bishops in formulating local catechism programs adapted to the cultural and other concerns of their locales. It is seen as an organic presentation of the Catholic faith in its entirety. *(CCC 18)*

catechumenate; catechumens   The period of instruction and involvement in the Catholic faith in preparation for the baptism of adults or for the reception of baptized non-Catholic Christians into the Catholic Church; the basic elements of the catechumenate are explained in the Rite of Christian Initiation of Adults (RCIA). *(CCC 1232)*

catechumens, oil of   See oils, holy.

cathedra   The chair, throne, or stool of a bishop in his cathedral church.

Catholic   From a Greek word meaning "universal," it is part of the official title or designation given to the body of Christian communities in union with the Bishop of Rome (the pope); it was used to describe the Church by Saint Ignatius of Antioch in approximately A.D. 107: "Wherever the Bishop shall appear, there let the people be, even as where Jesus is, there is the Catholic Church." The word is now used in a variety of ways: for example, to describe the universality of the Church itself as intended for all human beings; to identify particular institutions of the Church (for example, "Catholic Press") and individual members of the Church (for example, "John Doe is a good Catholic"). *(CCC 830–831)*

celibacy   In general, the unmarried state of life; in Christian teaching, celibacy is a vocation in which one freely chooses to be unmarried "for the sake of the kingdom of heaven" (Matthew 19:12), a vocation that may be lived in the lay state or in a religious institute publicly recognized by the Church; according to the Code of Canon Law for the Latin rite, celibacy is required of candidates for the priesthood. *(CCC 1579)*   See **chastity.**

cenacle   The upper room where the Last Supper was celebrated.

censer   A container, usually covered and suspended by chains, in which incense is burned at liturgical services.

censure   An ecclesiastical penalty for a grave sin. Excommunication, interdict, and suspension are three types of censure.

chalice   The cup containing the wine which in the Eucharistic sacrifice is changed into the precious blood of Christ. It must be constructed of appropriate materials and should be blessed by a bishop or priest. *(CCC 1574)*

chancellor   A priest appointed by the bishop of a diocese to be in charge of the diocesan governing office.

chancery   The administrative office of the diocese where the ordinary business of the diocese is conducted, records kept, meetings held, and the like.

chant, ecclesiastical   A simple melody, usually characterized by single notes, used in liturgical services. The Western Church uses Gregorian chant of which the Ambrosian, Dominican, and Carthusian are various forms.

chapel   A semi-enclosed part of a larger church building or a small addition to it that often has a special purpose, such as a shrine or place for relics.

chaplet   A circular string of beads for keeping count of prayers.

charism   Extraordinary gifts or graces of the Holy Spirit given to individuals for the sake of others. Saint Paul lists nine of these graces (1 Corinthians 12:4–11); he also insists that the virtue of charity is above all other charisms (1 Corinthians 13). *(CCC 799–801)*

Charismatic Renewal movement   Also known as the Catholic Pentecostal Movement, this movement originated in 1967, and believes there is a new outpouring of the Holy Spirit in the Catholic Church, a need to reawaken Catholics to the gifts of the Holy Spirit and to the baptism of the Holy Spirit, that is, to a personal experience of the graces already sacramentally received. Generally, charismatic communities have weekly meetings consisting of Scripture readings and teachings, prayer, singing of hymns, sharing of experiences, and fellowship.

charity   One of the theological (God-given and God-directed) virtues infused into the soul with sanctifying grace, providing the ability and inclination to love God above all things and to love others for the sake of God; it is the greatest of all the virtues. *(CCC 1822–1829)* See **sanctifying grace.**

charm (amulet)   An object, word, or act thought to have magical power over others, especially when they call on the aid of demons or have the intent of harming another. The Church warns the faithful against such practices. *(CCC 2117)*

chastity   The virtue that moderates and regulates the sexual appetite according to the principles of right reason and the law of God; this virtue applies to all, both married and single, but is expressed differently according to one's state of life. This virtue, according to the Vatican's Declaration on Sexual Ethics, "increases the human person's dignity and enables him [or her] to love truly, disinterestedly, unselfishly and with respect for others" (§12).

   The vow of chastity is one of the evangelical counsels (see Matthew 19:11) and one of the three vows (together with obedience and poverty) professed by religious in the Church. *(CCC 915, 2337)*   See **religious life; religious.**

choir   Members of the Church who assist at the liturgy through the ministry of song. *(CCC 1143)*

choirs of angels   The nine ranks of angels, from the lowest to the highest: angels, archangels, principalities, powers, virtues, dominations, thrones, cherubim, and seraphim.

chrism   An aromatic oil consecrated by the bishop in the Mass of Chrism on Holy Thursday and distributed to the churches for use in baptism (to signify the gift of the Holy Spirit on the newly baptized), confirmation, and ordination. *(CCC 1183, 1241)*   See **oils, holy.**

chrismation   The act of anointing. The name for the sacrament of confirmation in the Eastern Churches. *(CCC 695)*

Christ   A title of Jesus meaning the Anointed One, identical to the Hebrew word for Messiah, that is, Savior or Deliverer. To acknowledge Jesus as the Christ is to acknowledge him as Savior. *(CCC 436–440)*

Christian   One who accepts the faith of Christ whether in full communion with the Catholic Church or separated from it.

Christmas   The feast of the Nativity of Jesus Christ, celebrated on December 25. The liturgy provides three different Masses for the feast (midnight, dawn, during the day), and priests are permitted to celebrate all three Masses. Many of the customs that have grown over the centuries to celebrate Christmas had their origin in the pagan celebration of the beginning of winter but have been "christened" with a religious significance. *(CCC 525)*

Church   The Church may be defined as that visible religious society founded by Jesus Christ, under one head (Saint Peter and his successors), whose purpose is to preserve and proclaim his teachings and to make present his sacrifice and sacraments for the salvation of all until the end of time. The Church is known by the marks that characterize it: it is one, holy, catholic, and apostolic. Vatican II (in the Dogmatic Constitution on the Church) offered many images and descriptions to try to communicate the total meaning of the Church: it is the new people of God; it is the Mystical Body of Jesus Christ, "the whole Christ, head and members"; it is a sacrament or sign of God's presence; it is a community of believers united with Christ, especially in and through the Eucharist; it is an assembly of the faithful, committed to carry forth the mission of Christ under the guidance of the Holy Spirit. *(CCC 763–766)*

circumcision   From a religious viewpoint, circumcision was very important to the people of Israel: it was a "mark of the covenant" between Yahweh and his people (see Genesis 17:10–14). Jesus himself was circumcised on the eighth day after his birth (Luke 2:21), and the early Christians were sometimes referred to as simply "the circumcised" (see Acts 11:2). It was soon recognized, however, that the Mosaic Law need not be imposed on gentile Christians and that circumcision was no longer a religious requirement for the baptized. "In Christ Jesus neither circumcision nor uncircumcision counts for anything; the only thing that counts is faith working through love" (Galatians 5:6; see also Galatians 6:15 and Romans 3:30). *(CCC 527)*

clairvoyance   A phenomenon in which a person is able to sense or know something about a person or event without using ordinary means of communication. Clairvoyance may proceed from diabolical, supernatural, or natural causes. *(CCC 2116)*

clergy   A title referring to those men who are ordained for the service of God and the Church, including deacons, priests, and bishops. A distinction may be made between diocesan clergy, that is, those ordained for a particular diocese and committed in obedience to a particular bishop; and regular (or religious) clergy, that is, those who belong to a religious institute in the Church and owe primary obedience to their religious superiors as well as pastoral obedience to the bishop in whose diocese they exercise their ministry. *(CCC 1562–1568)*

cloister   An enclosed place in a convent or a monastery set aside exclusively for the use of religious. A body of laws govern who may enter and leave these areas. The word is also used to refer to covered walkways, from the fact that these were often found in religious institutions.

collectivism   An economic system by which property is owned by the state. The Church views unrestricted collectivism as undermining the autonomy of the individual. *(CCC 1885)*

College of Cardinals   According to the Code of Canon Law, "The cardinals of the Holy Roman Church constitute a special college whose responsibility is to provide for the election of the Roman Pontiff in accord with the norm of special law; the cardinals assist the Roman Pontiff collegially when they are called together to deal with questions of major importance; they do so individually when they assist the Roman Pontiff especially in the daily care of the universal Church by means of the different offices which they perform" (Canon 349).

collegiality   In a strict sense, this term refers to the fact that all the bishops of the Church in union with and subordinate to the pope, the Bishop of Rome, possess supreme teaching and pastoral authority over the whole Church. This authority is exercised most clearly in ecumenical councils, but also in other ways sanctioned by the pope. Collegiality is considered an essential element of the Church as instituted by Christ; it is explained at length in Vatican II's Dogmatic Constitution on the Church. In a wide sense, this term is often used to describe other forms of coresponsibility in various ecclesiastical communities, such as the diocese, the parish, or the religious community. *(CCC 877)*

commandments of God   A term often applied to the Decalogue or Ten Commandments as given by God to Moses on Mount Sinai (see

Exodus 20:1–21 and Deuteronomy 5:2–33) and interpreted by Jesus Christ (see Matthew 5:17–48). As given in the Book of Exodus, the Ten Commandments are as follows:

I am the LORD your God....You shall have no other gods before me....

You shall not take the name of the LORD your God in vain.

Remember the sabbath day, to keep it holy....

Honor your father and your mother....

You shall not kill.

You shall not commit adultery.

You shall not steal.

You shall not bear false witness against your neighbor.

You shall not covet your neighbor's house....

You shall not covet your neighbor's wife....

(CCC 2056–2063)

commandments of the Church   See **Precepts of the Church.**

common good   A broad concept that may be described as the sum total of social conditions that allow individuals, families, and organizations to achieve complete and efficacious fulfillment. *(CCC 1905–1912)*

communion of saints   One of the articles of the Apostles' Creed is "I believe in...the communion of saints," a term which describes the spiritual bond that exists between all the members of the Church: the saints in heaven, the souls in purgatory, and the faithful still living on earth. According to Catholic teaching, all are united with Christ and with one another in grace, prayer, and good works. *(CCC 946–948)*   See **purgatory.**

Communion, spiritual   A deep desire to receive the Blessed Sacrament when one is actually unable to do so.

concelebration   The simultaneous saying of Mass by more than one priest where all consecrate the same bread and wine. This practice was common in the West until the Middle Ages, and was restored in modern times by Vatican II.

concordat   An agreement between the Holy See and a secular government regarding religious matters.

concubinage   A term given to the cohabitation of two persons without benefit of marriage. *(CCC 2390)*

concupiscence   A tending toward sin, an inordinate desire for material things. *(CCC 418)*

confession   See **penance, sacrament of.**

confirmation   One of the seven sacraments described thus by the Church: "The sacrament of confirmation impresses a character and by it the baptized, continuing on the path of Christian initiation, are enriched by the gift of the Holy Spirit and bound more perfectly to the Church; it straightens them and obliges them more firmly to be witnesses to Christ by word and deed and to spread and defend the faith" (Canon 879).

This sacrament is conferred through anointing with chrism on the forehead, which is done by the imposition of the hand, and through the words: "Be sealed with the Gift of the Holy Spirit." The ordinary minister of Confirmation is a bishop, though there are cases when a priest is authorized to confirm. The general norm of canon law is that this sacrament should be conferred "at about the age of discretion," but the conference of bishops may determine another age. In the United States, most dioceses seem to favor an older age. The person to be confirmed should ordinarily be suitably instructed and prepared for this sacrament. As far as possible each person being confirmed should have a sponsor; the same norms apply to the sponsor at confirmation as those governing the sponsor at baptism; it is desirable that the person who was sponsor at one's baptism be sponsor for one's confirmation as well. *(CCC 1315–1321)*   See **baptismal sponsors.**

conscience   A dictate of practical reason or a personal judgment which decides, on the basis of general moral values and principles, that an act one is about to do is morally good or evil because it does or does not conform to God's law of love. Vatican II spoke of conscience in many ways: "Deep within his conscience man discovers a law which he has not laid upon himself but which he must obey. Its voice, ever calling him to love and to do what is good and to avoid evil, tells him inwardly at the right moment: do this, shun that. For man has in his heart a law inscribed by God. His dignity lies in observing this law, and by it he will be judged. His conscience is man's most secret core, and his sanctuary. There he is alone with God whose voice echoes in his depths. By conscience, in a wonderful way, that law is made known which is fulfilled in the love of God and of one's neighbor" (Pastoral Constitution on the Church in the Modern World, §16). *(CCC 1776–1782)*

conscience, examination of   The act of reflecting on one's moral state and its conformance to the will of God; a preliminary to confession. *(CCC 1454)*

conscientious objector   One who refuses to take an active or direct part in a war on the grounds of conscience. In the event of an undoubtedly unjust war, a Catholic would be bound to decline participation. *(CCC 2311)*

consecration   The act of making a person, place, or thing holy and sacred, and setting it aside for the service of God. The bread and wine are consecrated at Mass, a permanent church building is consecrated, as are those who receive holy orders. *(CCC 1377, 1538)*

consistory   A meeting of the cardinals presided over by the pope and called to conduct important Church business, such as the appointing of bishops or the creation of new dioceses.

consummation at the end of time   The moment at the end of time when the kingdom of God will come in all its glory. *(CCC 1042–1048)*

contemplation   A form of interior, affective prayer in which one admires or rests in the knowledge and love of God. In the words of Saint John of the Cross, "Contemplation is the science of love, which is an infused knowledge of God." In its purest form contemplation is a gift of the Holy Spirit. *(CCC 2709–2719)*   See **quiet, prayer of.**

contraception   The deliberate and positive interference with sexual intercourse in order to avoid conception. The constant teaching of the Church, even from earliest times, is that contraception is morally wrong. In modern times this teaching has been strongly restated by Pope Paul VI and by Pope John Paul II in a number of places. According to Pope Paul VI, "Each and every marriage act must remain open to new life" and, as a consequence, "every action which, either in anticipation of the conjugal act, or in its accomplishment, or in the development of its consequences, proposes, whether as an end or a means, to render procreation impossible" must be excluded as a licit means of regulating births (*Humanae Vitae*, §14). *(CCC 2370, 2399)* See **natural family planning.**

contracts   An agreement between two or more parties to transfer a right or a benefit for sufficient consideration. Contracts must be strictly observed to the extent that their provisions are morally just and are in accord with a strict respect for the rights of each party. *(CCC 2410–2411)*

contrition; conversion   In the words of the Council of Trent, contrition is "heartfelt sorrow and aversion for the sin committed along with the intention of sinning no more." In the sacrament of penance, contrition is the most important act of the penitent. A theological distinction may be made between perfect contrition and imperfect contrition (also called attrition). Perfect contrition is sorrow for sin arising out of the motive of love of God, while imperfect contrition is sorrow for sin arising out of some lesser motive, such as fear of the anticipated loss of heaven or condemnation to hell. *(CCC 1451–1454)* See **penance, sacrament of.**

contumely The unjust treatment of another person by way of ridicule and contempt. It offends against charity and justice.

conversion In the New Testament the Greek word *metanoia*, often translated as conversion or repentance, means something very profound and personal: not merely a change of manners but a change of heart, a turning away from sin, a return to the Father's love. "We can only approach the kingdom of God in Christ by metanoia (conversion). This is a profound change of the whole person by which one begins to consider, judge, and arrange his or her life according to the holiness and love of God, made manifest in his Son in the last days and given to us in abundance." *(CCC 1427–1429)*

corporal works of mercy The seven actions that show respect for the body as a temple of the Holy Spirit. They are as follows: feeding the hungry, giving drink to the thirsty, clothing the naked, sheltering the homeless, tending the sick, visiting the imprisoned, and burying the dead.

correction The act of prudently admonishing a sinner in order to encourage a change in behavior. This reproof must be done out of charity; and there must be a reasonable chance that the admonition will do some good and that no one else can or will give it. *(CCC 1829)*

cosmos The visible universe that will be transformed at the end of time. *(CCC 1147)*

council, ecumenical An assembly of the Catholic bishops from around the world called by the pope who sets the council's agenda and approves its decisions. These meetings are held to consider matters of concern to the universal Church. *(CCC 884)*

counsel One of the seven gifts of the Holy Spirit whose effect is to enable one to identify what is the right course of action in a given circumstance and to urge a person to pursue that right action. *(CCC 1831)*

counsels, evangelical These are the counsels of perfection: poverty, chastity, and obedience.

covenant   A word meaning a formal agreement, pact, or contract; in religious terms it describes the special relationship between God and his people. The Old Testament gives many examples of God's covenant with the Israelites: for example, with Abraham (see Genesis 15 and following), with Noah (see Genesis 6:18), with Moses (see Deuteronomy 5, 6, 7). In the covenant, God promised to be faithful to his people; and they, in turn, promised to be faithful to him, to worship him alone, and to keep his commandments. One of the dominant themes of the Old Testament is that while God is always faithful to his part of the covenant, the Israelites are not always faithful to theirs. The New Testament describes the new covenant: that is the special relationship between God the Father, Jesus his beloved Son, and each Christian in and with Jesus. The new covenant does not annul the old but, in Jesus, brings it to fulfillment (see Galatians 3:15–29). In the new covenant, Jesus expresses unconditional love for his people, instructs them, forgives them, and lays down his life for them, thus sealing the new covenant in his blood: "This cup is the new covenant in my blood. Do this, as often as you drink it, in remembrance of me" (1 Corinthians 11:25). *(CCC 1961–1974)*

creation   The act of producing something from nothing. The story of the Creation of the world and its inhabitants by God is told in the book of Genesis. *(CCC 302, 325)*

creed   A summary of the principal truths of the Church in the form of a profession of faith. Two of the most important creeds are the Apostles' Creed and the Nicene Creed. *(CCC 193–195)*   See **Apostles' Creed, Nicene Creed.**

cremation   The disposal of the dead by reducing the body to ashes. The Church strongly condemned cremation in the past because the practice was associated with the denial of the Christian doctrine of the resurrection of the dead. The present teaching of the Church, as expressed in canon law, is as follows: "The Church earnestly recommends that the pious custom of burying the bodies of the dead be observed; it does not, however, forbid cremation unless it has been chosen for reasons which are contrary to Christian teaching" (Canon 1176, §3). *(CCC 2301)*   See **burial, Christian.**

crosier   A symbol of authority and jurisdiction, shaped like a shepherd's staff, conferred on bishops and some abbots at the time of their consecration.

cross   A term that describes the instrument of suffering on which Christ died for the salvation of the world; thus, the cross is a symbol of Christ's redeeming love, profoundly respected by Christians throughout the world. Also, a term that describes the suffering or mortification of a Christian, especially when accepted lovingly in union with the sufferings of Christ: "If any want to become my followers, let them deny themselves and take up their cross and follow me" (Mark 8:34). *(CCC 616–617)*

crucifix   A cross bearing the image of Christ either as suffering Savior or as risen Lord. A crucifix must be on or over the altar where Mass is celebrated. Among Catholics, a blessed crucifix is a revered object of private and public devotion.

cult   A term that in modern times refers to particular religious or semireligious groups noteworthy for esoteric beliefs, rituals, and practices.

cura animarum   The obligation of an ordained priest to give instruction in the faith, administer the sacraments, and perform other pastoral duties.

Curia, Roman   All the organized bodies that assist the pope in the governance of the Church.

Cursillo movement   An intense, three-day experience of Christian renewal involving community living, presentations on Christian doctrine by laypersons and priests, participating in group discussions, liturgical prayer, and the like. The Cursillo is followed by a post-Cursillo program focusing on weekly meetings of small groups and larger reunions (called Ultreyas) in which participants share prayer and insights. The Cursillo movement originated in Spain in 1949; it was introduced in the United States in 1957.

D

damage, unjust   Willful infliction of harm on another without material benefit to the person doing the harm. Willful damage to public or private property is also contrary to moral law. Unjust damage requires restitution. *(CCC 2409)*

Daniel, Book of   A book of the Old Testament, containing 14 chapters, written between 167 and 164 B.C., a time of persecution of the Jews. The overall purpose of this book was to give comfort and reassurance during this persecution. The Book of Daniel belongs to a type of literature known as "apocalyptic"; this literature emphasizes that Yahweh is the Lord of history, that he will ultimately vindicate his people, and that the kingdom of God will eventually be victorious against persecutors.

David The second, and perhaps the greatest, king of the Israelites, a major recipient of the messianic promises, David ascended the throne about 1000 B.C. after having been the armor-bearer of King Saul. (His engaging story is told especially in 1 Samuel 16 and following and 2 Samuel.) Among his greatest accomplishments was seizing the city of Jerusalem from the Jebusites, defeating the Philistines, and transforming the disparate tribes of Israel into an organized and united nation. He was a religious poet who wrote a number of the psalms (though by no means all of them) and a religious man who desired to serve the Lord in obedience; his grave sins (adultery and murder) are described in the Bible, but so also is his repentance. The promises made to him and his descendants are fulfilled in Jesus. *(CCC 2579)* See **Psalms.**

deacon; diaconate A man who is ordained for service to the people of God. In apostolic times the ministry of deacon was to serve various corporal and spiritual needs of the community (Acts 6:1–7) and to assist in preaching the word of God (Acts 8:40). Because of his important ministry, the deacon was expected to be a man of religious and moral integrity (see 1 Timothy 3:8–11). In the Church there are two kinds of deacons: those who receive the order as they advance to the priesthood and those who receive the order and remain in it permanently. In 1967, following the desire expressed by the bishops of Vatican II, Pope Paul VI decreed that (1) qualified unmarried men twenty-five years of age or older may be ordained permanent deacons, but may not marry after ordination; (2) qualified married men thirty-five years of age or older, with the consent of their wives, may be ordained permanent deacons. Of these deacons Vatican II declares: "Strengthened by sacramental grace, in communion with the bishop and his group of priests they are dedicated to the People of God, in conjunction with the bishop and his body of priests, in the service of the liturgy, of the Gospel and of works of charity" (Dogmatic Constitution on the Church, §29). *(CCC 1569–1571)*

Dead Sea Scrolls A collection of manuscripts and fragments of manuscripts discovered in 1947 at the site of the ancient Qumram community west of the Dead Sea. They have been dated from approximately 100 years before and after Christ. Among the scrolls are portions of many Old Testament books and writings about the Essene community (an ascetical community or sect living in Palestine during the first century A.D.). The scrolls, which are still being studied, have been of great value to biblical scholars in reconstructing the textual history of the Old Testament.

death; dying   According to Christian teaching, death (that is, the cessation of life, or the separation of the soul from the body) is considered a punishment for Adam's sin: "Therefore, just as sin came into the world through one man, and death came through sin, and so death spread to all because all have sinned..." (Romans 5:12). At the same time, however, Christian faith affirms that the power of death is not eternal but, because of the victorious Resurrection of Christ, yields to a new and eternal life: "If, because of the one man's trespass, death exercised dominion through that one, much more surely will those who receive the abundance of grace and the free gift of righteousness exercise dominion in life through the one man, Jesus Christ" (Romans 5:17). *(CCC 1010–1014)*

defense, legitimate   The lawful protection of one's right to life or that of one's family or of the state. Someone who defends a life is not guilty of murder even if the aggressor is dealt a death blow. *(CCC 2263)*

deism   A view holding that God created the universe but abandoned it after this initial act. This view does not accept Christianity as a supernatural religion and thus also does not accept grace, miracles, and mysteries. *(CCC 285)*

deposit of faith   A term used to describe the sum of revelation and tradition entrusted to the Church and its teaching office (magisterium) to be safeguarded and explained to the people of God. "The Roman Pontiff and the bishops, by reason of their office and the seriousness of the matter, apply themselves with zeal to the work of enquiring by every suitable means into this revelation and of giving apt expression to its contents; they do not, however, admit any new public revelation as pertaining to the divine deposit of faith" (Dogmatic Constitution on the Church, §25). *(CCC 66–67, 84)*

desires, disordered   The wish for something we do not possess that exceeds the limits of reason and drives us to covet unjustly what is not ours, for example, the desire to amass earthly goods without limit or the immoderate desire to acquire a neighbor's goods. *(CCC 2520)*

despair   The deliberate abandonment of hope of salvation and trust in God's providence. This act interferes with one's willingness to serve God.

detachment   A liberation from any inordinate attachment to another object, person, or emotion.

detraction   The act of revealing something about another that is true but that harms the other person's reputation. The fact that something is true does not necessarily allow it to be disclosed.

devil; satan   An evil spirit or fallen angel; specifically, the term often applies to Lucifer or Satan, the chief of the fallen angels (see Matthew 12:24), who tempts the human person to sin. In his teaching and ministry, Jesus Christ opposes the evil spirit with the Spirit of God. *(CCC 391–395)*

devotions   Any public or private prayer and/or worship that is not part of the Church's official public worship. Such devotions may include the Stations of the Cross, novenas, the rosary, and so forth.

diocese   According to the Code of Canon Law, "A diocese is a portion of the people of God which is entrusted for pastoral care to a bishop with the cooperation of the presbyterate so that, adhering to its pastor and gathered by him in the Holy Spirit through the gospel and the Eucharist, it constitutes a particular church in which the one, holy, catholic and apostolic Church of Christ is truly present and operative" (Canon 369). Only the Holy See is authorized to erect a diocese. *(CCC 833)*

discalced   From a Latin word meaning "without shoes," this term is applied to religious organizations whose members wear sandals. The Discalced Carmelites are an example.

disciple   A word which means "learner," it is used to describe those who hear and follow the teaching of Jesus (Matthew 10:1), not only in New Testament times but in every age. *(CCC 645, 647)*

disciplina arcani   Latin words meaning "discipline of the secret," which refer to the custom in the early Church of concealing from unbelievers certain mysteries and rites, and of educating catechumens very slowly in order to prevent profanation.

dispensation   A relaxation of an ecclesiastical law in a particular instance by an authority who has the power to do so, for example, a dispensation for the observance of Sunday Mass.

dissension   A vice which Christians must avoid if they are to enter into communion with God at the end of time. A catalog of vices is listed in Galations 5:19–21. *(CCC 1852)*

divination   Foretelling the future through calling on evil spirits or by other magical or satanic means. These practices are to be rejected. *(CCC 2116)*

Divine Office   The name formerly used for the public prayer of the Church designed to sanctify the hours of the day. The revision of this prayer is known as the Liturgy of the Hours.

divinity of Christ   It is the solemn teaching of the Church that Jesus Christ is a divine Person, true God as well as true man, the second Person of the Blessed Trinity. *(CCC 653)*   See **Holy Trinity.**

divorce   The teaching of the Church, based on the teaching of Christ himself (see Mark 10:2–12 and Luke 16:18), is that "a ratified and consummated marriage cannot be dissolved by any human power or for any reason other than death" (Canon 1141). Thus, although civil law may claim to dissolve the bond of marriage and render a person free to marry again, the Church maintains that the civil law has no power to do this. For serious reasons (such as adultery, serious danger to spirit or body of the other spouse or of the children), a spouse may have a legitimate cause for separation "in virtue of a decree of the local ordinary, or even in his or her own authority if there is danger in delay" (Canon 1153, §1). *(CCC 1650–1651, 2384–2386)* See **annulment.**

Docetism   A heresy of the early Church that holds that Christ only appeared to be human, that his material body was only an illusion. Gnosticism and Pelagianism were Docetic heresies. *(CCC 465)*

Doctor of the Church   A title conferred on ecclesiastical writers of eminent learning and outstanding holiness because of their contribution to the explanation and defense of Catholic doctrine. There are presently 32 such Doctors of the Church, including two women, Saint Catherine of Siena (died 1380) and Saint Teresa of Avila (died 1582).

dogma   A teaching or doctrine authoritatively and explicitly proposed by the Church as revealed by God and requiring the belief of the people of God. A dogma may be proposed by the Church in a solemn manner (for example, the dogma of the Immaculate Conception) or through the ordinary magisterium (for example, the truth that innocent human life is inviolable). *(CCC 88–90)*

doubt, involuntary and voluntary   The inability of an individual to accept a certain proposition as true. In terms of a person's faith, involuntary doubt refers to hesitation in believing or a difficulty in overcoming objections connected with a particular truth. Voluntary doubt is an outright refusal to hold what God has revealed and the Church proposes as true. *(CCC 2088)*

dove A common symbol for the Holy Spirit who appeared in the form of a dove at our Lord's baptism. *(CCC 701)*

doxology A hymn or prayer of glory and praise to God; notably, the "Glory to God in the highest" often prayed at Mass; the "Through him, with him, in him, etc.," that concludes the Eucharistic Prayer; the "Glory to the Father and to the Son and to the Holy Spirit...." *(CCC 2641, 2760)*

drugs, morality of Psychotropic (or psychoactive) drugs are chemicals that influence the working of mind and alter behavior, mood, and mental functioning. These drugs may be distinguished into two main categories: therapeutic and nontherapeutic. The use of therapeutic drugs is considered morally justified provided they are used under the direction of a competent physician and are believed to be for the total good of the patient. The use of nontherapeutic drugs is considered morally unjustified when they seriously impair one's health or human functioning or when there is danger of addiction. *(CCC 2291)*

dualism A system of belief which holds that the universe is the work of two opposing principles, Good and Evil, Light and Darkness, locked in eternal conflict. *(CCC 285)*

dulia The reverence given to saints and angels on account of their union with God. Dulia is distinguished from latria, which is the adoration due to God, and hyperdulia, which is the special honor given to the Blessed Virgin Mary.

E

Easter A movable feast, celebrated on a Sunday between March 22 and April 25, commemorating the Resurrection of Jesus Christ from the dead (see Mark 16:1–7). It is considered the greatest of all Christian feasts and holds a central place in the liturgical year. Liturgically, the celebration of Christ's Resurrection continues for a period of 50 days, that is, from Easter Sunday to the feast of Pentecost. *(CCC 638–640, 1169)* See **year, liturgical.**

Easter duty A popular term for the obligation thus described in the Code of Canon Law: "All the faithful, after they have been initiated into the Most Holy Eucharist, are bound by the obligation of receiving Communion at least once a year.

"This precept must be fulfilled during the Easter season unless it is fulfilled for a just cause at some other time during the year" (Canon 920, §§1–2).

In the United States the Easter season, for purposes of fulfilling this precept, has traditionally been understood to extend from the First Sunday of Lent until Trinity Sunday (eight weeks after Easter).

Easter Vigil   Called the "mother of all holy vigils," the Easter Vigil is celebrated after sundown on the night before Easter. The Easter Vigil service includes ceremonies that were held in the early Christian communities and highlights some of the most precious symbols of the Church. The Vigil consists of four parts: Service of the Light, Liturgy of the Word, Liturgy of Baptism, and Liturgy of the Eucharist. *(CCC 1095)*

Easter water   The water that is blessed at the Easter Vigil celebration. It is used for the renewal of baptismal promises and in some places is taken home to be used by the faithful in private devotions.

Eastern Churches, Catholic   These are Catholic Churches (whose members number approximately twelve million throughout the world) who follow the Eastern rites. Originally, they were the patriarchates of Constantinople, Alexandria, Antioch, and Jerusalem. Today the five principal rites are the Byzantine, Alexandrian, Antiochene, Armenian, and Chaldean. Best represented in the United States is the Byzantine rite with nine dioceses serving its Ruthenian and Ukrainian rite adherents. Vatican Council II, in its Decree on Eastern Catholic Churches, says: "The Catholic Church values highly the institutions of the Eastern Churches, their liturgical rites, ecclesiastical traditions and their ordering of Christian life. For in these churches, which are distinguished by their venerable antiquity, there is clearly evident the tradition which has come from the apostles through the Fathers and which is part of the divinely revealed, undivided heritage of the Universal Church" (§1).   See **Byzantine rite.**

Eastern Churches, separated   These are the Eastern Churches that are not in union with Rome. Their separation occurred in 1054 in what is often historically referred to as the Eastern Schism. The Orthodox Churches are the largest of these separated Eastern Churches. They hold in common with their Eastern Catholic counterpoints many matters of faith and morals, valid orders and sacraments, and a rich liturgy. They accept, however, only the first seven ecumenical councils of the Church, and do not acknowledge or hold communion with the pope. Since Vatican Council II there has been a continuing ecumenical dialogue between the separated Eastern Churches and the Catholic Church. *(CCC 838)*

Ecclesiastes, Book of   One of the Wisdom Books of the Old Testament, written by an unknown author around 250 B.C. Its essential theme is the vanity of all human efforts and achievements in relationship to lasting happiness; the wise person is the one who fears the Lord and keeps his commandments.

ecclesiastical province   A name given to a group of neighboring dioceses under the supervision of a metropolitan archbishop. The bishops of these groupings can meet in synods or provincial councils. *(CCC 887)*

ecclesiology   That part of theology which studies the nature, members, structure, and mission of the Church.

economy   The activities of the members of a particular group as they pertain to the management of the material means of production. Economic life ought to be at the service of the common good and should be conducted in a moral and just way so as to follow God's plan for human beings. *(CCC 2431)*

economy of salvation   The great plan of God by which his will and work is accomplished even without the help of human beings. This plan of salvation is described in Ephesians 1:3–14.

ecumenical council   The word *ecumenical* means "general" or "universal"; an ecumenical council is an assembly of all Catholic bishops ("the college of bishops") together with and under the authority of the Bishop of Rome, the pope. According to the Code of Canon Law: "The college of bishops exercises power over the universal Church in a solemn manner in an ecumenical council" (Canon 337, §1). The authority of the pope in regard to ecumenical councils is stated thus by the Code of Canon Law: "It is for the Roman Pontiff alone to convoke an ecumenical council, to preside over it personally or through others, to transfer, suspend or dissolve it, and to approve its decrees" (Canon 338, §1). There have been 21 ecumenical councils in the history of the Church. *(CCC 883–885)*   See **Trent, Council of; Vatican Council I; Vatican Council II.**

ecumenism   The movement which seeks to bring about the unity of all Christians. According to Vatican Council II, "The term 'ecumenical movement' indicates the initiatives and activities encouraged and organized, according to the various needs of the Church and as opportunities offer, to promote Christian unity" (Decree on Ecumenism, §4). *(CCC 820–822)*

ejaculation   A brief prayer that can be said from memory. Examples are "My Lord and my God" and "Jesus, have mercy on me."

ember days   A three-day cycle of prayer observed every quarter during which public thanks to God and prayers for the needs of all the people are offered. Before 1969, ember days were considered penitential in nature.

embryo   The human being in the first six weeks of development. The embryo must be treated as a person from the moment of conception. *(CCC 2274)*

Emmanuel   A Hebrew word (sometimes spelled Immanuel) which literally translates as "God with us." It is found as a prophecy in Isaiah 7:14, and as part of the angelic message in Matthew 1:23:
> "Look, the virgin shall conceive and bear a son,
> and they shall name him Emmanuel,"
> which means "God is with us."
> *(CCC 712)*

encyclical   A "circular letter" addressed by the pope to all members of the Church or to a specific group in the Church or, as is common for recent popes, to all men and women of good will. The subject matter of an encyclical is traditionally serious and important, a matter of doctrine or morals or discipline in the Church or a matter of grave importance (for example, peace and justice) to the whole world. For Catholics, the teachings in encyclicals "belong to the ordinary magisterium of the Church" (Pope Pius XII) and therefore demand internal assent and external respect.   See **magisterium.**

enmity   A sin of the flesh, cataloged in the Letter to the Galatians, that prevents a person from inheriting the kingdom of God. *(CCC 1852)*

envy   One of the capital or "deadly" sins, it is sadness or melancholy at the gifts (natural and supernatural), good fortune, or success of another precisely because they are seen as a loss to oneself or a diminishment of one's own excellence; it is a violation of the virtue of charity. *(CCC 2538)*

eparchy   A term used in the Eastern Church to signify a diocese. *(CCC 833)*

epiclesis   Intercessory prayer in which the priest asks God the Father to send down the Holy Spirit so that the bread and wine at Mass may be changed to the body and blood of Jesus Christ. *(CCC 1105)*

Epiphany   A liturgical feast celebrated on January 6 (or in the United States on a Sunday between January 2 and January 8) commemorating the manifestation of Christ to the Gentiles in the person of the magi and his divinity manifested at his baptism as well as at the marriage feast of Cana. It is a feast of ancient origin, especially in the East, and in many countries is the occasion for special celebrations and the exchange of gifts. *(CCC 528)*

episcopal conferences   An assembly of the bishops of a region or a country who join together to address issues of mutual concern. Vatican II recommended the establishment of episcopal conferences for the entire Church. *(CCC 887)*

episcopate   The office of a bishop or the period of time during which a bishop serves in that office.

epistles   See **letters (New Testament)**.

eschatology   *Eschata* is Greek for "last things"; eschatology is that part of theology which studies "the last things," such as death, judgment, heaven, hell, purgatory, the resurrection of the body, the Second Coming of Christ. *(CCC 1020–1041)*

eternal life   Participation in the state of endless happiness which comes to fullness in heaven.

ethics   The laws of right conduct.

Eucharist   One of the seven sacraments of the Church, indeed the greatest of the sacraments, described by the Church in this way: "The Most Holy Eucharist is the most august sacrament, in which Christ the Lord himself is contained, offered and received, and by which the Church constantly lives and grows. The Eucharistic Sacrifice, the memorial of the death and resurrection of the Lord, in which the sacrifice of the cross is perpetuated over the centuries, is the summit and the source of all Christian worship and life; it signifies and effects the unity of the people of God and achieves the building up of the Body of Christ. The other sacraments and all the ecclesiastical works of the apostolate are closely related to the Holy Eucharist and are directed to it" (Canon 897).

Although the Eucharist is one sacrament, there are three essential aspects to which the Church points: (1) It is a sacrifice; in the words of Vatican Council II: "At the Last Supper, on the night when he was betrayed, our Savior instituted the Eucharistic sacrifice of his Body and Blood. This he did in order to perpetuate the sacrifice of the Cross throughout the ages until he should come again…" (Constitution on the Sacred Liturgy, §47). (2) It is a communion: Christ himself, the Bread of Life, is really and truly present under the appearances of bread and wine and comes to the believer in Holy Communion as spiritual food. (3) It is real presence; for Christ himself is present in the Eucharistic species and abides among us, and is worthy of our adoration, gratitude, and love.

The Church calls the faithful to respond in faith to these three aspects of the Eucharist: "The faithful are to hold the Eucharist in highest honor, taking part in the celebration of the Most August Sacrifice, receiving the sacrament devoutly and frequently, and worshiping it with supreme adoration...." (Canon 898). *(CCC 1322–1327)* See **Mass.**

Eucharistic celebration   The central celebration of the Church's life by which the sacrifice of Christ on the cross is made present. *(CCC 1341–1344)*

Eucharistic Congress   A national or international conference held to promote devotion to the Holy Eucharist. The first Eucharistic Congress was held in France in 1931.

Eucharistic ministers   Persons who preside or assist at the Eucharistic assembly. Christ is always the principal agent of the Eucharist, but priests acting in his stead represent him. Other Eucharistic ministers include readers, those who bring up the offerings, and those who give Communion. *(CCC 1348)*

euthanasia   From a Greek word which means "easy death," euthanasia is now defined in a variety of ways. According to the Congregation for the Doctrine of the Faith in its Declaration on Euthanasia (1980), a strict definition is as follows: "By euthanasia is understood an action or an omission which of itself and by intention causes death, in order that all suffering may in this way be eliminated." Concerning the morality of euthanasia defined in this way, the Declaration says: "It is necessary to state firmly once more that nothing and no one can in any way permit the killing of an innocent human being, whether a fetus or an embryo, an infant or an adult, an older person or one suffering from an incurable disease, or a person who is dying. Furthermore, no one is permitted to ask for this act of killing, either for himself or herself or for another person entrusted to his or her care, nor can he or she consent to it, either explicitly or implicitly. Nor can any authority legitimately recommend or permit such an action. For it is a question of the divine law, an offense against the dignity of the human person, a crime, against life, and an attack on humanity." *(CCC 2276–2279)*

evangelical counsels   These are voluntary poverty, chastity, and obedience, seen as a means to the attainment of perfection and which are to be practiced in keeping with each person's vocation. *(CCC 914–915)*

evangelization   The proclamation of the Gospel, especially to those people who have never heard it; concretely, according to Pope Paul VI in his letter on evangelization, "Evangelizing means to bring the good news into all the strata of humanity, and through its influence transforming humanity from within and making it new....But there is no new humanity if there are not first of all new persons renewed by baptism, and by lives lived according to the Gospel" (Evangelization, §18).

evil   The absence of perfection: physical evil exists as when creation has not reached perfection, as in blindness; moral evil enters the world as a product of sin. In no way is God the cause of moral evil. *(CCC 309)*

evolution   The scientific theory of organic evolution holds that existing forms of vegetable, animal, and human life developed from more primitive organisms; this theory has not been completely proven, and many questions remain. Even if it were to be proven beyond a shadow of a doubt, however, it does not necessarily stand in opposition to the Bible or Christian faith. While some Christian theologians and communities teach that evolutionary theory cannot be accepted by a Christian, others (including many Catholics) affirm that the theory may be judged on its own merits as long as there is no denial of the basic truth of revelation: namely, that God is the immediate Creator of the human soul. *(CCC 362–368)*   See **soul.**

ex cathedra   From the Latin meaning "from the chair." When the pope speaks ex cathedra in matters of faith and morals, he is infallible.

examination of conscience   A methodical and prayerful review of one's life and actions to determine how they conform to God's will. Usually a preliminary to confession.

excommunication   A penalty imposed by the Church for serious offenses; by force of this penalty, as the Code of Canon Law points out, "An excommunicated person is forbidden: 1° to have any ministerial participation in celebrating the Eucharistic Sacrifice or in any other ceremonies whatever of public worship; 2° to celebrate the sacraments and sacramentals and to receive the sacraments; 3° to discharge any ecclesiastical offices, ministries or functions whatsoever, or to place acts of governance" (Canon 1331, §1). *(CCC 1463)*

Exodus, Book of   The second book of the Bible; the word means "departure," and this book describes the departure of the Israelites from Egypt and their wandering through the desert to Mount Sinai. Five parts are discernible in this book: events in Egypt before the Exodus, leaving Egypt and journeying to Mount Sinai, the promulgation of the Mosaic Law, reconciliation and renewal of the covenant, and construction of the tabernacle.

exorcism   The public rite of driving out evil spirits in the name of Jesus Christ according to the form authorized by the Church. In a simple form, exorcism is performed at baptism. *(CCC 1673)*

exposition of the Blessed Sacrament   A ceremony of Scripture readings, hymns, prayers, and silent meditation in which the consecrated host is displayed, usually in a monstrance, for all the faithful to see. Exposition of the Blessed Sacrament has traditionally been part of Benediction, Corpus Christi processions, perpetual adoration, and Forty Hours devotion.

extravagance   Excessive and wasteful expenditures which are seen as violations of respect for other persons and their goods. *(CCC 2409)*

extreme unction   See **anointing of the sick.**

F

faith   One of the three theological (God-given and God-directed) virtues or powers, infused into the soul with sanctifying grace, by which, in the words of Vatican Council I, "a person is enabled to believe that what God has revealed is true—not because its intrinsic worth is seen with the rational light of reason—but because of the authority of God who reveals it, that God who can neither deceive nor be deceived." This definition is amplified by the description of faith given by Vatican Council II: "'The obedience of faith' (see Romans 1:5; Romans 16:26; 2 Corinthians 10:5–6) must be given to God as he reveals himself. By faith man freely commits his entire self to God, making 'the full submission of his intellect and will to God who reveals,' and willingly assenting to the Revelation given by him. Before this faith can be exercised, man must have the grace of God to move and assist him; he must have the interior helps of the Holy Spirit, who moves the heart and converts it to God, who opens the eyes of the mind and 'makes it easy for all to accept and believe the truth.' The same Holy Spirit constantly perfects faith by his gifts, so that Revelation may be more and more profoundly understood" (Dogmatic Constitution on Divine Revelation, §5). *(CCC 1814–1816)*

faith, professions of   Summaries and symbols of the essential elements of the Church's principal truths. The first profession of faith is made at baptism. Different articulations of faith, or creeds, have been formulated in different eras; for example, the Apostles' Creed, the Nicene Creed, the Athanasian Creed. *(CCC 186–199)*

faithful, the   Those members of the Church who have been united in baptism to Christ and to other members of the Mystical Body. Because of their membership, the faithful have certain rights and obligations. *(CCC 871–873)*

faithfulness   One of the fruits of the Holy Spirit as listed in Galatians 5:22–23. *(CCC 1832)*

Fall, the   A term used to describe the original sin of Adam and Eve as described in Genesis. *(CCC 55)*   See **original sin.**

family, Christian   Considering the family from a Christian viewpoint, Pope John Paul II, in his encyclical *Familiaris consortio* (On the Family), points out that the family is (1) a community of persons: a community which must strive for ever deeper communion through the power of love; (2) a school of humanity where each member learns to take care of the others and where mutual service is highlighted; (3) a place of reconciliation where conflict and division can be healed; (4) a vital cell of society where young citizens learn the values of justice, respect, and charity. *(CCC 2204–2206)*

family planning, natural   See **natural family planning.**

family, rights of   The family is a natural society in its own right. As such it possesses certain fundamental rights which should be respected both by other natural societies and by individuals. After the Roman Synod of 1981, at which bishops from different parts of the world shared their views on the family, Pope John Paul II issued "a charter of family rights." These rights are as follows:

- The right to exist and progress as a family, that is, the right of every human being, even if he or she is poor, to found a family and to have adequate means to support it.
- The right to exercise its responsibility regarding the transmission of life and to educate children.
- The right to the intimacy of conjugal life.
- The right to the stability of the bond and the institution of marriage.

- The right to believe in and profess one's faith and to propagate it.
- The right to bring up children in accord with the family's own traditions and religious values, with the necessary instruments, means, and institutions.
- The right, especially of the poor and sick, to obtain physical, social, political, and economic security.
- The right to housing suitable for living family life in a suitable way.
- The right to expression and representation, either directly or through associations, before the economic, social, and cultural authorities.
- The right to form associations with other families and institutions in order to fulfill the family's role suitably.
- The right to protect minors by adequate legislation from harmful drugs, pornography, and the like.
- The right to wholesome recreation of a kind that also fosters family values.
- The right of the elderly to a worthy life and a worthy death.
- The right to emigrate as a family in search of a better life.

(CCC 2207–2213)

famine Extreme starvation sometimes resulting in death. The acceptance by human society of widespread famine is a grave injustice. *(CCC 2269)*

fast, Eucharistic Abstention from food and drink (except water) for one hour before the reception of Holy Communion. This fast may be shortened to as much as fifteen minutes for those who are sick or who have a similar compelling reason.

fasting A traditional form of penance among religious people, seen as a way of purifying the spirit or of sacrificing some good to the Lord; it consists of one's free choice to limit the kind or quality of food or drink. The Gospel emphasizes, especially, the motivation for fasting: namely, that it be done not for vain display but as an expression of interior religious attitudes (Matthew 6:1–18). According to the general law of the Church, Catholics (from the completion of their fourteenth year to the completion of their fifty-ninth) are obliged to fast on Ash Wednesday and on Good Friday. The law of fasting allows only one full meal a day, but does not prohibit taking some food at breakfast and lunch. *(CCC 1434, 1438)* See **abstinence**.

Fathers of the Church   Saintly, orthodox writers of the early Church (from the first to approximately the end of the seventh century); their writings had a major impact on the doctrinal development of the Church. They are usually divided into the Latin Fathers, including such giants as Saint Irenaeus (130–200), Saint Ambrose (340–397), Saint Augustine (354–430), and the Greek fathers, including Saint Clement of Alexandria (150–215), Saint Athanasius (297–373), Saint John Chrysostom (347–407). *(CCC 250)*

Fátima   See **shrines of Our Lady.**

fear   Disturbance of the mind because of impending evil. Grave fear can invalidate marriage vows or ordination, and can lessen responsibility for one's actions. *(CCC 1746)*

fear of God   A gift of the Holy Spirit whose attainment results in an attitude of respect and awe toward God. *(CCC 1831)*

feast days   Popularly, a day set aside to honor God, Mary, the saints, or angels. In liturgical terms, a feast is one category of liturgical observance, with a solemnity being a festival of higher observance, and a memorial being a lower order of observance.

Filioque   A Latin word meaning *and from the son* which signifies the theological view that the Holy Spirit proceeded from both the Father and the Son. This phrase was added to the Nicene Creed in the sixth century; the Greek Orthodox Church strongly objected to its inclusion. This point of contention between Eastern and Western Churches still exists. *(CCC 246)*

fire   A symbol of transforming energy and purification. It signifies Holy Spirit. *(CCC 696, 7110)*

First Communion   The solemn observance of one who is receiving the Eucharist for the first time. For children, this usually occurs on reaching the age of reason.

First Fridays   A devotion in honor of the Sacred Heart in which a person receives Holy Communion for nine consecutive first Fridays of each month. According to a promise made to Saint Margaret Mary Alacoque, a person following this observance will have the grace of a final repentance.

fisherman's ring   The papal ring engraved with a picture of Saint Peter fishing from a boat and the pope's name. It is destroyed on the death of the pope.

font, baptismal   A container for holding the baptismal water; it is usually made of durable material and properly ornamented. Every parish church is to have a baptismal font. In recent years the baptismal font has been given a prominent and visible place in the church building.   See **baptistery.**

forgery   Falsely producing another's signature or work and claiming it as genuine for personal gain. Forgery is morally illicit and corrupts the common good. *(CCC 2409)*

fornication   Sexual intercourse between a man and a woman who are not married. According to Christian tradition, clearly stated in the New testament (see, for example, Ephesians 5:1–7 and 1 Thessalonians 4:3–8), fornication is morally wrong. This tradition was aptly summarized by the American Catholic bishops in their pastoral reflections on the moral life, To Live in Christ Jesus:

"Our Christian tradition holds the sexual union between husband and wife in high honor, regarding it as a special expression of their covenanted love which mirrors God's love for His people and Christ's love for the Church. But like many things human, sex is ambivalent. It can be either creative or destructive. Sexual intercourse is a moral and human good only within marriage; outside marriage it is wrong" (§50). *(CCC 2353)*   See **chastity.**

fortitude   One of the four cardinal (or "hinge") virtues and one of the gifts of the Holy Spirit; it is courage in doing good despite the dangers or difficulties that stand in one's way. *(CCC 1808)*

fortunetelling   Unhealthy seeking of knowledge of the future through recourse to horoscopes, astrology, palm reading, consultation with mediums, tea leaves, and so on. All these practices conceal a false desire for power over future events and contradict the confidence with which we should put ourselves into the hands of divine Providence. *(CCC 2116)*

Forty Hours devotion   An approximately three-day period of worship before the Blessed Sacrament as it is exposed in a monstrance and displayed on an altar of reservation. The forty hours commemorates the length of time that Jesus lay in the tomb. Forty Hours devotion originated in Milan about 1527.

Franciscan crown   A rosary of seven decades introduced in 1422, and said in honor of the seven joys of the Blessed Virgin. This rosary is also known as the seraphic rosary.

fraternal harmony   Right relationships among groups and members of groups so that good will is maintained. *(CCC 2213)*

fraud   In moral theology, fraud may be defined as deception or trickery by which the contractual rights of another are harmed. It is a violation of justice and truth. *(CCC 2409)*

freedom, human   According to the teaching of the Church, the human person, made in the image and likeness of God, is not subject to determinism but possesses true moral freedom of choice: that is, the human person, when acting in a truly human way, is able to choose or not to choose a certain course of action or is able to choose freely between two alternative courses of action. The importance of human freedom is emphasized in Vatican II: "Only in freedom that man can turn himself towards what is good...But that which is truly freedom is an exceptional sign of the image of God in man....Man's dignity therefore requires him to act out of conscious and free choice, as moved and drawn in a personal way from within, and not by blind impulses in himself or by mere external constraint" (Pastoral Constitution on the Church in the Modern World, §17). *(CCC 1731–1732)*

freedom of conscience   The dignity of the human person consists in the fact that he or she can intelligently and freely choose God's will and God's law. On a practical level, conscience plays a critical role in this choice. Conscience should be free from all external constraints and force. According to Vatican II: "...man sees and recognizes the demands of the divine law. He is bound to follow this conscience faithfully in all his activity so that he may come to God, who is his last end. Therefore he must not be forced to act contrary to his conscience. Nor must he be prevented from acting according to his conscience, especially in religious matters" (Declaration on Religious Liberty, §3). *(CCC 1732, 1782)*

freedom, religious   In matters of religious conviction and worship of God the human person should be free to follow the dictates of his or her conscience and should not be forced by civil authority to act against these dictates nor be restrained from acting in accord with them, provided there is no serious danger to the common good. Vatican II in its Declaration on Religious Liberty says that the right to religious freedom in civil society "means that all men should be immune from coercion on the part of individuals, social groups and every human power so that, within due limits, no body is forced to act against his convictions nor is anyone to be restrained from acting in accordance with his convictions in religious matters in private or in public, alone or in associations with others..." (§2). *(CCC 2108)*

Freemasonary   A secret organization founded in England on the traditions of the guild of masons. Aspects of this organization have

.long been associated with hostility to the Catholic Church, and thus membership in Masonic lodges is prohibited to Catholics.

free will   The human faculty to choose among several courses of action and thus the underlying basis for moral responsibility.

friar   A member of one of the mendicant orders who pursue an ideal of poverty. Friars are distinct from monks because they pursue a pastoral ministry and can move around according to need. Dominicans and Franciscans are examples of orders of friars.

friendship   A gift of self to others that mirrors the generous friendship of our Lord for each of us. In a spiritual sense, such relationships include mutual affection, service, and conversations that help one another achieve spiritual communion. *(CCC 1939)*

fruits of the Holy Spirit   Qualities that are activated in human beings through the workings of the Holy Spirit: charity, joy, peace, patience, kindness, goodness, faithfulness, gentleness, and self-control. *(CCC 1832)*

fundamentalists   This term is used to refer to a variety of Protestant individuals or communities; generally speaking, fundamentalists are conservative evangelicals who insist on the literal interpretation of the Scriptures, place great emphasis on the "born again" experience, the Second Coming of Christ, and personal missionary activity. They tend to be critical of liberal Protestant churches and of the Catholic Church.

funeral rites   The liturgical ceremonies that the Church provides for her deceased members, including the Mass of Christian Burial, the final commendation, and prayers at the grave; the emphasis is on Christian hope, resurrection, and eternal life. *(CCC 1684–1690)*   See **burial, Christian; cremation; wake.**

G

Galatians   See **letters (New Testament).**

gambling; games of chance   In Catholic moral theology, gambling is considered a kind of contract (technically, an aleatory contract, from the Latin word *alea* meaning "chance"). It is a contract by which the participants in a game of chance agree that the winner receives a certain prize or sum of money. Though some Christian churches condemn gambling absolutely, the Catholic tradition has held that it may be morally justified provided the following conditions are observed: (a) the stakes belong to the one who gambles and may be freely used by him or her; (b) there is no fraud or deceit involved, such as marked cards, loaded dice, collusion with the operator; (c) there is equal risk and equal opportunity for all participants; (d) there is no just prohibition by the civil authorities. At the same time, Catholic moralists warn that gambling may give rise to serious abuses, especially for those who are compulsive or addictive gamblers. *(CCC 2413)*

Gehenna   A valley south of Jerusalem known for its worship of the god, Moloch. It is used in the New Testament to denote hell.

generosity   One of the twelve traditional fruits of the Holy Spirit as listed in Galatians, generosity encourages a sense of values and a willingness to do what may not be popular. *(CCC 1832)*

Genesis, Book of   The first book of the Bible; the first eleven chapters treat of the origin of the world and the human race, the original state of innocence and the Fall, the promise of salvation, the Deluge, and the Tower of Babel; the remaining chapters treat the early history of Israel, especially outstanding leaders, such as Abraham, Isaac, Jacob, and Joseph. *(CCC 289)*

genocide   The extermination of a people, nation, or ethnic minority which is an unprincipled and inexcusable act. *(CCC 2313)*

gentleness   An emotional state in which one shows a forbearance of the acts of others. It is one of the twelve fruits of the Holy Spirit. *(CCC 736)*

Gentiles   A word used frequently in the Bible, it means "pagans" or "foreigners" or simply people who were not Jews. In the Old Testament there is evidence of hostility and distrust between Jews and Gentiles. In the New Testament it is clear that Jesus first directed his disciples to preach the Good News only to "the lost sheep of the house of Israel" (Matthew 10:6), but gradually extended their mission to the Gentiles—"all nations"—as well (Matthew 28:19). The extension of the Church to Gentiles is spoken of in Acts of the Apostles (see chapters 8–12) and in many of the New Testament letters. *(CCC 58, 60)*

genuflection   A bending of the knee as a sign of adoration and reverence; it is a Catholic practice to genuflect when entering a church where the Blessed Sacrament is reserved or when passing before the Blessed Sacrament. *(CCC 1378)*

Gethsemani   A garden at the foot of the Mount of Olives where Jesus suffered the agony in the garden and where he was betrayed.

gift of tongues The ability to speak in a language that is not known to the speaker. Mentioned in Acts and Corinthians, speaking in tongues is a means of praising God and an indication of his approval.

gifts of the Holy Spirit According to Catholic teaching, the gifts of the Holy Spirit are supernatural graces freely given to the soul with sanctifying grace and enable the graced person to respond freely and promptly to the inspirations of God. The seven gifts are wisdom, understanding, counsel, fortitude, knowledge, piety, and fear of the Lord. *(CCC 1831)*

gluttony One of the capital or deadly sins, it is an unreasonable, disordered desire for food and drink, usually expressed by eating and drinking to excess. *(CCC 1866)* See **temperance.**

Gnosticism A heresy which teaches that the body is corrupt and that salvation comes through hidden knowledge. *(CCC 285)*

God Catholic teaching on the nature of God and his divine attributes is admirably expressed by Vatican I: "The holy, Catholic, apostolic Roman Church believes and professes that there is one true, living God, the Creator and Lord of heaven and earth. He is almighty, eternal, beyond measure, incomprehensible, and infinite in intellect, will and every perfection. Since he is one unique spiritual substance, entirely simple and unchangeable, he must be declared distinct from the world, perfectly happy in himself and by his very nature, and inexpressibly exalted over all things that exist or can be conceived other than himself." In the fullness of revelation, moreover, it is known that the one God subsists in three equal persons, the Father and the Son and the Holy Spirit. *(CCC 199–221)* See **Holy Trinity.**

godparent See **baptismal sponsor.**

good That which is of the higher ethical worth and value.

Good Friday The Friday in Holy Week that commemorates the Passion and death of Jesus Christ. It is the one day of the year on which Mass is not celebrated; the three-part Good Friday ceremony consists of the reading of the Passion from the Gospel of John, the Veneration of the Cross, and a Communion service. The Eucharist consumed on Good Friday was consecrated on Holy Thursday.

goodness One of the twelve traditional fruits of the Holy Spirit by which one grows in positive thoughts, feelings, and words. *(CCC 1832)*

Gospel From an Old English word *god-spel*, that is, good news, a Gospel is one of the four divinely inspired accounts of the life, teaching, suffering, death, and Resurrection of Jesus Christ. It is customary to describe the Gospels of Matthew, Mark, and Luke as "synoptic Gospels" because they give a "synopsis" or similar view of the life and teaching of Jesus; the Gospel of John reflects a different apostolic tradition. The Gospels are held in high esteem by the Church; passages from them are read in the Eucharistic Liturgy and in the formal celebration of all the sacraments. *(CCC 125–127)*

grace A biblical and theological term used in a wide variety of ways. According to Catholic teaching, grace is a supernatural gift of God bestowed upon a person with a view to salvation and sanctification. Understood in this sense, there are three kinds of grace: (1) uncreated grace refers to the abiding presence of the Holy Trinity in the souls of the just; (2) created or sanctifying grace is a created sharing or participation in the life of God himself; (3) actual grace is a transient help of God which enlightens the mind and strengthens the will to do good and avoid evil. Grace is given to human beings through the merits of Jesus Christ and is communicated by the Holy Spirit. The principal means of growing in grace are prayer, the sacraments (especially the Eucharist), and good works. Sanctifying grace is lost by the commission of mortal sin. *(CCC 1996–2005)*

Guadalupe, Our Lady of See shrines of Our Lady.

guilt A state or condition of mind and soul that follows upon a personal, free, deliberate transgression of God's law; awareness that one has done wrong gives rise to what are often referred to as "guilt feelings," that is, feelings of spiritual unrest and discomfort. Guilt feelings, in their turn, urge the sinful person to repent and to seek reconciliation, and thus once again to experience inner peace. In contrast to true guilt which follows upon actual sin, false or neurotic guilt seems to arise from a general lack of self-worth or a scrupulous conviction that one is almost always in sin. *(CCC 1420–1421)*

H

habit A disposition to some thought or act facilitated by repetition. Habit makes resistance to the performance of an act more difficult and thus is one of the factors to be taken into account in evaluating the morality of an act. *(CCC 1735)*

hagiography Research into and writing about the lives of the saints.

Hail Mary The best-known and most popular prayer in honor of the Blessed Virgin Mary, it is composed of verses from the Gospel of Luke (see Luke 1:28, 42) and a centuries'-old petition formulated by the Church. "Hail Mary, full of grace. The Lord is with thee. Blessed art thou among women, and blessed is the fruit of thy womb, Jesus. Holy Mary, Mother of God, pray for us sinners, now and at the hour of our death. Amen." *(CCC 2676–2677)*

hair shirt   An inner garment made usually of goat's hair and worn next to the skin as a form of penance. This form of mortification is no longer practiced in favor of other forms of self-discipline.

halo   The circle of light around the head of saints, the Blessed Virgin Mary, and Jesus Christ as used in various artistic representations.   See **aureole.**

happiness   True happiness is not found in riches, power, fame, or well-being but in God alone. *(CCC 45, 1024)*

hatred   In moral theology, hatred is deliberately desiring harm or evil on another person. It is contrary to charity, indeed the direct opposite of love of one's neighbor and love of one's enemies as taught by Jesus in the Sermon on the Mount (see Matthew 5:44–45). *(CCC 2303)*

health   In moral theology, a basic moral principle is that the human person has a moral responsibility to take reasonable care of his or her health; health is used in the holistic sense, that is, the care of and harmony between one's physical, mental, and spiritual capacities. *(CCC 2288–2290)*

Heart of Jesus, adoration of   The Church venerates and honors the Heart of Jesus as a symbol of his love for us. *(CCC 2669)*

heaven   The dwelling place of God and the angels and the place of eternal happiness for all those who have been saved; it consists primarily in the beatific vision, the face-to-face vision of God, the possession of eternal life and peace; in addition, the blessed in heaven rejoice in the knowledge, love, and enjoyment of creatures. *(CCC 326, 1023–1029)*

Hebrews, Letter to the   See **letters (New Testament).**

hell   The dwelling place of Satan and the evil spirits and of all those who die deliberately alienated from God. The primary punishment of hell is the pain of loss: the deprivation of the face-to-face vision of God and eternal happiness with him. There is also the pain of sense caused by an outside agent, described as fire in the New Testament (see Matthew 25:41 and Mark 9:43). Hell is the dire destination for one who freely chooses his or her own will against the will of God. *(CCC 1033–1037)*

heresy   Formal heresy is the deliberate and obstinate denial by a baptized person of any truth which must be believed as a matter of divine and Catholic faith; it is a grave sin and incurs the penalty of excommunication (see Canon 1364, §1). Reference is sometimes made to "material heresy" as the condition of those baptized persons who, in good faith and through no fault of their own, accept heretical doctrine; but, since they are in good faith, in reality there is no sin and no excommunication. *(CCC 2089)*   See **excommunication.**

hermit   One who follows a solitary life marked by prayer and austerity. Hermits were the forerunners of monks who today lead a communal life.   See **anchoress; anchorite.**

heroic act of charity   The offering to God of a person's works, prayers, and sufferings for the benefit of the souls in purgatory. This action can be revoked at will.

hierarchy   This term, as applied to the systematic arrangement of authority within the Catholic Church, is used in two ways: (1) the hierarchy of holy orders: namely, those ordained as bishops, priests, or deacons to carry out the sacramental and pastoral ministry of the Church; and (2) the hierarchy of jurisdiction: namely, the pope and the bishops in communion with him to carry out, by divine institution, the teaching and governing office in the Church. Vatican II treats of this entire matter in chapter 3 of the Dogmatic Constitution on the Church. *(CCC 874–887)*

holiness   A state of spiritual progress that is marked by an ever more intimate union with Christ. All Christians are called toward this fullness of Christian life. *(2013)*

holy days of obligation   Days especially set aside for the worship of God: notably, each Sunday of the year and other feast days designated by the Church. According to the Code of Canon Law: "Sunday is the day on which the paschal mystery is celebrated in light of the apostolic tradition and is to be observed as the foremost holy day of obligation in the universal Church. Also to be observed are the day of the Nativity of Our Lord Jesus Christ, the Epiphany, the Ascension and the Most Holy Body and Blood of Christ, Holy Mary Mother of God and her Immaculate Conception and Assumption, Saint Joseph, the apostles Saint Peter and Paul, and finally, All Saints" (Canon 1246, §1). The Code then goes on to note this practical principle: "However, the conference of bishops can abolish certain holy days of obligation or transfer them to a Sunday with prior approval of the Apostolic See" (Canon 1246, §2). The holy days to be observed in the United States are the Nativity of Our Lord Jesus Christ (December 25), Solemnity of Mary the Mother of God (January 1), Ascension of the Lord (sixth Thursday after Easter), Assumption of the Virgin Mary (August 15), All Saints (November 1), Immaculate Conception of the Virgin Mary (December 8). (In Canada, Christmas and New Year's Day are holy days. Others formerly specified have either been made nonobligatory or transferred to the Sunday following.)

The obligation of Catholics on these days is as follows: "On Sundays and other holy days of obligation the faithful are bound to participate in the Mass; they are also to abstain from those labors and business concerns which impede the worship to be rendered to God, the joy which is proper to the Lord's Day, or the relaxation of mind and body" (Canon 1247). *(CCC 2180–2188)*

Holy Land   The land in which Christ lived, died, and rose from the dead. This expression came into use in the Middle Ages.

holy orders   One of the seven sacraments of the Church, it is defined thus in the Code of Canon Law: "By divine institution some among the Christian faithful are constituted sacred ministers through the sacrament of orders by means of the indelible character with which they are marked; accordingly they are consecrated and deputed to shepherd the people of God, each in accord with his own grade of orders, by fulfilling in the person of Christ the Head the functions of teaching, sanctifying and governing" (Canon 1008). "The orders are the episcopacy, the presbyterate [priesthood], and diaconate" (Canon 1009, §1). *(CCC 1536, 1546–1547)*   See **bishops; priest; deacon.**

Holy See   A term used to designate the pope as head of the universal Church and all those associated with him who assist in its administration.

Holy Spirit   The third person of the Holy Trinity, distinct from the Father and the Son but coequal and coeternal with them. The ancient faith of the Church concerning the Holy Spirit—professed in all of the Christian creeds—is beautifully summarized in Pope Paul VI's Credo of the People of God:

"We believe in the Holy Spirit, who is Lord and giver of life, who is adored and glorified with the Father and the Son. He spoke to us by the prophets; he was sent by Christ after his Resurrection and his Ascension to the Father; he illuminates, vivifies, protects and guides the Church." *(CCC 687–688, 691–701)*

Holy Trinity The most sublime and central doctrine of the Christian faith, namely, that there are three Persons—Father, Son, Holy Spirit—in one God. This doctrine is indicated in the Scriptures (see, for example, Matthew 28:18–20) and expressed in all of the Christian Creeds. The Catholic Church celebrates the feast of the Holy Trinity on the Sunday after Pentecost. *(CCC 249–256)*

holy water Water that is blessed by a priest for use by the people of God, ordinarily while one is blessing oneself with the sign of the cross; it is a symbol of spiritual cleansing and by custom is used in time of physical or spiritual dangers; it is used in all of the Church's blessings. *(CCC 1668)* See **blessing; sacramentals.**

Holy Week The week before Easter, it is called the "great week" of the Church's liturgical year; it begins with Passion (Palm) Sunday, celebrating Christ's entrance into Jerusalem to accomplish his paschal mystery (see John 12:12), and also includes the Easter Triduum: Holy Thursday, commemorating the institution of the Holy Eucharist and the institution of the priesthood; Good Friday, commemorating the Passion and death of Jesus Christ; and the Easter Vigil, celebrating his Resurrection. *(CCC 1168–1171)* See **Easter Vigil.**

Holy Year A year which the pope proclaims as a special time for pilgrimage and other holy acts that result in plenary indulgences. A Holy Year usually occurs every 25 years.

homily An integral part of the Mass, it is an instruction or sermon preached after the readings from Scripture; its purpose is to explain the Word of God and also to make application of that word to the lives of people today. *(CCC 2033)*

homosexuality, morality of Homosexuality is defined as sexual attraction to or relationship with members of one's own sex; concerning the moral dimensions of homosexuality, Catholic teaching distinguishes between homosexual orientations and homosexual activity, a distinction expressed in the American bishops' letter on the moral life: "Some persons find themselves through no fault of their own to have a homosexual orientation. Homosexuals, like everyone else, should not suffer from prejudice against their basic human rights. They have a right to respect, friendship, and justice. They should have an active role in the Christian community. Homosexual activity, however, as distinguished from homosexual orientation, is morally wrong. Like heterosexual persons, homosexuals are called to give witness to chastity, avoiding, with God's grace, behavior which is wrong for them, just as nonmarital sexual relations are wrong for heterosexuals" (To Life in Christ Jesus, §52). *(CCC 2357–2359)*

honor   The recognition by others of one's human dignity. Every person enjoys a natural right to name and reputation. *(CCC 2479)*

hope   One of the theological (God-given and God-directed) virtues or powers, infused into the soul with sanctifying grace, by which we are able confidently to expect eternal life, the fullness of glory with God, and all the means to attain it, because God is faithful to his promises. *(CCC 1817–1821)*   See **faith; charity.**

horoscope   A diagram of the planets and the signs of the zodiac used to tell the future. Serious and unhealthy reliance on horoscopes is not consonant with a belief in God's providential care. *(CCC 2116)*

hosanna   A word from the Hebrew meaning "save us, we pray"; it occurs during Mass, and during the blessing of the palms and the procession on Palm Sunday.

host, sacred   A term for the Eucharistic bread. The word *host* comes from the Latin "victim," and thus commemorates Christ's sacrifice for all.

hostages, taking of   The taking of other persons against their will in order to obtain concessions is an act of terror that subjects victims to intolerable pressures. Hostage-taking is a grave violation against charity and justice. *(CCC 2297)*

humility   The moral virtue by which one recognizes his or her absolute dependence on God, appreciates all of one's abilities and talents as gifts of God, and strives to use them in accord with his will and purpose. *(CCC 2540)*   See **pride.**

hyperdulia   The special honor given to the Blessed Virgin Mary in her role as the mother of God.

hypostasis   A term used to describe the substance of the Holy Trinity wherein the Father, Son, and Holy Spirit are distinct but united. *(CCC 252, 464–469)*

hypostatic union   Theologically speaking, a term indicating that the two natures of Jesus Christ (the divine and the human) are united to form one person.

I

icon   The Greek word for "image." An icon is an image of our Lord, our Lady, or one of the saints, painted or glazed on a flat surface and used in Eastern Churches in place of statues. *(CCC 1159–1162)*

iconoclasm   A heresy that arose in the eighth century declaring that the religious veneration of pictures and images was sacrilegious and advocating "image breaking" as a solution to the problem; in 787, at the Second Council of Nicea, the Church, while defining the distinction between adoration to be given to God alone and veneration to be paid to Mary or the other saints, declared that such veneration is, in reality, an act of piety not toward the image but toward the person represented.

idolatry   Giving to any creature the worship that is due to the one true God alone; it is a violation of the first commandment. *(CCC 2112–2114)*

Ignatius Loyola, Saint   Born in 1491, he was a Spanish soldier wounded in the battle of Pamplona in 1521; during his recuperation he received an extraordinary grace of conversion, gave up his military career, and committed himself in a special way to Christ and the Church; he founded the Society of Jesus (Jesuits) in 1534 and composed the world-famous Spiritual Exercises; he died in 1556 and was canonized in 1622; his feast day is celebrated on July 31.

ignorance   Lack of knowledge on the part of someone who is capable of having such knowledge. Ignorance can diminish a person's responsibility for a particular action or even nullify it. *(CCC 1735)*

IHS   A shortened form of the Greek for "Jesus."

Immaculate Conception   A belief of ancient origin in the Church, defined as a dogma in 1854 by Pope Pius IX in these words: "We declare, announce, and define that the doctrine which states that the Blessed Virgin Mary was preserved, in the first instant of her conception, by a singular grace and privilege of God omnipotent and because of the merits of Jesus Christ the Savior of the human race, free from all stain of original sin, is revealed by God and must be believed firmly and with constancy by all the faithful." The feast of Mary's Immaculate Conception is celebrated on December 8 and is a holy day of obligation for the universal Church. *(CCC 490–493)*

immortality of the soul   That characteristic of the soul by which it is free from death. The immortal or undying soul, reunites with the body at the final resurrection, and both share the eternal life of those who have been saved by the same sacrifice.

impediments to marriage   An impediment is an obstacle; according to the Code of Canon Law there are certain obstacles to a valid marriage. These are called "diriment impediments." The Code defines a diriment impediment in this way: "A diriment impediment renders a person incapable of contracting marriage validly" (Canon 1073). The Code lists these impediments in Canons 1083 to 1094. Ordinarily, a person may receive a dispensation from impediments arising from ecclesiastical (Church) law, provided there is sufficient reason, by requesting it from one's diocesan bishop; in several cases, however, only the Holy See can grant a dispensation. Impediments arising from natural law (for example, impotence) cannot be given a dispensation.

impotence   The inability to perform the sexual act of intercourse; it is called antecedent impotence when it existed before the marriage; it is called perpetual when it cannot be corrected without serious danger to health or life. According to the Code of Canon Law, "Antecedent and perpetual impotence to have intercourse, whether on the part of the man or of the woman, which is either absolute or relative, of its very nature invalidates marriage" (Canon 1084, §1).

imprimatur   An official approval, usually by a diocesan authority, to publish a book or a pamphlet. This sanction is given to catechetical works, theology texts, and works dealing with Sacred Scripture according to canon law.

impurity   A term used for unlawful acts of sexual pleasure. Sins against purity can be committed in thought or action. *(CCC 1852)*

inadvertence   Unintentional lack of knowledge occurring when one knows a thing but is not able to think of it in the circumstances. Inadvertence can diminish a person's responsibility for an act. *(CCC 1735)*

incardination   The act by which a cleric is subordinated to his diocese and bishop or a religious to his community superiors.

Incarnation   The basic Christian doctrine which affirms that Jesus Christ, the eternal Son of God, the second Person of the Holy Trinity, took human flesh from his human mother Mary and that he is at one and the same time fully God and fully man. There are two natures, human and divine, permanently united in one divine Person, Jesus Christ. *(CCC 461–463)*

incense   A grainy substance made from the resins of various plants that gives off an aromatic odor when burned; used in divine worship as a symbol of the ascent of prayer to God. *(CCC 2581)*

incest   Intimate sexual relations between relatives or in-laws within a degree that prohibits marriage between them. In both Scripture (see 1 Corinthians 5:1, 4-5) and moral theology this is considered an especially grave moral evil because of its severe impact on family relationships. *(CCC 2388–2389)*

incredulity   Unbelief in a revealed truth when one knowingly neglects to make a reasonable inquiry into it or when one willingly refuses to assent to it. *(CCC 2089)*

indifference   Neglect of the practices of religious life and unconcern about observing the Precepts of the Church. *(CCC 2994)*

indulgence   According to the Code of Canon Law: "An indulgence is a remission before God of the temporal punishment for sin the guilt of which is already forgiven, which a properly disposed member of the Christian faithful obtains under certain and definite conditions with the help of the Church which, as the minister of redemption, dispenses and applies authoritatively the treasury of the satisfactions of Christ and the saints" (Canon 992). The Code also notes that "an indulgence is either partial or plenary in as far as it frees from the temporal punishment due to sin either partly or totally" (Canon 993) and that "the faithful can gain partial or plenary indulgences for themselves or apply them for the dead by way of suffrage" (Canon 994). The most complete modern teaching of the Church on indulgences is found in the Apostolic Constitution on Indulgences issued by Pope Paul VI after Vatican Council II (1967). *(CCC 1471–1473)* See **purgatory; temporal punishment.**

indult   Special permission given by the Holy See, usually for a specific period of time, to bishops or others to do something not usually permitted by the general law of the Church.

inerrence of Scripture   The teaching of the Church concerning the truth of the Sacred Scriptures, expressed by Vatican Council II in this way: "Since, therefore, all that the inspired authors, or sacred writers, affirm should be regarded as affirmed by the Holy Spirit. We must acknowledge that the book of Scripture, firmly, faithfully, and without error, teach that truth which God, for the sake of our salvation, wished to see confided to the sacred Scriptures" (Dogmatic Constitution on Divine Revelation, §11). *(CCC 106–107)* See **inspiration, biblical.**

infallibility   A doctrine of the Church, that the Church, through the power of God, is preserved from the possibility and liability of error in teaching matters of faith and morals. This charism is present in a singular way in the Bishop of Rome—the pope—and in the college of bishops. The doctrine is carefully described by Vatican Council II in its Dogmatic Constitution on the Church:

"This infallibility, however, with which the divine redeemer wished to endow his Church in defining doctrine pertaining to faith and morals, is co-extensive with the deposit of revelation, which must be religiously guarded and loyally and courageously expounded. The Roman Pontiff, head of the college of bishops, enjoys this infallibility in virtue of his office, when, as supreme pastor and teacher of all the faithful—who confirms his brethren in the faith (see Luke 22:32)—he proclaims in an absolute decision a doctrine pertaining to faith or morals. For that reason his definitions are rightly said to be irreformable by their very nature and not by reason of the assent of the Church, in as much as they were made with the assistance of the Holy Spirit promised to him in the person of blessed Peter himself; and as a consequence they are in no way in need of the approval of others, and do not admit of appeal to any other tribunal. For in such a case the Roman Pontiff does not utter a pronouncement as a private person, but rather does he expound and defend the teaching of the Catholic Church as the supreme teacher of the universal Church, in whom the Church's charism of infallibility is present in a singular way. The infallibility promised to the Church is also present in the body of bishops when, together with Peter's successor, they exercise the supreme teaching office. Now, the assent of the Church can never be lacking to such definitions on account of the same Holy Spirit's influence, through which Christ's whole flock is maintained in the unity of the faith and makes progress in it" (§25). *(CCC 889–891)*

infant baptism   See **baptism of infants.**

infused virtues   The virtues of faith, hope, and charity that are infused in the soul through sanctifying grace. These virtues are not acquired by any human effort so that even baptized infants possess the infused virtues.

ingratitude   Failure or refusal to acknowledge divine love and to return this love in measure. *(CCC 2094)*

Inquisition   Historically, a legal court of the Church whose purpose was to investigate and prosecute persons guilty of formal heresy. The Inquisition came into existence in 1232; its main purpose was to call those professing heresy to repentance. There were a number of safeguards for the accused, including the right to counsel. If the heretic repented, an ordinary penance such as fasting was imposed. If the heretic did not repent, he then received a more severe penance such as the confiscation of goods or imprisonment or even death at the stake. Unfortunately—and this was especially true of the Spanish Inquisition toward the end of the fifteenth century—the rights of the accused were not always respected; and penalties, including death, seemed to be imposed too rashly. Some modern historians believe that the abuses of the Inquisition crept into the process because the Church was too closely affiliated with the state. See **heresy.**

INRI   An abbreviation that stands for the Latin words "Jesus of Nazareth, King of the Jews," which was the phrase Pontius Pilate had ordered affixed to Jesus' cross.

inspiration, biblical   The teaching of the Church, as expressed in Vatican II, that "the divinely revealed realities, which are contained and presented in the text of sacred Scripture, have been written down under the inspiration of the Holy Spirit. For Holy Mother Church relying on the faith of the apostolic age, accepts as sacred and canonical the books of the Old and the New Testaments, whole and entire, with all their parts, on the grounds that, written under the inspiration of the Holy Spirit (see John 20:31; 2 Timothy 3:16; 2 Peter 1:19–21; 3:15–16), they have God as their author, and have been handed on as such to the Church herself. To compose the sacred books, God chose certain men who, all the while he employed them in this task, made full use of their powers and facilities so that, though he acted in them and by them, it was as true authors that they consigned to writing whatever he wanted written, and no more" (Dogmatic Constitution on Divine Revelation, §11). *(CCC 106)*

intercommunion   An agreement between two religious bodies that permits their respective members to receive communion in either denomination regardless of doctrinal differences.

interdict   A penalty of canon law that prohibits interdicted individuals from taking part in services or receiving the sacraments.

intinction   The practice of giving Holy Communion by dipping the consecrated bread into the consecrated wine.

irony   The use of words to mean the opposite of the literal meaning of what is being said or written. The use of irony is an offense against truth when one maliciously disparages another by characterizing some aspect of a person's behavior.

irreligion   A positive refusal to offer the worship due to God. Irreligion is forbidden by the first commandment. *(CCC 2110)*

Isaiah, Book of   Perhaps the best-known and greatest of the prophetic books of the Old Testament; Isaiah of Jerusalem was born about 760 B.C., and his careers spanned the reign of three Judean kings; this book is beautifully written, contains many poems and oracles and outstanding prophecies, especially those concerning Immanuel (chapters 6–12). Chapters 40 to 55 are often referred to as Second Isaiah because they were written at a later date not by Isaiah of Jerusalem, but by one of his followers; this section contains the four famous Servant Songs which the Church sees as applying to Jesus the Messiah. *(CCC 702)*

Islam   The religion initiated by Mohammed (A.D. 570–632). Followers of Islam are sometimes known as Muslims.

Israelites   The name given to the descendants of Jacob, collectively, the twelve tribes. *(CCC 62–64, 218, 839)*

itinerarium   The prayer of the Church for those about to set out on a journey.

J

Jansenism   A body of heretical doctrine developed by Cornelius Jansen (1585–1638), a Catholic theologian and bishop, and his followers; in his book, *The Augustinus*, Jansen taught that when God first created human beings he made them good, but after the Fall human nature became a slave of sin and could no longer do any good on its own; the necessary grace to do good, however, was given only to the elect few (the predestined) for whom Jesus died; the sign that one belonged to the elect was a spirit of fear that kept the person from approaching the sacraments or feeling at peace with God. The followers of Jansen became extreme rigorists, taught that the average Catholic cannot keep some of the commandments and is practically always unworthy of receiving Holy Communion. This harsh and inhuman heresy was condemned by Pope Innocent X in 1653, but it exercised a strong negative influence on the pastoral life of the Church for centuries to come.   See **Alphonsus Liguori, Saint.**

jealousy   Resentment or intolerance of another usually because that person possesses some good, such as wealth, popularity, social status, or so on, of which the jealous person wishes to be the exclusive possessor. *(CCC 1852)*

Jeremiah, Book of   One of the prophetic books of the Old Testament, written by Jeremiah who was born about 650 B.C. Jeremiah's writings express a keen awareness of the idolatry and infidelity on the part of the Israelites and the external threats from their enemies; about the time Jerusalem was being destroyed (587 B.C.), Jeremiah uttered the great oracle of the "new" covenant (31:31–34), Yahweh's tender and consoling promise to his people; after the fall of Jerusalem, Jeremiah was forced into Egyptian exile and was probably murdered by people from his own country. *(CCC 61, 64)*

Jerusalem   An ancient city in Palestine that became the religious and political center of Israel, chosen by King David as his capital; three great temples were built in Jerusalem before the coming of Christ who, together with his apostles, ministered in Jerusalem; the city and the temple were destroyed in A.D. 70. The Church is sometimes referred to in the liturgy as the New Jerusalem. *(CCC 557–560)*

Jesus   The name of our Lord, derived from a Hebrew name meaning "Yahweh is salvation"; given by divine command to Jesus "for he will save his people from their sins" (Matthew 1:21). *(CCC 430–435)* See **Christ.**

Jesus Prayer   A popular invocation to Jesus, based on the urgent request of the blind man in the Gospel: "Lord Jesus Christ, Son of God, have mercy on me, a sinner!" (See Matthew 9:27; Mark 10:48.) *(CCC 451)*

Jews   The children of Israel and the people chosen by God to receive his revelation. After the destruction of Jerusalem by the Romans in 70 A.D., the Jews were dispersed throughout the world. This dispersal is called the *diaspora.*

Job, Book of   One of the Wisdom Books of the Old Testament, written by an unknown author between 600 and 400 B.C. Job is the chief character in several dialogues with his friends on the profound question of human suffering and how this evil can be reconciled with the goodness of God; the religious truth of this book is that, while there is no adequate human explanation of the mystery of evil or suffering, faith in God and submission to his will make them bearable.

John the Baptist   Precursor of Jesus, John the Baptist was the son of Zechariah and Elizabeth. An account of his birth is given in the Gospel of Luke. After conducting a ministry of preaching and baptizing, John incurred the anger of Herod Antipas and was executed by him. *(CCC 523, 719)*

John, Gospel of   One of the four divinely inspired accounts of the life, teaching, death, and Resurrection of Jesus Christ; written about A.D. 95, its author was traditionally considered to be John, the beloved apostle, but in the light of modern research the author is commonly considered to be one of John's disciples; it is the most theological of the Gospels, emphasizing the messiahship and divinity of

Jesus, and rooting the belief and practice of Christians in the person of Jesus who is the Word, the Way, the Truth, the Life, the Light. *(CCC 125–127)*

Joseph, Saint   Spouse of the Virgin Mary and foster father of Jesus; most of what we know about him is from the Gospel accounts, especially of Matthew and Luke, where he is described as a just and holy man; he has long been held in veneration by the Church, is honored as her universal patron on the feast of Saint Joseph, March 19, and as the special patron of working people on the feast of Saint Joseph the Worker, May 1. *(CCC 497)*

journalists   Those who report and interpret the events of daily life even as they happen. The basic responsibility of journalists is to serve the truth and not to offend against charity in disseminating information. *(CCC 2477)*

joy   A feeling of pleasure caused by the possession of something one cherishes. *(CCC 301, 523)*

Judaism   The oldest known religion of the Western world, it was revealed by God and originated with the Mosaic covenant (see Exodus 19:5–6) and was identified with the land of Israel (see Deuteronomy 11:8–9); Judaism does not have a formal creed, but traditionally expresses belief in God who reveals himself through the law, the prophets, and the events of history; the faithful Jew is one who lives justly according to the law and who worships God by prayer, reflection upon the sacred writings, and the observance of Sabbath and other festivals. According to Vatican Council II, there is a relationship between the Church and the Jewish people, "That people to which the covenants and promises were made and from which Christ was born according to the flesh (see Romans 9:4–5)...for the sake of the fathers, for the gifts of God are written repentance..." (Dogmatic Constitution on the Church, §16). *(CCC 62–64)*

judgment   According to Catholic teaching, there is a distinction between General Judgment and the particular judgment. The General, or Last or Final Judgment, is the judgment of the human race by Jesus Christ (see Matthew 25:31; 2 Thessalonians 2:3–10) who "will come in glory to judge the living and the dead" (Nicene Creed). The particular judgment is the judgment that takes place immediately after an individual's death and determines whether the individual is worthy of heaven (after purification in purgatory, if necessary) or hell. *(CCC 678–679)*

judgment, rash   The act of assuming that another's actions or motives are immoral without sufficient foundation. *(CCC 2477)*

jurisdiction   The power to govern as exercised within the Church for the spiritual well-being of her members.

justice   One of the principal (cardinal) moral virtues; in the strictest sense, it is the virtue by which one person renders to another that which is his or her due, or the virtue which urges one to give to others what is theirs by right (commutative justice). Justice is required not only between persons but also between individual persons and the community (legal justice) and likewise between the leaders of the community and the community itself (distributive justice). *(CCC 2411)*   See **social justice.**

justification   The process by which a sinner is made right with God; in the teachings of Saint Paul, God makes a person "just," free from sin and pleasing to God through grace, attested by faith (see Romans 3:20–30); according to Catholic teaching as expressed by the Council of Trent: "Justification is the change from the condition in which a person is born as a child of the first Adam into a state of grace and adoption among the children of God through the second Adam, Jesus Christ our Savior." Thus, justification includes a true removal of sin by the power of God and a true supernatural sanctification through the gift of sanctifying grace or participation in the life of God. *(CCC 1266)*

just wage   See **wage, just.**

just war   See **war, morality of.**

K

kerygma   From the Greek word for "proclamation"; in the Christian sense, it refers especially to the preaching of the Good News of salvation, the proclaiming of the essential elements of God's salvific plan in Christ, the passing on of the "core message" of the Gospel. *(CCC 2–3)*   See **Gospel.**

keys   The symbol of spiritual power and authority conferred on Saint Peter and his successors by Jesus Christ: "I will give you the keys of the kingdom of heaven" (Matthew 16:19). The "power of the keys" is an expression used to describe the authority of the Bishop of Rome, the pope, over all the faithful and all the Churches. It is also used to describe the Church's authority to "bind" and "loose" (forgive or retain) sins in the sacrament of penance. *(CCC 551–553)*   See **pope; primacy, papal.**

kidnapping The abduction of another person by force and without consent. It is morally wrong. *(CCC 2295)*

killing The unjust taking of one's own life (suicide) or that of another. Killing is forbidden by the fifth commandment. *(CCC 2262–2268)*

kindness Listed in the tradition of the Church as one of the fruits of the Holy Spirit; these are perfections that the Holy Spirit forms in us as "the first fruits of eternal glory"; kindness is an aspect of charity which is the distinguishing mark of the disciples of Jesus. *(CCC 736, 1832)*

kingdom of God A rich biblical term, often translated as "the reign of God"; the coming of the kingdom of God was foretold in the Old Testament and was especially revealed in the very person of Christ, Son of God and Son of Man (see Mark 1:15; Matthew 4:17); in the words, works, and miracles of Christ, the kingdom is described (see, for example, Luke 11:20 and Matthew 12:28). The mission of the Church, in the words of Vatican II, is "of proclaiming and establishing among all peoples the kingdom of Christ and of God, and she is, on earth, the seed and the beginning of that kingdom. While she slowly grows to maturity, the Church longs for the completed kingdom and, with all her strength, hopes and desires to be united in glory with her king (Dogmatic Constitution on the Church, §5). The Church celebrates the feast of Christ the King on the final Sunday of the liturgical year. *(CCC 543–546)*

Kings, Books of The first Book of Kings and the second Book of Kings are historical books of the Old Testament, probably completed in the sixth century B.C. and covering a broad sweep of the history of Israel; included in these books are a description of the last days of David, the reign of Solomon, the building of the Temple, stories concerning the prophets Elijah and Elisha, and the destruction of Jerusalem and the Temple. One of the theological themes running through these books is that the tragedies which occurred among the people were due to their weak faith and their lack of fidelity to God's law.

Knights of Columbus A fraternal society of Catholics originating in 1882 in New Haven, Connecticut. One purpose of the organization was an insurance feature designed to protect widows and their families. Another purpose was to attract young Catholic men who may have entered the Masons, a society prohibited by the Church.

Knights of Malta A common name for the military and religious order known as the military Hospitaler Order of St. John of Jerusalem, of Rhodes, and of Malta. This organization has a long history of hospice work dating from at least the twelfth century.

knowledge   A gift of the Holy Spirit that assists us in appraising the spiritual value and use of created things. *(CCC 1831)*

knowledge of God   Human beings are capable of knowing God through the exercise of reason, but such knowledge is extended through grace and revelation. *(CCC 31–32)*

Koran   The holy scriptures of Islam consisting of the revelations made to the prophet Muhammad.

Kyrie Eleison   Three Kyrie eleisons ("Lord, have mercy"), three Christe eleisons ("Christ, have mercy"), and three Kyrie eleisons are part of the introductory penitential rite in the Eucharistic Liturgy.

L

laicization   The process by which a priest is returned to the status of a layperson.

laity   All members of the Church belong to the people of God, the Christian faithful. According to the Code of Canon Law, "The Christian faithful are those who, inasmuch as they have been incorporated in Christ through baptism, have been constituted as the people of God; for this reason, since they have become sharers in Christ's priestly, prophetic and royal office in their own manner, they are called to exercise the mission which God has entrusted to the Church to fulfill in the world, in accord with the condition proper to each one" (Canon 204, §1). Among the Christian faithful the laity are all the faithful except those in holy orders (clergy) and those who belong to a religious state approved by the Church (religious). According to Vatican Council II's Decree on the Apostolate of the Laity, §8, the special mission of the laity is to renew the temporal order and to witness to Christ in a special way amid secular affairs. *(CCC 897–900)*

La Salette   See shrines of Our Lady.

Last Supper   The traditional name given to the Passover meal which Jesus ate with his apostles in Jerusalem on the night before he died (see Mark 14:15; Luke 22:12). According to Catholic teaching, it was on this occasion that Jesus instituted the Holy Eucharist and the holy priesthood. The Church celebrates the Lord's Supper on Holy Thursday evening. *(CCC 610–611)*

Lauds   The Morning Prayer in the office of the Liturgy of the Hours, forming one of the chief or "hinge" hours of each day. Vespers is considered the other hinge hour of prayer.

law   As used in Catholic theology, the term "law" is used in several senses, the most important of which are as follows:

The Eternal Law: that is, the plan of divine wisdom insofar as it directs all activity and change toward a final end; the eternal and universal law whereby, in the words of Vatican II, "God orders, directs and governs the whole world and the ways of the human community according to a plan conceived in his wisdom and love" (Declaration on Religious Liberty, §3).

The Natural Law: that is, the sharing of the rational creature in the eternal law of God, for as Vatican II expresses it, "God has enabled man to participate in this law of his so that, under the gentle disposition of divine providence, many may be able to arrive at a deeper and deeper knowledge of unchangeable truth" (Declaration on Religious Liberty, §3).

The Divine Positive Law: The eternal law of God is manifested in a fuller and clearer way through divine revelation: through "the law and the prophets" in the Old Testament and "in these final days, he has spoken to us by a Son" (Hebrews 1:2).

Ecclesiastical (Church) Law: the norms that govern the Church organized as a social and visible structure.

Civil Law: usually defined as an ordinance of reason promulgated by authority for the common good; ideally, every civil law should be consistent, just, observable, and useful. *(CCC 1950–1953)*   See **natural law; canon law.**

law of nature   In one sense, this is the moral law that is knowable by all humans and that is universally binding. In another sense, this is the law that contains the physical ordering of the universe, such as the law of gravity. *(CCC 341)*

laying on of hands   A ceremonial imposition of the hands on a person or thing in order to convey some spiritual power. The laying on of hands accompanies confirmation, ordination, the anointing of the sick, as well as some sacramentals. *(CCC 1288, 1507, 1538)*

lectern   A high stand used to support sacred books during the Liturgy of the Word. *(CCC 1184)*

lectio divina   Sacred readings, such as the Scriptures, read so as to become prayer. *(CCC 1177, 2708)*

lectionary   A book approved by the Church, containing a three-year cycle of Scripture readings for Sundays and solemn feasts, a two-year weekday cycle, a one-year cycle for the feasts of saints, and readings for ritual Masses and Masses for particular intentions. The present lectionary was approved in 1970; a second edition (substantially the same as the first) was published in 1981.   See **sacramentary.**

lector   One who reads scriptural and other passages during liturgical worship. *(CCC 1143)*

Legion of Decency   An organization established in 1934 by the bishops of the U.S. to promote high moral standards in films and to encourage discriminating viewing of films.

Lent   The penitential season of the Church's year, beginning on Ash Wednesday and ending with the Mass of the Lord's Supper on Holy Thursday; it has six Sundays, the sixth of which is called Passion (Palm) Sunday and marks the beginning of Holy Week. The time of Lent is a penitential time throughout the universal Church; fast and abstinence are observed on Ash Wednesday and Good Friday; in the United States, all the Fridays of Lent are days of abstinence from meat. Lent is also a season in which prayer, the reception of the sacraments, charity and almsgiving are emphasized. *(CCC 1095, 1163)*

letters (New Testament)   The Letters or Epistles form a large part of the New Testament. These letters are commonly divided into two general categories: the Pauline Letters and the Catholic Letters. The Pauline Letters were written by Saint Paul himself or by his disciples; they were written not long after the death and Resurrection of Christ (roughly between A.D. 54 and A.D. 80); they are rich firsthand sources of the development of Christian theology and practice. Included in the Pauline Letters are: Romans, 1 Corinthians, 2 Corinthians, Galatians, Ephesians, Philippians, Colossians, 1 Thessalonians, 2 Thessalonians, 1 Timothy, 2 Timothy, Titus, Philemon. (The Letter to the Hebrews is by an unknown author.) The Catholic Letters (so named because they were thought to be addressed not so much to particular communities but to a more general or universal audience) were written by various authors from approximately A.D. 65 to approximately A.D. 95; included in the Catholic Letters are: James, 1 Peter, 2 Peter, 1 John, 2 John, 3 John, Jude, and Revelation. *(CCC 120)*

lie   A statement, sign, or action by which one expresses to another something contrary to what one believes to be true, usually with the intention to deceive another. A lie is a violation of the eighth commandment, a perversion of the faculty of speech, and a barrier to mutual trust and confidence in human relationships. *(CCC 2482–2487)*

life   The vital principle given by God to human beings. It must be protected from its very inception. *(CCC 2260)*

light   A symbol of the illuminating power of the Holy Spirit and Christ, the Light of the World. *(CCC 697)*

limbo   See **unbaptized, fate of.**

litany   From the Greek word meaning "supplication," a litany is a form of prayer in which a person makes fixed responses to a series of petitions. Example of litanies are the Litany of the Saints and the Litany of the Precious Blood.

Little Office of the Blessed Virgin Mary   A fixed form of prayers modeled on the Divine Office (now the Liturgy of the Hours) and said in honor of the Blessed Virgin Mary.

liturgical art   Images, signs, and symbols created for the purpose of giving glory to God. Such art should be noble, worthy, and beautiful.

liturgy   The public worship of the Church, including the celebration of the sacrament and sacrifice of the Eucharist, the celebration of the other sacraments, and the Liturgy of the Hours or the Divine Office, which is a set form of hymns, psalms, readings, and prayers recited at particular times of the day. Vatican II, in its Constitution on the Sacred Liturgy, teaches that "...it is through the liturgy, especially the divine Eucharistic Sacrifice, that 'the work of redemption is exercised.' The liturgy is thus the outstanding means by which the faithful can express in their lives, and manifest to others, the mystery of Christ and the real nature of the true Church" (§2). *(CCC 1067–1070)*

Liturgy of the Eucharist   See **Mass.**

Liturgy of the Word   See **Mass.**

Lord   A customary title of God in the Old Testament, one of the titles given to Jesus in the New Testament, still frequently used in the prayers of the Church (for example, at the beginning—"Lord, Jesus Christ"—or at the conclusion—"through Christ our Lord").

Lord's day   See **holy days of obligation.**

Lord's Prayer   A term used to describe the prayer that Jesus taught his disciples: see Matthew 6:9–13; used frequently both in the liturgical prayer of the Church and informally by individual Christians; also called the Our Father. Part Four, Section Two of the *Catechism of the Catholic Church* is a commentary on this prayer. *(CCC 2759–2760, 2765–2766)*

Loreto, House of   A shrine to the Blessed Virgin Mary located in the Italian city of Loreto. This house is said to be the structure in which the Annunciation took place and was transported by angels to its site at Loreto.

Lourdes   See **shrines of Our Lady.**

Luke, Gospel of   One of the four divinely inspired accounts of the life, teaching, death, and Resurrection of Jesus Christ; written around A.D. 80, the author is Luke, a fellow missionary with Saint Paul and also the author of the Acts of the Apostles; his Gospel is directed especially to gentile Christians, provides insights into the Christian way of life, emphasizes the compassion and forgiveness of Jesus, highlights the role of women in the life and ministry of Christ.   See **Acts of the Apostles.**

lukewarmness   Tepidity, hesitation, or lack of enthusiasm in responding to the love of God. *(CCC 2094)*

lust   One of the capital or deadly sins, it is disordered and unrestrained seeking of sexual pleasure. *(CCC 2351)*

M

magi   The wise men who were led by the stars to pay homage to the infant Jesus in Bethlehem. They brought gifts of gold, frankincense, and myrrh, and by tradition are named Gaspar, Melchior, and Balthasar.

magic   A belief that certain forms of ritual can achieve supernatural ends or the invocation of evil spirits. The practice of magic is forbidden by the Church, but the kind of magic based on sleight of hand and used for entertainment is a different matter entirely. *(CCC 2138)*

magisterium   A Latin word meaning "teaching authority"; according to Catholic doctrine, this teaching authority is vested in the pope, the successor of Saint Peter and the head of the Church, and in the bishops together and in union with the pope. This teaching authority is at times infallible, and then demands from the Christian faithful the assent of faith. At other times this teaching authority, though not explicitly infallible, does express authentic Christian Catholic teaching and demands from the Christian faithful the loyal submission of the will and the intellect. Vatican Council II explains the matter in this way: "Bishops who teach in communion with the Roman Pontiff are to be revered by all as witnesses of divine and Catholic truth; the faithful, for their part, are obliged to submit to their bishops' decision, made in the name of Christ, in matters of faith and morals, and to adhere to it with a ready and respectful allegiance of mind. This loyal submission of the will and intellect must be given, in a special way, to the authentic teaching authority of the Roman Pontiff, even when he does not speak *ex cathedra* in such wise, indeed, that his supreme teaching authority be acknowledged with respect, and that one sincerely adhere to decisions made by him, conformably with his manifest mind and intention, which is made known principally either by the character of the documents in question, or by the frequency with which a certain doctrine is proposed, or by the manner in which the doctrine is formulated" (Dogmatic Constitution on the Church, §25). *(CCC 83–88)*   See **infallibility**.

Magnificat   The prayer of praise hymned by Mary on her visit to Elizabeth. The name comes for the first word of the Latin version.

Mandatum   It was customary in eastern countries in ancient days to wash the road dust from the feet of a guest. In imitation of this gesture of courtesy Jesus washed the feet of the apostles at the Last Supper. Today, in an optional foot-washing rite during the Holy Thursday Liturgy after the homily, the presider goes to selected people, pours water over each one's feet, and dries them with a towel. Any number of persons who are representative of the assembly are chosen for the rite. This ceremony is called Mandatum because of the Scripture "I give you a new commandment..." (John 13:34). Washing the feet of another is an important gesture of humility and charity that brings about reconciliation and symbolizes Jesus' call to service.

Manichaeism   A doctrine of dualism that takes its name from Mani (216–276). This heresy teaches that two opposing principles of good and evil existed from the beginning, out of which the world developed. Believers renounced war, work, hunting, business, property, agriculture, and sex. They believed that all matter was intrinsically evil. *(CCC 285)*

market economy   An economic system in which the outcomes of production are freely bought and sold and market forces guide these exchanges. In a market economy the main task of the state is to guarantee individual freedom, private property, a stable monetary system, and efficient public services so that those who work may enjoy the fruits of their labor. *(CCC 2431)*

Mark, Gospel of   One of the four divinely inspired accounts of the life, teaching, death, and Resurrection of Jesus Christ; the first of the Gospels, and the shortest, it was written around A.D. 65 and was directed especially to gentile Christians; it provides many details about the ministry and miracles of Jesus, and shows that Jesus is the Messiah, the Son of God, and Savior. *(CCC 125–127)* See **Gospel.**

marks of the Church   Four essential characteristics of the Church that mark it as the true Church of Christ. These are that the Church is one, holy, catholic, and apostolic.

marriage, Christian   One of the seven sacraments defined thus by the Church: "The matrimonial covenant, by which a man and a woman establish between themselves a partnership of the whole of life, is by its nature ordered toward the good of the spouses and the procreation and education of offspring; this covenant between baptized persons has been raised by Christ the Lord to the dignity of a sacrament" (Canon 1055, §1). In light of this teaching, the Church emphasizes that "a matrimonial contract cannot validly exist between baptized persons unless it is also a sacrament by that fact" (Canon 1055, §2).

Marriage is marked by two essential properties: "The essential properties of marriage are unity and indissolubility, which in Christian marriage obtain a special firmness in virtue of the sacrament (Canon 1056).

Marriage is effected by true consent: "Marriage is brought about through the consent of the parties, legitimately manifested between persons who are capable according to law of giving consent; no human power can replace this consent" (Canon 1057, §1). This consent "is an act of the will by which a man and a woman, through an irrevocable covenant, mutually give and accept each other in order to establish marriage" (Canon 1057, §2). Because true consent is so fundamental to the Church's understanding of marriage, there is an entire section of canon law dedicated to defining and explaining it (see Canons 1095 to 1107). In brief, this consent must be rational, free, true, and mutual; it can be invalidated by an essential defect, substantial error, the influence of fear or force, or the presence of a condition or intention contrary to the true nature of marriage.

Because marriage is a sacrament, the Church has detailed norms governing the form of its celebration. For Catholics, the basic norm is: "Only those marriages are valid which are contracted in the presence of the local ordinary or the pastor or a priest or deacon delegated by either of them, who assist, and in the presence of two witnesses..." (Canon 1108, §1). *(CCC 1621–1632)* See **annulment; contraception; divorce; impediments to marriage; mixed marriages; natural family planning.**

Marriage Encounter   A program of marriage enrichment developed in Spain which consists of a retreat weekend marked by prayer, discussion, private reflection, and the Mass.

marriage tribunal   An ecclesiastical court before which is brought cases concerning the validity of marriage.

martyr   From the Greek word for "witness," a martyr is one who voluntarily suffers death for the sake of his or her faith or in defense of some virtue; from the earliest times the Church has held the martyrs in high esteem, honoring their memory and prizing relics of them. *(CCC 2473–2474)*   See **baptism of blood; relic.**

martyrology   A chronological list of the feast days of saints with all the names given for each date. A martyrology gives some biographical information for some saints listed. The best-known martyrology is the Roman Martyrology, which first appeared at the end of the Middle Ages.

martyrdom   The act of being put to death or dying of one's sufferings as a consequence of refusing to renounce one's faith.

Mary, Blessed Virgin   Catholic teaching on the Blessed Virgin Mary is extremely rich; only the highlights can be treated here. Mary was the daughter of Joachim and Anne, a native of Nazareth who could trace her lineage to the royal house of David; she was conceived without sin; she was betrothed to Joseph; she was chosen by God to be the Mother of Jesus; she carried this good news to her cousin, Elizabeth, who greeted her as "the mother of my Lord" and prompted Mary's hymn called the *Magnificat*; she went with Joseph to Bethlehem for a census and there gave birth to Jesus; in due time she presented Jesus in the Temple according to the law; later, she, Joseph, and the Child Jesus fled to Egypt to escape the evil designs of Herod; she and Joseph took Jesus to the Temple when he was twelve years old, and there the family became separated for three days. At the beginning of the public ministry of Jesus, Mary was with him at the wedding feast of Cana, where he performed his first miracle; she was at the foot of the cross when Jesus died; she was present with the apostles in the upper room at Pentecost (Acts 1:14); after completing this earthly life, she was assumed body and soul into heaven.

The Church teaches that Mary was conceived without sin, that she remained sinless throughout her life, that she was truly the Mother of God, that she was always a virgin, and that she is able to make intercession for us before God. The Church honors Mary with many liturgical feasts, the most notable being the Immaculate Conception, December 8; the Nativity of Mary, September 8; the Annunciation,

March 25; the Purification, February 2; and the Assumption, August 15. The faithful pray to Mary with confidence and honor her in many ways. *(CCC 487–507)*   See **Immaculate Conception; Annunciation; virgin birth; Assumption; Hail Mary; rosary; shrines of Our Lady.**

Mass   A popular name for the Eucharistic sacrifice and banquet, the memorial of the death and Resurrection of the Lord, in which the sacrifice of the Lord is perpetuated over the centuries, the summit and source of all Christian worship and life.

The Mass consists of two main parts: the Liturgy of the Word and the Liturgy of the Eucharist. In addition, there are introductory rites (greeting, penitential rite, the Glory to God hymn on certain occasions, opening prayer) and concluding rites (final greeting, blessing, dismissal).

The Liturgy of the Word features the proclamation of the Word of God; on Sundays and other feasts there are three readings (usually including a first reading from the Old Testament, a second reading from the New Testament, and the third reading from one of the Gospels); on other days there are two readings, the final one is always from one of the Gospels. Between the readings is a responsorial psalm, and an acclamation is sung before the reading of the Gospel. After the Scripture readings there is a homily on the scriptural or liturgical theme of the Mass with an application to one's Christian life; then follows the Creed on Sundays and other feasts, after which come the general intercessions or prayers of the faithful.

The Liturgy of the Eucharist focuses on the central act of sacrifice in the consecration and on the Eucharistic banquet in Holy Communion. The Liturgy of the Eucharist begins with the presentation of the gifts of bread and wine and prayers of offering by the priest; then follows the Eucharistic Prayer or Canon, the central portion of which is the act of consecration by which the bread and wine are changed into the Body and Blood of Christ. The Eucharistic Prayer closes with a doxology. The Communion rite begins with a communal praying of the Lord's Prayer, a prayer of deliverance, a prayer for peace and the exchange of some sign of peace, the Lamb of God, and the receiving of Holy Communion by the priest and people, thus completing the sacrifice-banquet of the Mass. A Communion song, period of silence, and prayer after Communion complete the Liturgy of the Eucharist. *(CCC 1345–1355)*   See **Eucharist; Canon of the Mass; doxology.**

Mass for the People   The celebration of the Holy Eucharist for the intention of all the faithful. Pastors and diocesan bishops are required by canon law to offer Mass for the people on Sundays and other holy days of obligation.

materialism   A belief that the world is merely matter and has always existed. In its more common use, materialism is an excessive attachment and concern for material goods and comfort. *(CCC 285)*

matrimony, sacrament of   See **marriage, Christian.**

Matthew, Gospel of   One of the four divinely inspired accounts of the life, teaching, death, and Resurrection of Jesus Christ; written in the 70s or 80s A.D., it was directed primarily to Jewish Christians and therefore emphasizes how Jesus is the promised Messiah, the fulfillment of the Old Testament; it gives great attention to the teaching of Jesus by citing many of his discourses and sermons, notably the Sermon on the Mount, chapters 5 through 7.

medals   Metal disks imprinted with the image of Christ, Mary, a saint, a sacred event, and so on. The Church provides a blessing for medals and has long encouraged the use of them as an aid to devotion and prayer; there are a large number of them approved by the Church. At the same time the Church warns against making them objects of superstition. *(CCC 1667–1670)*   See **sacramentals.**

media   Modern methods of communication (newspapers, film, radio, television, computers, and so on) that are major factors in contemporary life. Information provided by the media should be at the service of the common good and should be based on truth, freedom, justice, and solidarity. *(CCC 2496–2499)*

medical treatment   The discontinuance of medical procedures that are burdensome, dangerous, extraordinary, or disproportionate to the expected outcome can be legitimate. Scientific, medical, or psychological experiments on humans are also legitimate in the eyes of the Church provided they do not offend the dignity of the human person. *(CCC 2292–2297)*

medicine   The uncontrolled use of pharmaceutical substances goes against the virtue of temperance. *(CCC 2290)*

meditation   Mental prayer consisting of reflections on a spiritual theme with the aim of moving the meditator toward some virtue. There are many different types of meditation. *(CCC 2705–2708)*

mercy, corporal and spiritual works of   The corporal works of mercy (flowing from the Gospel, especially Matthew 25:31–46) are to feed the hungry, give drink to the thirsty, cloth the naked, visit the imprisoned, shelter the homeless, visit the sick, and bury the dead. The spiritual works of mercy, also rooted in the Scriptures, are to counsel the doubtful, instruct the ignorant, admonish sinners, comfort the afflicted, forgive offenses, bear wrongs patiently, pray for the living and dead. *(CCC 2447)*   See **almsgiving; alms.**

mercy, divine   An attitude of God toward his creatures which causes him to forgive out of his love and goodness.

merit   The just reward or punishment owed to a person on account of his or her actions. With regard to God, there is no strict right to merit on the part of human beings. *(CCC 2006)*

Messiah   See **Christ.**

midrash   A Jewish commentary on the Old Testament clarifying a passage from a legal, homiletic, or narrative point of view. Midrashim is the plural form of midrash.

millenarianism   A belief that Jesus Christ and the saints will return to establish a thousand-year reign in the temporal sphere. This belief is based on a reading of the Book of Revelation, especially chapter 20. The Church has rejected this literal interpretation of the text. *(CCC 676)*

ministry   From the word *minister* which means "to render service"; in the viewpoint of Catholic theology, there is one essential ministry—the ministry of Jesus Christ; his ministry is extended, however, through the members of his Body, the Church. In the Church, the term is used in a variety of ways, among which are the following:

1. *Ordained ministry:* the service of the people of God by those who have received the sacrament of holy orders (that is, bishops, priests, deacons) and who have specific functions determined by the teaching of the Church itself.   See **bishops; priests; deacons.**

2. *Nonordained ministry:* the service of the people of God undertaken by baptized Catholics either (a) with a formal commission from the Church (for example, lector, catechist, acolyte, Eucharistic minister) or (b) without a formal commission from the Church (for example, performing the corporal and spiritual works of mercy).

Vatican Council II calls attention to both the variety and the unity of ministries in the Church: "In the Church not everyone marches along the same path, yet all are called to sanctity and have obtained an equal privilege of faith through the justice of God (see 2 Peter 1:1). Although by Christ's will some are established teachers, dispensers of the mysteries and pastors for the others, there remains, nevertheless, a true equality between all with regard to the dignity and to the activity which is common to all the faithful in the building up of the Body of Christ" (Dogmatic Constitution on the Church, §32). *(CCC 873–879, 1590–1596)*

miracle   An occurrence that alters or goes against the laws of nature and is a sign of God's presence in the world. Christ promised to continue the display of miracles in his Church, but the Church admits a miracle only on the basis of evidence and investigation.

miracles of Christ   The Gospels recount a large number of miracles performed by Jesus Christ: for example, miracles of healing, miracles of raising the dead, and miracles exhibiting control over natural forces. In the New Testament sense, they are signs and wonders—events that are naturally unexplainable—which serve as a motive of credibility by manifesting the power of Christ and inviting those who witness them to faith in Christ himself (see John 2:11). *(CCC 517, 1507)*

Miraculous Medal   A medal of the Blessed Virgin Mary, oval in form, which was revealed to Saint Catherine Labouré in a vision. On one side it bears the words: "O Mary, conceived without sin, pray for us who have recourse to thee," and the image of the Blessed Virgin Mary. On the other side is an image of a cross, the initial M, and a representation of the hearts of Jesus and his mother. Its designation as "miraculous" arises from its origin rather than with any miracles attributed to its devotional use.

misappropriation of funds   Dishonest application of funds under one's care–an act that is against the seventh commandment. *(CCC 2409)*

missal   The liturgical book that contains all the prayers for the liturgy of the Mass. Since Vatican II the missal consists of two books: the Roman Missal (called the Sacramentary in the U.S. and Canada), which contains the texts for the celebration of the Mass, and the Lectionary for Mass, containing a three-year cycle of Scripture readings and chants for Sundays and a two-year cycle of first readings and Gospels for the weekday liturgy. Readings for other feasts and for votive Masses are also included.

mission   A term used in several different senses, among which are the following:
The mission of Christ: that is, the exercise of redemptive love, the salvation of the human race: "The Son of Man came not to be served but to serve, and to give his life a ransom for many" (Mark 10:45); see John 16:27–28.

The mission of the Church: As the Father sent the Son into the world, so the Son sent his apostles and their successors (see John 20:21) into the world to carry on the mission of Christ.

A mission territory: a geographical location where the Gospel has not yet been preached or where the response to the Gospel has not yet been sufficient for the local Church community there to be considered self-sustaining.

A parish mission: a special series of spiritual exercises, with emphasis on the preached word, conducted in a parish to bring about fundamental conversion and renewal of faith among those who attend. *(CCC 849–856)*

mixed marriage   A marriage between a Catholic party and a party who is not Catholic. The basic discipline of the Catholic Church in regard to mixed marriages is explained in the Code of Canon Law: "Without the express permission of the competent authority, marriage is forbidden between two baptized persons, one of whom was baptized in the Catholic Church or received into it after baptism and has not left it by a formal act, and the other of whom is a member of a church or ecclesial community which is not in full communion with the Catholic Church" (Canon 1124). The express permission called for in this Canon may be granted by the local ordinary (bishop) for a just and reasonable cause; according to Canon 1125, he is not to grant this permission, however, unless the following conditions have been fulfilled: "1° the Catholic party declares that he or she is prepared to remove dangers of falling away from the faith and makes a sincere promise to do all in his or her power to have all the children baptized and brought up in the Catholic Church; 2° the other party is to be informed at an appropriate time of these promises which the Catholic party has to make, so that it is clear that the other party is truly aware of the promise and obligation of the Catholic party; 3° both parties are to be instructed on the essential ends and properties of marriage, which are not to be excluded by either party." The Catholic party is bound to the form of marriage (that is, marriage in the presence of the local ordinary [bishop] or the pastor or a priest or deacon delegated by either of them, who assist, and in the presence of two witnesses); but for serious reasons the local ordinary has the right to dispense from the form in individual cases. It is the responsibility of the Catholic party to request this dispensation in due time before the marriage. *(CCC 1633–1637)*

modesty   Moderation in a person's personal life, attitudes, speech, dress, and so forth, relative to one's culture and circumstance. Modesty is part of a temperate attitude toward one's intimate inner self and fosters harmonious social relationships. *(CCC 2521–2524)*

monastery   A place of residence where a community of men or women reside under a common rule. In general, a monastery is made up of a church, a chapter house, a cloister, refectory, work area, and individuals cells or a dormitory.

monasticism   The way of life followed by those who set themselves apart from society to devote themselves to the service of God. Saint Anthony is considered to be the father of monastic life, and Saint Benedict of Nursia and Saint Augustine have written rules that are followed in a monastic way of life.

monk   Strictly, a member of one of the monastic orders in the Church, such as Benedictines, Cistercians, Carthusians; popularly, the term is sometimes applied to men who belong to religious communities but who are not monks in the strict sense.

Monophysitism   An heretical view held by those claiming that, after the Incarnation, Jesus Christ had only one nature, that his humanity is entirely absorbed by his divinity.

monotheism   Belief in one, personal, and transcendent God instead of many.

monstrance   The sacred vessel which holds the consecrated host when it is exposed for adoration or carried in procession; it is constructed of precious metals and in such a way that the consecrated host is clearly visible.

morality   In Catholic moral theology, usually defined as the relationship between the human act and the norm of morality; the goodness or badness of a human act deriving from its conformity to or lack of conformity to the norm established by God. The objective norm of morality is especially the eternal law of God, embracing both the natural law and the divine positive law. The subjective norm of morality is the conscience of the individual person formed in harmony with the divine norm. *(CCC 1749–1754)* See **law; conscience.**

Mormons   Members of the Church of Jesus-Christ of the Latter-day Saints, founded by Joseph Smith who announced that he had received divine revelations which he put down in *The Book of Morman.* While acknowledging the divine nature of Jesus Christ, Mormans maintain that believers can become gods through Morman baptism and by living according to the laws of the Morman Church.

mortal sin　From the Latin word meaning "deadly," the term *mortal* is synonymous in Catholic teaching with "grave" or "serious." A mortal (grave, serious) sin is a personal sin involving a fundamental choice against God in a serious way, a free and willing turning away from his love and law in a grave matter; or, in the words of Saint Thomas Aquinas, "when our acts are so deranged that we turn away from our last end, namely God, to whom we should be united by charity, then the sin is mortal." Traditionally, Catholic theology has emphasized three conditions for mortal sin: (1) that the matter be grave or serious; (2) that there be sufficient reflection or advertence or awareness of the seriousness of the choice one is making; (3) that there be full consent of the will, that is, that one freely chooses to do what one knows is seriously wrong even though one could stop from doing it. According to Catholic teaching, mortal sin brings about the loss of sanctifying grace or friendship with God; grace and friendship are regained especially through the sacrament of penance, for "Individual and integral confession and absolution constitute the only ordinary way by which the faithful person who is aware of serious sin is reconciled with God and with the Church" (Canon 960). *(CCC 1854–1861)*　See **penance, sacrament of.**

mortification　From the Latin word which means "death"; the Christian ideal (see Luke 9:23–24 and Galatians 5:24) of "dying to self" through the deliberate restraint of unruly passions and appetites; the struggle against one's evil inclinations so as to bring them in conformity with the will of God. Spiritual writers often distinguish between external mortification (that is, the discipline of the senses by way of fasting, abstinence, control of the tongue, modesty of the eyes) and internal mortification (that is, control over errant passions, emotions, and feelings). *(CCC 2015)*

moto proprio　Name given to a document originating from the pope himself and written at the pope's own discretion.

music, Church　That liturgical song and music which are characterized by beauty, holiness, appropriate solemnity and unanimity through participation of the whole assembly. *(CCC 1156–1158)*

Muslims　Followers of the teaching of Islam, a religion founded by Muhammad.

mutilation of self　Partial destruction of the human being by depriving one's self of an important bodily organ or its use. It is a form of murder. *(CCC 2297)*

myron　The Greek name for the chrism consecrated by the bishop at the Mass of Chrism on Holy Thursday and used throughout the diocese for the administration of confirmation and to consecrate churches and altars.

mysteries of faith Doctrines of faith, such as the Blessed Trinity and the Incarnation, that are products of divine Revelation but cannot be totally understood by reason alone.

mystagogy Initiation into the mystery of Christ through special instruction in the sacramental life which takes place immediately after initiation into the Christian community. *(CCC 1075)*

mystery As used in Catholic theology, a mystery is a divinely revealed truth whose existence cannot be known without revelation by God and whose inner essence cannot be wholly understood by the human mind even after revelation; for example, the mystery of the Trinity, the mystery of the Eucharist. A mystery, in this sense, is said to be above reason but not contrary to reason; even though it cannot be fully understood, it can be understood to some degree, and for that reason the Church encourages all to reflect upon and study the mysteries God has revealed. See **theology.**

Mystical Body A term used to describe the Church. Saint Paul speaks of the Church as the Body of Christ; Christ is the Head and we are the members (see Colossians 1:18 and 1 Corinthians 12:27). In 1943 Pope Pius XII wrote a complete encyclical, The Mystical Body of Christ, in which he traced this image of the Church through the Christian centuries and in which he concluded: "If we would define and describe the true Church of Jesus Christ—which is the one, holy, catholic, apostolic Roman Church—we shall find nothing more noble, more sublime, or more divine than the expression 'the Mystical Body of Christ'—an expression that flows spontaneously from the repeated teaching of the sacred Scriptures and the holy Fathers." Vatican II also explains this image of the Church at length in the Dogmatic Constitution on the Church (§8). *(CCC 787–795)*

mysticism An immediate and experiential knowledge of God attained in this present life through religious experiences, especially prayer; it is the fruit of God's freely given grace and results in an intimate union with God as well as a desire to live in his love and to do his will as completely as possible. *(CCC 2709–2719)* See **contemplation.**

N

name of God   From a biblical viewpoint, the name signifies more than the external person; it describes also his or her basic personality; thus the name of God signifies God himself. The Israelites held the name of God in such high reverence that they did not even say "Yahweh" but used "Adonai" (the Lord) instead. Likewise, the first Christians held the name Jesus in great reverence (see Philippians 2:9–10). The second commandment inculcates this spirit of reverence: "You shall not make wrongful use of the name of the LORD your God, for the LORD will not acquit anyone who misuses his name" (Exodus 20:7). *(CCC 203–209, 2160–2164)*   See **Yahweh; Jesus.**

National Conference of Catholic Bishops (NCCB)   An ecclesiastical body mandated by Vatican Council II and described thus in the Code of Canon Law: "The conference of bishops, a permanent institution, is a grouping of bishops of a given nation or territory whereby, according to the norm of law, they jointly exercise pastoral functions on behalf of the Christian faithful of their territory in view of promoting that greater good which the Church offers humankind, especially through forms and programs of the apostolate which are fittingly adapted to the circumstances of time and place" (Canon 447). The National Conference of the American Bishops was established in 1966, has its own bylaws and officers, and meets in plenary session at least annually. Its offices are in Washington, D.C. Its service agency is the United States Catholic Conference. *(CCC 887)*   See **United States Catholic Conference.**

National Council of Catholic Men (NCCM)   Organized in 1920, this group of American Catholic laymen concentrates its activities on issues involving family life, social action, and leadership at the local level.

National Council of Catholic Women (NCCW)   This organization of Catholic laywomen focuses its efforts on issues of international peace, housing, and leadership.

natural family planning   The controlling of conception by limiting the marital act to the infertile periods of the woman. According to Catholic teaching, as expressed by Pope Paul VI, "It is licit to take into account the natural rhythms immanent in the generative function, for the use of marriage in the infertile periods only, and in this way to regulate birth without offending the moral principles which have been recalled earlier" (*Humanae Vitae*, §16). The methods of natural family planning are constantly being refined; two of the methods widely used are: the Sympto-Thermal Method and the Billings Method. *(CCC 2370)* See **contraception; Christian marriage.**

natural law The law inherent in the very nature of rational creatures whereby they rightly ordered their basic conduct with respect to God, others, and themselves. Saint Paul speaks of "the law...written on their hearts" (Romans 2:15). Saint Thomas Aquinas defines the natural law as "the participation of the rational creature in the eternal law of God" and argues that all men and women, through the light of reason, are able to arrive at a basic moral code, embracing at least the principle that good must be done and evil avoided. *(CCC 1954–1960)* See **law.**

natural sciences The science or knowledge of the workings of the physical world. *(CCC 284)*

nave That part of a church building between the sanctuary and the entrance where those in attendance sit or stand.

neighbor, love of Love of neighbor is one of the two great summarizing commandments of Jesus Christ. In this sense, Christ enlarges the word to mean all human beings everywhere. *(CCC 2196)*

New American Bible A comprehensive translation of the Bible from the original languages with critical use of all the ancient sources by members of the Catholic Biblical Association of America and sponsored by the Bishops' Committee on the Confraternity of Christian Doctrine; it was begun in 1944 and completed in 1970; it is a translation of the Bible highly respected and widely used by American Catholics and others. *(CCC 131)*

New Covenant A sacred agreement between God and his people established by Jesus Christ and completing the Old Covenant established between God and Moses. *(CCC 1965–1974)*

New Testament One of the two general divisions of the Bible made up of 27 books, including the Gospels, the Epistles, the Acts of the Apostles, and the Apocalypse. *(CCC 120)*

Nicene Creed A summary of the truths of faith that emerged from the Council of Nicea (A.D. 325) and the Council of Constantinople (A.D. 381). It contains a fuller expression of Catholic doctrine, especially on the Holy Trinity, than the Apostles' Creed. The Nicene Creed is the one used in the Profession of Faith recited after the homily in the Eucharistic Liturgy of Sundays and other special feasts. *(CCC 195)*

217

non-Christian religions   Vatican Council II issued a Declaration on the Relation of the Church to Non-Christian Religions; in that Declaration, the Council Fathers referred specifically to the religion of Hindus, Buddhists, Muslims, and especially Jews. According to that Declaration, "The Catholic Church rejects nothing of what is true and holy in these religions. She has a high regard for the manner of life and conduct, the precepts and doctrines which, although differing in many ways from her own teaching, nevertheless often reflect a ray of that truth which enlightens all men" (§2). Recognizing that Christians and Jews "have a common spiritual heritage," the Council encouraged "mutual understanding and appreciation" between them. In a summary statement Vatican II eloquently insisted that "the Church reproves, as foreign to the mind of Christ, any discrimination against people or any harassment of them on the basis of their race, color, condition in life or religion" (§5). *(CCC 839–845)* See **Buddhism; Judaism.**

North American College   Founded in 1859 by the bishops of the United States to provide a central location for those priests and seminarians studying theology in Rome.

novena   A word signifying "nine" and referring to a public or private devotion that extends for nine consecutive days or, in less common usage, for nine consecutive weeks, with the devotion being held on a particular day for those nine weeks. The Church approves of such devotional practices, provided that there is no superstition connected with the number nine and that such externals are used as a help to prayer.

novice   According to the Code of Canon Law, novices are those who begin a period of trial and formation in the novitiate of a religious institute in order to "better recognize their divine vocation" and to "experience the institute's manner of living" (Canon 646). The novice is helped to discern his or her vocation, and is formed both in the essentials of the Christian life and in the charism and spirit of the particular institute. (See Canon 652.) This period must last for 12 months and may be extended to 24 months; at the end of it the novice either leaves or is admitted to temporary vows of poverty, chastity, and obedience. *(CCC 915–916)*   See **religious life; vow.**

nun   Popularly, this term is used to describe a woman who belongs to a religious institute, that is, to any "Sister"; technically, the title "nun" applies in the strict sense only to those women who belong to a religious order with solemn vows.   See **sister; vow.**

Nunc Dimittis The canticle of Simeon beginning "Now let your servant depart in peace," which is sung at Night Prayer.

nuncio A legate sent by the Holy See to serve as an ambassador to a civil government and who also represents the pope to various churches in that nation.

nuptial Mass The Mass at which a Catholic is married; it includes a choice of readings, prayers, and blessings that have special relevance to Christian marriage. The nuptial blessing is a formal blessing of the newlywed couple and is given after the Our Father at the nuptial Mass. *(CCC 1621)*

O

oath The act of invoking God's name in witness to the truth of a statement.

obedience The moral virtue which inclines one to submit to the law of God in all of its manifestations, including the eternal law, the natural law, the divine positive law, ecclesiastical law, and civil law. Obedience is also one of the evangelical counsels or vows which religious publicly profess in the Church. *(CCC 944, 1900, 2342)* See **law; religious life, religious.**

occasions of sin Extrinsic circumstances (persons, places, or things) which tend to lead one to sin. Theologians make a number of distinctions about occasions of sin, the most important of which are occasions that are voluntary (that is, of one's own choosing and therefore easily avoidable) and occasions that are necessary (that is, those that cannot be easily avoided); occasions that are proximate (that is, those that frequently lead one to sin) and occasions that are remote (that is, those that seldom lead one to sin.) There is a definite moral obligation to avoid voluntary proximate occasions of sin; and to take precautions against those which are remote. Most moral theologians hold that to place oneself in a voluntary proximate occasion of sin is itself a sin. See **sin.**

octave The practice of extending the celebration of a major feast for eight consecutive days. Christmas and Easter both have octaves in the liturgical year.

Office, Divine The Liturgy of the Hours; according to Vatican II, this is the public prayer of the Church for praising God and sanctifying the day. "The divine office, in keeping with ancient Christian tradition, is so devised that the whole course of the day and night is made holy by the praise of God. Therefore, when this wonderful song of praise is correctly celebrated by priests and others deputed to it by the Church, or by the faithful praying together with a priest in a the approved form, then it is truly the voice of the Bride herself addressed to her Bridegroom. It is the very prayer which Christ himself together with his Body addresses to the Father" (Constitution on the Sacred Liturgy, §84). *(CCC 1174–1178)*   See **breviary.**

oikonomia   A Greek word meaning "economy" and referring to all the works by which God reveals himself and communicates his life. *(CCC 236)*

oils, holy   A general term for the various kinds of oils used for religious purposes, especially (1) the oil of catechumens used at baptism; (2) the oil of chrism used at baptism, at confirmation, at the ordination of a priest or bishop, in the dedication of churches and altars; and (3) oil of the sick used in the anointing of the sick. The oils are usually blessed by the bishop at the Mass of Chrism on Holy Thursday (though in case of necessity they may be blessed at another time or by a priest if the bishop is not available). Traditionally, olive oil has been the oil of preference, but for a good reason the Church allows other oils (from plants, seeds, or coconuts). *(CCC 1241)* See **chrism.**

Old Catholics   A name given to several sects who refuse to accept the infallibility of the pope. Old Catholics are found in Holland, Germany, and the United States. They also reject fast days, indulgences, the veneration of saints, and a celibate clergy.

Old Covenant   The sacred agreement between Yaweh and the Jews. It is expressed in God's revelation to Moses.

Old Testament   See **Bible.**

Opus Dei   An international association made up of lay members and priests founded by Blessed Josemaria Escrivá de Balaguer in Spain in 1928. Members of Opus Dei seek personal sanctification and that of society as well.

oratory   A place of worship divided into public, semipublic, and private classifications. Oratories are not meant for public use, but for religious communities, schools, families, or individuals.

orders, religious   A general term commonly used to describe what in the laws of the Church are called "institutes of consecrated life"; this consecrated life is thus described in the Code of Canon Law: "Life consecrated by the profession of evangelical counsels is a stable

form of living by which faithful, following Christ more closely under the action of the Holy Spirit, are totally dedicated to God who is
loved most of all, so that, having dedicated themselves to His honor,
the upbuilding of the Church and the salvation of the world by a
new and special title, they strive for the perfection of charity in service to the Kingdom of God and, having become an outstanding sign
of the Church, they may foretell the heavenly glory" (Canon 573,
§1). There are in the Church a large number of institutes of consecrated life; they have different purposes and charisms, stemming from
the intention of the founders and the different gifts of grace that
have been given to them. All of these institutes of consecrated life
have goals and norms expressed in their constitutions and all are in
some way under the competent authority of the Church (see Canon
576). *(CCC 925–927)*

orders, sacrament of holy   See holy orders.

ordinariate   An ecclesiastical unit similar to a diocese but which is
not based on geographic boundaries. Most often used to refer to military dioceses.

ordinary   A title for a certain class of officeholders, among them
bishops, major religious superiors, vicar generals, and so on.

ordination   The act of conferring or receiving the sacrament of holy
orders which initiates candidates into the priesthood.

organ transplants   From a moral viewpoint, two types of organ
transplants are of import: (1) the transplant of an organ from a dead
person to a living person, for example, a liver transplant; there is no
moral objection to this type of transplant provided, of course, the
donor is truly dead; and (2) the transplant of an organ from one
living person to another living person, for example, a kidney transplant; the following norm expresses the Catholic moral position on
this type of transplant: "The transplantation of organs from living
donors is morally permissible when the anticipated benefit to the
recipient is proportionate to the harm done to the donor, provided
that the loss of such organ(s) does not deprive the donor of life itself
nor of the functional integrity of [the] body" (Ethical and Religious
Directives for Catholic Health Facilities, §30). *(CCC 2296)*

original justice   A term used to describe the presinful state of Adam
and Eve before the Fall. *(CCC 379)*

original sin   The sin that occurred at the origins of the human race;
the personal sin of Adam, as described in Genesis 2:8—3:24, passed
on to all persons (with the certain exception of Jesus Christ and the

Blessed Virgin Mary) as a privation of grace; original sin is not a personal sin actually committed by each individual but, rather, in the words of Pope Paul VI, "it is human nature so fallen, stripped of the grace that clothed it, injured in its natural powers and subjected to the dominion of death, that is transmitted to all men, and it is in this sense that every man is born in sin" (Credo of the People of God). Original sin means, therefore, that each descendant from Adam is created without sanctifying grace and is subject to concupiscence (that is, the tendency of fallen human nature to act contrary to reason and grace) as well as the punishment of death. Yet human nature is not completely corrupt or incapable of good choices; fallen human nature is capable of receiving sanctifying grace through the death and Resurrection of Jesus Christ (See Romans 5). *(CCC 388–395)*

O Salutaris Hostia Latin words for "O Saving Victim," a hymn written by Saint Thomas Aquinas for the Feast of Corpus Christi, now celebrated as the Solemnity of the Body and Blood of Christ.

Osservatore Romano, L' The semiofficial daily newspaper of the Vatican.

Oxford Movement An effort to reform the Anglican Church which began at Oxford University in 1833. It attacked secularism, liberalism, and the state as a final authority in religious matters.

P

pacifism The moral conviction that all war is intrinsically evil and that it is forbidden by the Gospel; historically, this position (sometimes called "absolute pacifism") has been a minority position among Christians, the more common position being that of the "just-war theory"; in recent times, the moral position that opposes not all war but the use of nuclear weapons is sometimes called "relative pacifism." *(CCC 2306–2308)* See **war, morality of.**

palliative care The term used to describe care for the dying that is aimed at alleviating suffering and making the sick person comfortable. It is a special form of disinterested love and should be encouraged. *(CCC 2279)*

palms, blessed Palm or other branches blessed and distributed to the faithful on Passion (Palm) Sunday, the sixth Sunday of Lent; the blessed palms are carried in procession to commemorate the triumphant entrance of Jesus into Jerusalem (Matthew 21:1–9) shortly before he died.

Pantheism A false view that believes that God is the universe and the universe is God. God then is the absolute essence of the world. Hinduism is a pantheistic set of beliefs. *(CCC 285)*

parable A short story drawn from everyday life, used to point out a spiritual lesson; Jesus used parables extensively (more than 30 are recorded in the Gospels) to express some truth about the reign of God (see Matthew 13:11); in reflecting upon parables, the main point—not the particular details—should be especially noted. *(CCC 546)*

Paraclete A word meaning "Consoler," "Defender," or "Advocate," it is used in the Gospel of John to refer either to Christ himself, who fulfilled this role for the disciples, or to the Holy Spirit who continues to fulfill this role in the community of the Church (see John 14:16). *(CCC 692)* See **Holy Spirit.**

paradise A word meaning "garden," with special reference to the Garden of Eden (see Genesis 2:15) and to the eternal abode of the just (Luke 23:24); often used as a synonym for heaven. See **heaven.**

parents Mothers and fathers of children whose duties are to provide for the physical, social, cultural, moral, and religious upbringing of their offspring. *(CCC 2221–2231)*

parish According to the Code of Canon Law, "A parish is a definite community of the Christian faithful established on a stable basis within a particular Church; the pastoral care of the parish is entrusted to a pastor as its own shepherd under the authority of the diocesan bishop" (Canon 515, §1). Though a parish is generally territorial, embracing all the faithful within a certain territory, it is also possible that other types of parishes be established "based upon rite, language, the nationality of the Christian faithful within some territory or even upon some other determining factor" (Canon 518). *(CCC 2179)* See **pastor.**

Parousia The Second Coming of Christ to earth (see 1 Corinthians 15:23), when his triumph over evil will be complete and his kingdom definitively established (see 1 Thessalonians 4:15–17; Luke 23:3–14). *(CCC 671–674)*

particular church A term used to describe the local church, which is the diocese or a community of Christian faithful under the guidance of their bishop ordained in apostolic succession. *(CCC 833)*

paschal A phrase referring to the passion, death, and Resurrection of Jesus Christ, the Lamb of God, by which he brought about salvation for all humankind; also, our way of participating in the dying and rising up of Jesus (see 2 Corinthians 4:10–12). *(CCC 571–573)*

paschal candle   Easter candle, marked with a cross, Alpha and Omega, and the numerals of the current year, stands as a symbol of Christ rising from the dead. The pascal candle is lit at the opening of the Easter Vigil.

paschal precept   Church law which requires the reception of the Eucharist during the Easter season, also called the Easter duty.

passion of Christ   The redemptive sufferings of Jesus as recorded in all four Gospels, featured in a special way during the liturgies of Holy Week. *(CCC 572)*   See **Holy Week.**

passions   Feelings, emotions, or movements of the sensitive appetite that dispose a person to act or not to act in regard to something believed to be good or evil. According to this definition, there are eleven passions; love, hate, desire, aversion, joy, sadness, hope, despair, courage, fear, and anger. *(CCC 1761–1766)*

Passover   A solemn Jewish feast, celebrated annually on the fifteenth of Nisan (the first month of the postexilic Hebrew calendar, occurring during our March and April), commemorating the deliverance of the Israelites from the bondage of Egypt (see Exodus 12); its main feature was the sacrificial meal, ending with eating the paschal lamb; in later days celebrated in conjunction with the weeklong feast of Unleavened Bread. The Christian Passover is the sacrifice of Christ, the Lamb of God, by which humankind was freed from the bondage of sin and led into the freedom of the sons and daughters of God. *(CCC 1164)*

pastor   According to the Code of Canon Law, "The pastor is the proper shepherd of the parish entrusted to him, exercising pastoral care in the community entrusted to him under the authority of the diocesan bishop in whose ministry of Christ he has been called to share; in accord with the norm of law he carries out for his community the duties of teaching, sanctifying and governing, with the cooperation of other presbyters or deacons and the assistance of lay members of the Christian faithful" (Canon 519). See **parish.**

patience   A virtue that enables its possessor to endure with composure all sufferings out of the love of God. Patience is sometimes called the root and guardian of all virtues. *(CCC 1832, 2219)*

patriarch   In the biblical sense, the father or founder of a tribe. In

Church organization, a prelate who presides over a larger grouping of particular churches. *(CCC 61, 205, 707)*

patriarchate   The territory governed by a patriarch. The pope is the Patriarch of the West. The five most ancient patriarchates are Rome, Constantinople, Alexandria, Antioch, and Jerusalem. *(CCC 887)*

patrology   The scientific study of the writings of the Fathers of the Church; also called patristics. *(CCC 8)*   See **Fathers of the Church.**

Paul, Saint   Born in Tarsus around A.D. 5 and originally named Saul; his family were Pharisees, and he was dedicated to persecuting Christians until his extraordinary conversion on the Damascus road (Acts 22:10); having experienced the call of Christ, he dedicated himself with equal fervor to the preaching of the Gospel and became known as the Apostle of the Gentiles during his three major missionary journeys; 13 New Testament letters bear his name; he was under house arrest for a two-year period and was beheaded outside the city of Rome around A.D. 67; he is buried near the present Roman basilica in honor of Saint Paul; feasts are celebrated in his honor on June 29 (with Saint Peter) and on January 25.

peace   A term used among Catholic Christians in several senses, among them: (1) right relationship between God and human beings, a fruit of fidelity to the covenant, a result of reconciliation; (2) right relationships between and among individuals and communities. Christ is the Prince of Peace (see Isaiah 9:5) and came to bring peace (Luke 2:14) and reconciliation (see Ephesians 2:14–17). True peace can be achieved only by extending the reign of Christ to all human relationships. *(CCC 2304–2305)*

peace, sign of   The sign of peace used at Mass today to symbolize renewal in Christ was originally a kiss. The form of this gesture in the Mass is left to the local episcopal conferences.

pectoral cross   A cross, sometimes made of precious metal and adorned with jewels, that is worn on a chain or silken cord by abbots, bishops, cardinals, and the pope.

penance, sacrament of   One of the seven sacraments of the Church described thus in the Code of Canon Law: "In the sacrament of penance the faithful, confessing their sins to a legitimate minister, being sorry for them, and at the same time proposing to reform, obtain from God forgiveness of sins committed after baptism through the absolution imparted by the same minister; and they likewise are reconciled with the Church which they have wounded by sinning" (Canon 959).

It is the teaching of the Church that "individual and integral confession and absolution constitute the only ordinary way by which the faithful person who is aware of serious sin is reconciled with God and with the Church; only physical or moral impossibility excuses the person from confession of this type, in which case reconciliation can take place in other ways" (Canon 960).

Only a priest is the minister of the sacrament of penance; the priest cannot validly absolve, however, unless he possesses the faculty to do so either from the law of the Church or from competent authority. The confessor acts as both judge and healer in the sacrament of penance; he is to act with prudence and in fidelity to the magisterium of the Church. The confessor's obligations under the sacramental seal are stated thus: "...it is a crime for a confessor in any way to betray a penitent by word or in any manner or for any reason" (Canon 983, §1). *(CCC 1440–1470)*   See **absolution; mortal sin; seal of confession.**

penance, works of Acts performed in satisfaction for personal sins or the sins of others. They can include prayers, alms, good works, acts of denial, service to one's neighbor, and so forth. *(CCC 1460)*

Pentateuch The collective name given to the first five books of the Bible. They are as follows: Genesis, Exodus, Leviticus, Numbers, and Deuteronomy. *(CCC 702)*

Pentecost A liturgical solemnity celebrated 50 days after Easter to commemorate the descent of the Holy Spirit upon the apostles and the baptism of some three thousand new Christians (see Acts 2:14); it is considered "the birthday of the Church," the day of its empowerment to bring the Good News of Jesus Christ to all nations. *(CCC 731–732)*

perjury Calling on God to witness to what one knows to be a lie; a public bearing of false witness when one is under oath. It dishonors God, is a violation of truth, and brings about many compromises in the application of justice. *(CCC 2476)*

permissiveness An attitude that allows for great personal latitude in moral decision making. In its excess this belief rests on an erroneous conception of human freedom. *(CCC 2526)*

Perpetual Help An ancient and well-loved picture of the Madonna and Child; it is a Byzantine picture and belongs to the "sorrowing" style meant to highlight the meaning of Christ's Passion and death; in the picture, on a background of gold, Mary's head is tilted toward Jesus, her hand loosely clasping his hand; Jesus seems frightened as he gazes into the future; his sandal seems to be falling from his foot; two angels in the upper corners of the picture carry the instruments of Christ's Passion; the original picture was entrusted to the Redemptorists by Pope Pius IX in 1866 and is now enshrined in the Redemptorist Church of San Alfonso in Rome; to honor Mary, the Redemptorists have established the worldwide Archconfraternity of Our Mother of Perpetual Help.

Peter, Saint Born in Bethsaida, his name was originally Simon, and he was a fisherman by trade; he was called by Christ, who changed his name to Cephas or Peter or "Rock" and made him the chief of the apostles and the rock on which the Church would be built; he is intimately associated with Jesus in the Gospels and was the first to preach in and around Jerusalem, where he established a Christian community; his name has been traditionally attached to two Catholic or general letters to the Christians in Asia Minor; he established his see in Rome, where he was martyred by crucifixion around A.D. 65 and is buried under what is now St. Peter's Basilica; his feasts are June 29 (with Saint Paul) and February 22. *(CCC 552–553)*

Peter's pence The annual contribution by the faithful from all over the world used to maintain the Holy See and to support the pope's charities.

Pharisees A religious sect of the Jews that sought to protect the Jews from contamination by foreign religions and that strove for strict separation from the Gentiles; they insisted on absolute loyalty to the Scriptures and to the traditions of the rabbis; by the time of Christ many (but not all) of the Pharisees had fallen into hypocrisy, and that is why Christ rebuked them so often (see Matthew 23:25; Luke 11:39); they were leaders in the opposition to Christ and his message.

piety A gift of the Holy Spirit which fosters in us duty, respect, and loyalty toward our parents, family, and country. *(CCC 1831)*

piety, forms of Expressions of fervor in the practice of religion. The forms of piety may include participation at the Holy Mass and other liturgical services, as well as acts of veneration of the saints. *(CC 575, 1674)*

pilgrim One who travels to a holy place to obtain some spiritual benefit. Rome, Lourdes, Jerusalem, and so on, are all places of pilgrimage.

plants While plants are by nature destined for the common good, humanity's dominion over them must be tempered by a concern for the quality of life of one's neighbor, as well as a religious respect for the integrity of creation. *(CCC 2415)*

politics   Activities revolving around public affairs that concern all the members of a community. The role of the Church in the political order is to defend the dignity of the human person. The Church may also comment on those political issues that have moral implications. *(CCC 2246)*

polygamy   The state of having more than one wife at a time. Polygamy is contrary to the unity and indissolubility of marriage. *(CCC 1610, 1645, 1664)*

polytheism   The belief in, and worship of, more than one God. The first commandment condemns polytheism. *(CCC 57, 2112)*

poor box   A collection box for donations to the needy, usually found at the rear of the church.

pope   Also known as the Bishop of Rome, the Vicar of Jesus Christ, the Successor of Saint Peter, the Supreme Pontiff, the Roman Pontiff, his role in the Church is thus described in the Code of Canon Law: "The bishop of the Church of Rome, in whom resides the office given in a special way by the Lord to Peter, first of the Apostles and to be transmitted to his successors, is head of the college of bishops, the Vicar of Christ and Pastor of the universal Church on earth; therefore, in virtue of his office he enjoys supreme, full, immediate and universal ordinary power in the Church, which he can always freely exercise" (Canon 331). *(CCC 882)*

pornography   The description or display of any person or action that is intended to stimulate immoral sexual feelings. *(CCC 2211, 2354)*

Portiuncula   A ruined church and the land around it given to Saint Francis of Assisi by a Benedictine monastery and which became the birthplace of his order. The church now stands in the midst of the basilica of Our Lady of the Angels and is an important place of pilgrimage.

possession, diabolical   The state of a person whose body, mind, or organs are controlled by a demon or demons. The New Testament records several instances of diabolical possession.

poverty   A term used by Christians in several senses, among them: (1) The state of being destitute or in need of the basic necessities of life; this state is opposed to human dignity and is the result of an unjust distribution of the goods of this world, and is seen as a moral and social evil; (2) The state of being "poor in spirit," having the attitude of Christ toward material possessions, that is, seeing them as gifts of God for one's own support, the support of one's family, and the support of those in need; (3) One of the evangelical counsels or vows professed by religious men and women in the Church; it involves the voluntary renunciation of the right to own property or, at least, the renunciation of the independent use and disposal of what one owns, the living of the common life, whereby one gives to the community what one earns and receives from the community what one needs; the details of the vow of poverty are regulated by the Code of Canon Law and by the constitutions of each religious institute. *(CCC 2443–2447)*

Prague, Infant of   A wooden statue of the Child Jesus given to the Carmelites of Our Lady of Victory Church in Prague in 1628. It has figured in the devotion to the childhood and kingship of Jesus ever since.

prayer   An act of the virtue of religion, a response of the intelligent creature to God; among the many definitions or descriptions is the well-known one of Saint Augustine: "Prayer is communication with God"; in the Christian tradition the basic purposes of prayer are to give adoration to God, to thank him for his blessings, to ask pardon for sins, to ask for his grace and help; there are many forms of prayer, for example: common prayer (with others) and private prayer (alone); common prayer may be liturgical or nonliturgical; private prayer may be vocal or mental. *(CCC 2559–2565)*   See **liturgy.**

prayer, difficulties in   Dryness and distraction are the most habitual difficulties in prayer. Vigilance and sobriety of heart are two defenses against distraction. Dryness is a feeling of spiritual aridity. It requires a sheer act of faith to overcome dryness in prayer. *(CCC 2728, 2754)*

prayer groups   An assembly of people whose purpose is both to pray together and to grow in the practice of prayer. *(CCC 2689)*

precept   An order given to an individual by an ecclesiastical superior. A precept usually enjoins a person to do or refrain from doing something.

Precepts of the Church   Obligations imposed on Catholics by the law of the Church; traditionally, six are listed: (1) to participate in Mass on all Sundays and holy days of obligation; (2) to fast and abstain on days designated by the Church; (3) to confess one's sins once a year; (4) to receive Holy Communion during Eastertime; (5) to contribute to the support of the Church; (6) to observe the laws of the Church governing marriage. In 1977 the National Catechetical Directory for Catholics of the United States added two other precepts, namely: "To study Catholic teaching in preparation for the sacrament of confirmation, to be confirmed, and then to continue to study and advance the cause of Christ" and "to join in the missionary spirit and apostolate of the Church." All of the traditional precepts of the Church have been reaffirmed in the revised Code of Canon Law, 1983. *(CCC 2041–2046)*   See **abstinence; Easter duty; fasting; holy days of obligation.**

prenatal diagnosis   Medical diagnosis of conditions existing in the human fetus or embryo while still in the womb. Such diagnosis is morally licit unless it is done with the possible thought of inducing an abortion. *(CCC 2274)*

presumption   A condition seen as the opposite of hope whereby a person expects to gain eternal life either totally without help from God or solely on God's power without personal effort. *(CCC 2091–2092)*

preternatural gifts   Exceptional gifts enjoyed by Adam and Eve before original sin. Among these gifts were immunity from suffering and death, integrity, control of the passions, and superior knowledge.

pride   One of capital or "deadly" sins, it is disordered love of self by which one takes personal credit for what are actually gifts of God and by which one seeks unreasonable acclaim for one's accomplishments. *(CCC 1866)*   See **humility.**

prie-dieu   A bench or kneeler suitable for kneeling in prayer. A prie-dieu usually has a place on which to rest a book.

priest   A man who, through the sacrament of holy orders, is ordained for the service of the people of God; he has the power to celebrate the Eucharistic sacrifice, to administer the sacraments, to preach the Word of God, and to perform pastoral functions according to the mandate of his ecclesiastical superior. *(CCC 1547–1553)* See **holy orders.**

primacy, papal   A charism of the pope as head of the Church, described in the Code of Canon Law in this way: "The Roman Pontiff, by virtue of his office, not only has power in the universal Church but also possesses a primacy of ordinary power over all particular churches and groupings of churches by which the proper, ordinary and immediate power which bishops possess in the particular churches entrusted to their care is both strengthened and safeguarded" (Canon 333, §1). *(CCC 882)*

prior; prioress The superior of some religious houses. There are several classes of priors and prioresses.

private revelations Revelations given by God to an individual for his own use or those of others. Private revelations do not belong to the deposit of faith. *(CCC 67)*

privilege A special favor bestowed by the grant of an ecclesiastical authority. Canon law sets down the conditions under which a privilege is granted or revoked.

proclamation of the Gospel Communicating Christ to the world by speaking, writing, and good example. This is the duty of every Christian. *(CCC 848)*

profession of faith A public recitation of the central doctrines of the faith, usually during the liturgy. Also, an obligation of those who hold high Church office to make a solemn declaration of faith before taking office.

profession, religious The public act by which one embraces the religious state by pronouncing the vows of poverty, chastity, and obedience and promising to live according to the rules and constitutions of a particular religious community. *(CCC 925)*

promises A voluntary and spontaneous action by which a person contracts to do or not to do something for another's benefit. Promises are binding on the basis of truth because truth requires actions to mirror words. *(CCC 2410)*

promoter of the faith An office within the Sacred Congregation for the Causes of Saints whose job it is to investigate any objections raised against a cause of beatification and to make sure that the procedures are followed.

Propagation of the Faith One of the major departments of the Roman Curia, technically known as the Sacred Congregation for the Evangelization of Peoples, with special responsibility for all of the Church's missions and missionary efforts throughout the world.

property Material things which a person owns. Private property is a right flowing from natural law since such a concept is useful to procure peace and to ensure order. *(CCC 2401–2403)*

prophecies of Saint Malachy Supposed prophecies that list characteristics attributed to 102 popes and 10 antipopes, erroneously ascribed to Saint Malachy, Bishop of Armagh. Actually this list was a forgery by an unknown writer in the sixteenth century and while some characteristics are fitting, others are wildly distorted.

prophecy   Communication from God through a human being, emphasized either prediction of the future or events.

prophets   In the Old Testament, those who wrote or spoke under divine inspiration to make known the will of God or to interpret his message; their message, insofar as it communicated the Word of God, related to both their own times and to the future; the prophets of the Old Testament (and the books they wrote) are Isaiah, Jeremiah, Baruch, Ezekiel, Daniel, Hosea, Joel, Amos, Obadiah, Jonah Micah, Nahum, Habakkuk, Zephaniah, Haggai, Zechariah, Malachi. *(CCC 702)*

prostitution   Engaging in sexual intercourse for money. It is injurious to all parties who engage in it and a violation of purity. *(CCC 2355)*

providence, divine   The ordering of things according to God's plan. Through his divine providence, God mercifully watches over all things that he has made.

prudence   A moral virtue which inclines a person to choose the most suitable means for attaining one's good purposes or for avoiding evil; it demands mature deliberation, taking advice if necessary, a wise judgment, and right execution of what one has decided. *(CCC 1805–1806)*

Psalms   The 150 prayer-songs contained in the Bible's Book of Psalms. *(CCC 2597)*

punishment   Penalty for wrongdoing inflicted by a proper authority. Punishment may have aspects of remediation, deterrence, and retribution. Following Saint Thomas, the Church holds that capital punishment is lawful in extreme cases. *(CCC 2266)*

purgatory   According to Catholic teaching, the state or condition of the elect (that is, those who have died in sanctifying grace or the friendship of God) still in need of purification before they see God; this purification is altogether different from the punishment of the damned. The faithful are encouraged to pray for the souls in purgatory, especially on the feast of All Souls, November 2. *(CCC 1030–1032)*   See **eschatology; All Souls.**

purity of heart   A term that refers to those who have attuned their minds and wills to the demands of God's holiness in the areas of charity, chastity, and love of truth. *(CCC 2518)*

pyx   A vessel or container used for carrying the Blessed Sacrament, especially to the sick.

Q

quiet, prayer of   A form of interior prayer described by Saint Teresa as a spiritual delight in the presence of God, the first step in mystical union with God. *(CCC 2715)*   See **mysticism.**

Quietism   A form of false mysticism that arose in the seventeenth century, sponsored especially by Michael Molinos, who taught that the human person achieves perfection by complete passivity before God and that once one has submitted to God there is no need to practice virtue, to resist temptation, to participate in the sacraments, or to desire salvation. Quietism was condemned as a heresy by Pope Innocent XI in 1687.

Qumram Scrolls   See **Dead Sea Scrolls.**

R

racism   A theory that holds that some human beings are inherently superior and others essentially inferior because of race. From the viewpoint of Catholic moral teaching, as expressed by the American bishops: "Racism is a sin: a sin that divides the human family, blots out the image of God among specific members of that family, and violates the fundamental human dignity of those called to be children of the same Father....It is the sin that makes racial characteristics the determining factor for the exercise of human rights" (Brothers and Sisters to Us, §9). *(CCC 1934–1935)*

rape   The act of forcing a person, against his or her will, to have sexual intercourse; the force may be physical or moral (for example, fraud, deceit). It is a serious violation of justice (violence against the person), as well as of the virtue of charity. *(CCC 2356)*

rash judgment   Attributing sins or faults to a person without sufficient reason; unfounded suspicion of another's conduct. It is a violation of justice and charity. *(CCC 2477)*

rationalism   A view requiring that all claims to truth be proven on a scientific basis. Rationalism stands in opposition to any religious tradition based on divine revelation and was condemned by Vatican I.

readers   See **lector.**

Real Presence   The teaching of the Church, as defined by the Council of Trent, that "in the sacrament of the most Holy Eucharist is contained truly, really, and substantially the body and blood, together with the soul and divinity, of our Lord Jesus Christ, and consequently the whole Christ." *(CCC 1373–1377)*   See **Eucharist.**

reason   The power of the intellect to distinguish truth. *(CCC 286)*

recollection   The practice of being aware of the presence of God or of "walking in the presence of God" so that one may grow in love and fidelity to him. *(CCC 1185)*

reconciliation   The act of reestablishing a damaged or destroyed relationship between two parties. Reconciling humankind to God was the primary work of Jesus Christ and is an essential part of the Good News (see 2 Corinthians 4:17–19). According to Catholic teaching, reconciliation with God after one has gravely sinned against him and reconciliation with the Church which is wounded by sin are basic results of the sacrament of penance. *(CCC 1468–1469)*   See **penance, sacrament of.**

reconciliation room   A place in most Catholic churches set aside for celebrating the sacrament of penance; the penitent is given the option of confessing anonymously behind a screen or conversing with the priest face to face. *(CCC 1185)*

Reformation, Protestant   A general term that describes the religious upheaval in the Catholic Church in the sixteenth century; some members of the Church, especially Augustinian monk Martin Luther (1483–1546) and John Calvin (1509–1564) opposed abuses in the Church (for example, in regard to indulgences) and challenged some of its basic teachings (for example, papal primacy); the result was a serious division within the Catholic community and the birth of Protestant churches. *(CCC 838)*   See **ecumenism.**

relativism   A view that holds that moral norms differ from culture to culture or that the rightness or wrongness of an action varies depending on the situation and one's motives. The Catholic view is that certain actions are always wrong despite cultural, psychological, or social conditions.

relic   Part of the physical remains of a saint or an object closely associated with a saint; according to Catholic teaching, authentic relics are worthy of veneration by the faithful; the relics of martyrs and other saints are placed in the altar stone of a fixed altar; according to Church law, "It is absolutely forbidden to sell sacred relics" (Canon 1190, §1).

religion   A moral virtue that inclines a person to give due reverence and worship to God as Lord and Creator; the authentic virtue of religion must be both internal (that is, the will or desire to give oneself wholeheartedly to the worship and service of God) and external (that is, the expression of this will or desire through the approved practices of religion—such as prayer, sacrifice, and communal worship. *(CCC 2095–2096)* See **liturgy; prayer; sacrifice.**

religious life; religious   According to the Code of Canon Law, a person who belongs to a religious institute, that is, "a society in which members, according to proper law, pronounce public vows either perpetual or temporary, which are to be renewed when they have lapsed, and live a life in common as brothers or sisters (Canon 607, §2). *(CCC 925–927)*   See **orders, religious; profession, religious.**

reliquary   A container used to display one or more relics.

reparation   Making amends for a morally wrong action that causes harm or results in a loss to another. *(CCC 1491)*

resistance   In moral theology, the right of the citizen in conscience not to follow the directives of civil authorities when they are contrary to the demands of the moral order or the fundamental rights of other persons. In New Testament teaching, there is a sharp distinction between serving God and serving "Caesar" or the political community when it opposes the law of God (see Matthew 22:21 and Acts 5:29). *(CCC 2242)*

responsibility   Accountability for one's actions to the extent that they are voluntary. *(CCC 1734–1735)*

restitution   Returning to its rightful owner whatever has been unjustly taken from him or her; restoring stolen goods or their equivalent; restitution obliges whenever commutative (person-to-person) justice has been violated; a sin of injustice cannot be forgiven unless the penitent intends to make restitution to the best of his or her ability. *(CCC 2412)*   See **justice.**

Resurrection of Christ   The fundamental Christian belief that Jesus Christ arose from the dead (see Mark 16:1–7); it is the cornerstone of the Christian faith, the central theme of apostolic preaching (see 1 Corinthians 15:13–14), the guarantee of the Christian's final resurrection with Christ (see Romans 6:5–8). The Resurrection of Christ is celebrated on the feast of Easter. *(CCC 648–655)*   See **Easter.**

resurrection of the body   The Christian belief (see 1 Corinthians 15:1–58), affirmed in all the major creeds ("I believe in…the resurrection of the body"), that before Final Judgment each individual soul will be united with its own body and that those who are judged as just will have their bodies glorified. *(CCC 997–1001)*

retreat   A special period of prayer, reflection, and solitude for deepening one's relationship with God and renewing one's living of the Christian life; priests and religious are required by Church law to spend some days in retreat each year, and laypeople are strongly encouraged to do so. *(CCC 2583)*

Revelation, Book of   The final book of the New Testament, written sometime after A.D. 90 and influenced by Johannine thought; it is a highly symbolic book dealing with things to come and the struggle between the Church and the powers of evil; though it contains dire warnings, it is fundamentally a message of hope to the Church concerning the final triumph of the Lord Jesus Christ. *(CCC 1137)*

revelation, divine   The manifestation of God and his plan of salvation to humankind; in Catholic theology, a distinction is sometimes made between the body of revealed truth given us by God ("divine revelation") and the process by which he has revealed it, especially through his Son, Jesus Christ, who in the words of Vatican II "perfected revelation" and "confirmed with divine testimony what revelation proclaimed…" (Dogmatic Constitution on Divine Revelation, §4); this revelation of God is found in the community of believers which is the Church, whose primary function, especially through its magisterium or teaching office, is to preserve it intact and hand it on to each new generation. *(CCC 74–79)*   See **Bible; magisterium; tradition.**

revenge   The desire to exact just punishment for a wrong committed. It becomes excessive when the person seeking it wants the undeserving to be punished or the guilty to be punished excessively. Revenge can take on the form of sinful anger. *(CCC 2262)*

rights, human   According to Catholic social teaching, each human person is endowed by God with certain fundamental and inalienable rights; perhaps the most complete enumeration and explanation of these rights is contained in Pope John XXIII's Peace on Earth (*Pacem in Terris,* 1963, especially §§14–27); among the more important listed are the right to life, to bodily integrity, to the means necessary for the development of life, to security in sickness or old age, to respect for one's person and good reputation, to a share in the benefits of one's culture, to the free exercise of religion, to freedom of choice in regard to one's state in life, to safe working conditions, to the ownership of private property, to freedom of assembly and association, to freedom of movement (emigration and immigration), to an active part in public affairs, and to just juridical protection. *(CCC 2458)*

rites   A term used to describe the forms and ceremonies in liturgical worship; the words and actions that belong to a religious ceremony, for example, the rite of baptism. The term is used also to group various communities within the Catholic Church in accordance with their official ritual usages, for example, Roman rite Catholics and Byzantine rite Catholics. *(CCC 1125, 1203)*   See **Eastern Churches, Catholic.**

ritual   A book, previously called the *Roman Ritual* and now called the *Book of Blessings,* that contains the prayers and ceremonies, other than the Mass, that are used in the administration of the sacraments and other functions.

rogation days   Special days in the liturgy marked by prayer, processions, and litanies. The time and manner of the celebration of rogation days is left up to the conference of bishops.

rosary   A popular devotion among Catholics, including meditation on the main mysteries of salvation as well as the recitation of certain vocal prayers. The mysteries are divided into three groups of five as follows: The Joyful Mysteries (the Annunciation, the Visitation, the Nativity, the Presentation in the Temple, the Finding in the Temple); the Sorrowful Mysteries (the Agony in the Garden, the Scourging, the Crowning With Thorns, the Carrying of the Cross, the Crucifixion); the Glorious Mysteries (the Resurrection, the Ascension, the Descent of the Holy Spirit, the Assumption of Mary Into Heaven, the Coronation of Mary). Meditation on each mystery is accompanied by the vocal praying of one Our Father, ten Hail Marys, and one Glory to the Father. To help in praying the rosary, a string of beads (a "rosary") is usually used. The Church strongly recommends the praying of the rosary, especially the family rosary. *(CCC 2708)*

Rota, Sacred Roman   An ecclesiastical court of the Holy See. It is best known as a court of appeals in marriage cases.

rubrics   From the Latin term meaning "red text," rubrics are directions for liturgical actions or gestures that are printed in red in order to distinguish them from the spoken texts which are printed in black.

S

Sabbath   The seventh day of the week (Saturday), prescribed in the Decalogue as a day to be kept holy, a day of rest and religious observance (see Deuteronomy 5:12–14), held in special reverence by religious Jews; the manner of observing it became a source of conflict between Jesus and the Pharisees (see Mark 2:27); in apostolic times Christians transferred the Sabbath to the first day of the week in honor of the Resurrection of Christ and called it the "Lord's day." *(CCC 2168–2173)*   See **holy days of obligation.**

Sacrament, Most Blessed   A term for the holy Eucharist that expresses the fact that this is the sacrament of sacraments. *(CCC 1374)*

sacramentals   The Church's understanding of the sacramentals is thus expressed in the Code of Canon Law: "Somewhat in imitation of the sacraments, sacramentals are sacred signs by which spiritual effects especially are signified and are obtained by the intercession of the Church" (Canon 1166). Some well-known sacramentals are blessings by a priest, blessed palms, blessed candles, blessed medals and scapulars, holy water. *(CCC 1667–1671)*   See **blessing.**

sacramentary   A part of the Roman Missal containing the prayers and directives (but not the Scripture readings) for the celebration of Mass and a number of sacramental formulas; it was revised in accord with the principles of Vatican II and approved by the Church in 1970. See **lectionary.**

sacraments   The Church's understanding of the sacraments, which are seven in number, is thus described by the Code of Canon Law: "The sacraments of the New Testament, instituted by Christ the Lord and entrusted to the Church, as they are actions of Christ and the Church, stand out as the signs and means by which the faith is expressed and strengthened, worship is rendered to God and the sanctification of humankind is effected, and they thus contribute in the highest degree to the establishment, strengthening and manifestation of ecclesial communion; therefore both the sacred ministers and the rest of the Christian faithful must employ the greatest reverence and the necessary diligence in their celebration" (Canon 840). *(CCC 1113, 1210–1211)*   See **baptism; confirmation; Eucharist; penance; holy orders; marriage, Christian; anointing of the sick.**

Sacred Heart of Jesus   The physical heart of Jesus as a sign and symbol of his immense love for human beings for whom he accomplished the work of redemption; the Church celebrates the solemnity of the Sacred Heart on the Friday after the second Sunday after Pentecost; the Church encourages the faithful to practice approved devotion in honor of the Sacred Heart. *(CCC 2669)*

Sacred Heart, promises of the   Twelve promises communicated by Christ to Saint Margaret Mary Alacoque: (1) all graces necessary to their state in life; (2) peace in their homes; (3) comfort in all afflictions; (4) secure refuge in life and death; (5) abundant blessings on all their undertakings; (6) infinite mercy for sins; (7) tepid souls turning fervent; (8) fervent souls mounting in perfection; (9) blessings everywhere a picture or image of the Sacred Heart is mounted; (10) gift to priests of touching the most hardened hearts; (11) promoters' names written in the Sacred Heart of Jesus; (12) grace of final penitence to those who receive Holy Communion on nine consecutive First Fridays.

Sacred Scripture   See **Bible**.

sacrifice   From a religious viewpoint, the form of worship by which a duly authorized minister offers a victim in recognition of God's supreme dominion; in the Old Testament true and authentic sacrifices were offered, but they were imperfect "for it is impossible for the blood of bulls and goats to take away sins" (Hebrews 10:4); in the New Testament Christ himself is the perfect sacrifice, who with his own blood "obtaining eternal redemption" (Hebrews 9:12). The sacrifice of Christ is perpetuated in the Eucharist. *(CCC 2099–2100)*   See **Eucharist**.

sacrilege   A violation or contemptuous treatment of a person, place, or thing that is publicly dedicated to the worship of God; in essence it amounts to a personal affront against God. *(CCC 2120)*

sacristy   A room annexed to a church used to store sacred vessels and other materials used in the liturgy, and to provide a place for priests and other ministers to vest and prepare for liturgical celebrations.

sadness   A state of unhappiness or depression. Sadness maybe as a result of a wrong done to us or to another person as a result of our own sin. Sadness may take on an unlawful form as in envy, which is sadness over the good fortune of another. *(CCC 2539)*

saint   In the wide sense, any person known for Christian holiness; in the strict sense, a person who has manifested heroic devotion during his or her life and who is officially honored by the Church as one who has attained heavenly glory and as one through whom God freely chooses to exhibit exceptional generosity. *(CCC 828, 2013– 2014, 2683–2684)*   See **canonization**.

saints, veneration of The ancient tradition of honoring and invoking the saints, explained by Vatican II in this way: "The Church has always believed that the apostles and Christ's martyrs, who had given the supreme witness of faith and charity by the shedding of their blood, are closely united with us in Christ; she has always venerated them, together with the Blessed Virgin Mary and the holy angels, with a special love, and has asked for the help of their intercession…" (Dogmatic Constitution on the Church, §50). *(CCC 956–957)*

salvation Deliverance from sin and eternal union with God in heaven made possible by the paschal mystery of Jesus Christ, Lord and Savior, and by its fruits offered in the Church, especially through the sacraments. *(CCC 169, 1088)*

sanctifying grace According to Catholic teaching, a created participation or sharing in the life of God himself; friendship with God. *(CCC 1996–2000)* See **grace.**

sanctuary That part of the church where the priest, servers, and other ministers have places to perform their functions. This area should be large enough to accommodate the liturgical rites and should be set off from the rest of the church by a raised floor, a special decoration, or so on.

Sanctus The prayer at the end of the preface at the Eucharistic Liturgy. It begins with the words "Holy, holy, holy."

satan See **devil.**

scandal An action, word, or omission which has at least the appearance of evil and is likely to lead another into sin; there is a distinction between direct scandal (that is, one person deliberately intends to lead another into sin) and indirect scandal (that is, one person foresees that his or her action or omission may lead another into sin but does not deliberately intend this). Direct scandal is always morally evil; indirect scandal may sometimes be permitted when one's actions are morally good and there is sufficient reason to allow the evil effect. *(CCC 2284–2287)*

scapular An outer garment worn by members of some religious orders, consisting of a shoulder-wide strip of cloth reaching almost to the floor front and back and symbolizing the yoke of Christ; also an adaptation of this (two small pieces of cloth connected by strings) worn around the neck by persons who do not belong to the religious order; a scapular approved by the Church is a sacramental. See **sacramental.**

scapular medal   A medal with an image of the Sacred Heart on one side and the Blessed Virgin on the other. It may be worn on a chain or carried in place of the scapular in which the wearer is invested.

schism   A formal break in Church unity through a refusal to submit to the authority of the pope or to hold communion with the members of the Church subject to him. *(CCC 2089)*

scholasticism   A philosophy that was prominent in the Middle Ages and personified by the work of Saint Thomas Aquinas.

science   The knowledge of physical principles observed through demonstration. The Church holds that science and scientific research is a significant expression of the human dominion over creation. *(CCC 2293–2294)*

Scribes   A class of government officials who in the time of our Lord had become interpreters of the law of Moses.

Scripture, Sacred   The written and authoritative word of God as inspired by the Holy Spirit. *(CCC 81)*

scruple   A fear arising in the mind by which a person sees a sin when there is none.

scrupulosity   A religious-moral-psychological state of more or less severe anxiety, fear, and indecision; an unreasonable and morbid fear of sin, error, and guilt.

seal of confession   The secrecy demanded of the confessor in the sacrament of penance; no reason whatever justifies the breaking of this seal, and the Church reserves grave penalties for any confessor who would dare to do so (see Canon 1388). *(CCC 1467, 2490)*

Second Coming   See **Parousia.**

secrecy   A secret is something known only to a certain person or persons (either because of their profession or because they have promised to keep a secret) and purposely kept from the knowledge of others; something that for one reason or another should not be made known to other people. The possessor of a secret has a moral responsibility to conceal his or her knowledge of the secret unless grave harm would come to the holder of the secret, to the community, or to an innocent third party. There is no exception to the confessional secret. *(CCC 2491)*   See **seal of confession.**

secular clergy   See **clergy.**

secular institutes   According to the Code of Canon Law, "A secular institute is an institute of consecrated life in which the Christian faithful living in the world strive for the perfection of charity and work for the sanctification of the world especially from within" (Canon 710). Persons who belong to an institute of consecrated life profess the evangelical counsels of chastity, poverty, and obedience according to the constitutions of their particular institute (see Canon 573). *(CCC 928–929)*

secularism A philosophy of life that in theory or in practice rejects the value of the supernatural in human life; it professes that human existence and destiny belong to this world only, with no reference to eternal realities.

self-control A fruit of the Holy Spirit marked by the quality of having one's desires under the control of the will and enlightened by right reason and faith. *(CCC 736)*

self-defense The moral right to use force against an unjust aggressor. *(CCC 1909)*

self-knowledge The act of understanding one's self, useful as a means for resisting temptation and in a full examination of conscience. *(CCC 2340)*

seminary A place where candidates for the priesthood (called seminarians) pursue their academic, apostolic, and spiritual formation.

Sermon on the Mount The comprehensive presentation of the teachings of Jesus as presented in the Gospel of Matthew, chapters 5, 6, 7; a brief version is found in the Gospel of Luke 6:20–49; it has been called the "Magna Carta of Christianity" and contains the teaching of Jesus on true discipleship, including an explanation of the beatitudes, the Lord's Prayer, and the relationship of the old law to the new law in Christ. *(CCC 2764)*

Servant of God Jesus Christ as Servant of the Lord who came in fulfillment of the servant poems in the Book of Isaiah. *(CCC 713)*

servers, altar Those who assist the celebrant at Mass and other liturgical rites.

seven last words of Christ Words spoken by Jesus on the cross: (1) "Father, forgive them; for they know not what they do"; (2) to the repentant thief, "Truly, I say to you, today you will be with me in paradise"; (3) to Mary and John, "Woman, behold your son....Behold your mother"; (4) "My God, my God, why hast thou forsaken me?"; (5) "I thirst"; (6) "It is finished"; and (7) "Father, into thy hands I commit my spirit."

sex education Instruction in the fundamental meaning of human sexuality and the right use of sex according to one's state in life; the Church has often spoken in favor of proper sex education and has given guidelines for it, as in the Educational Guidance in Human Love: Outlines of Sex Education issued by the Vatican Congregation for Catholic Education in December 1983. *(CCC 369–373, 2343–2345)*

sexual abuse Rape, sexual assault, or sexual molestation, especially any sexual abuse perpetrated by adults on children entrusted to their care. *(CCC 2389)*

shrines of Our Lady Holy places where apparitions of the Blessed Virgin Mary are believed to have taken place; because of their reputation as places where moral and physical miracles have been granted, they are centers of pilgrimages; among the outstanding shrines of the Blessed Virgin Mary, the following four (in alphabetical order) are especially noteworthy:

1. Fátima, Portugal: Between May 13 and October 13, 1917, Mary appeared six times to three children near Fátima, north of Lisbon. After intense study, Church authorities pronounced these apparitions worthy of belief in 1930. The message of Mary at Fátima included an exhortation to frequent recitation of the rosary, works of mortification on behalf of sinners, the consecration of the people of Russia to her under the title of the Immaculate Heart, and the observance of the first Saturday of each month by receiving Holy Communion in reparation for sin.

2. Guadalupe, Mexico: In 1531, Mary appeared four times to Juan Diego on Tepeyac Hill near Mexico City; a life-size figure of Mary was miraculously painted on Juan Diego's mantle; this painting is now enshrined in the basilica of the shrine; the Church has accepted the apparition as authentic and celebrates the feast of Our Lady of Guadalupe (the "Mother of the Americas") on December 12.

3. La Salette, France: In September 1846, Mary appeared to two peasant children; in 1851 Church authorities declared the apparition worthy of belief, and devotion to Our Lady of La Sallette was approved. The chief message of our Lady was the necessity of penance on the part of the faithful.

4. Lourdes, France: Between February and July, 1858, Mary (identifying herself by saying, "I am the Immaculate Conception") appeared 18 times to a young woman, Bernadette Soubirous. After four years of intense study, Church authorities approved the apparitions as authentic in 1862. Mary's message was a solemn exhortation to

prayer and penance for the conversion of peoples. The feast of Our Lady of Lourdes is celebrated on February 11. *(CCC 971)*

shroud of Turin   The cloth or winding sheet housed in the cathedral of Turin, Italy, is thought by many to have covered the body of Jesus in the tomb. This shroud bears an imprint of a crucified man and has been the subject of many investigations. The Church, however, has made no ruling on the authenticity of the relic.

sickness   Illness or disease can lead humans to anguish, despair, and even revolt against God, or can provoke a search for God and a return to him. *(CCC 1500–1505)*

sign of the cross   A gesture in the form of a cross by which one professes his or her faith in the holy Trinity; it is made in several ways: (1) one "blesses oneself," for example at the beginning and end of one's prayers, by touching the fingers of one's right hand to one's forehead, breast, left shoulder, and right shoulder while saying, "In the name of the Father, and of the Son, and of the Holy Spirit"; (2) one forms a small cross on one's forehead, lips, and breast before the proclamation of the Gospel; (3) one authorized to give blessings in the Church makes a large cross with the right hand over the person or object to be blessed. *(CCC 1671–1672)*   See **blessing.**

signs   Things that point to other things beyond themselves. The liturgy of the Church is built on signs. Jesus refers to his miracles as signs, and the sacraments are signs that manifest the special presence of God. *(CCC 1145–1151)*

signs of the times   A phrase used in Vatican II's Pastoral Constitution on the Church in the Modern World which declares that "the Church has always had the duty of scrutinizing the signs of the times and of interpreting them in the light of the gospel."

simony   Intentional buying or selling of something spiritual (for example, grace, a sacrament) or something closely connected with the spiritual (for example, a relic); both the law of God and the law of the Church forbid such buying and selling because it is a violation of the honor due to God and the things of God. *(CCC 2121)*   See **sacrilege.**

sin   In Catholic theology, a term used to describe two separate realities: original sin and actual sin. Original sin is the sin of Adam that brought about evil effects on the human race. Actual (or personal) sin is a fundamental choice against God, a free and willing turning away from his love and his law. Actual sin may be either mortal or venial. *(CCC 388–395, 1854–1864)*   See **original sin; mortal sin; venial sin.**

sins against the Holy Spirit   Sins considered especially repugnant to the third Person of the Blessed Trinity. These six sins are despair, presumption, envy, obstinacy in sin, final impenitence, and deliberate resistance to the known truth.

sins, forgiveness of   Only God forgives sins. Christ has willed that the Church be the sign and instrument of this forgiveness that reintegrates forgiven sinners into the community of the people of God. *(CCC 1441)*

sins that cry to heaven for vengeance   These sins are willful murder, perversion, oppression of widows, orphans, or the poor, and defrauding workers of their wages.

sister   Popularly, a title given to any woman who belongs to a religious institute; strictly, the title belongs to a woman who belongs to a religious institute that professes simple, not solemn, vows.   See **nun; vows.**

slander   See **calumny.**

slavery   The bondage of one person to another that allows human beings to be bought, sold, or exchanged like merchandise or animals. It is an offense against the dignity of persons and the natural law. *(CCC 2414)*

sloth   One of the capital or deadly sins, it is a kind of spiritual laziness or boredom in regard to the things of God, frequently leading to a neglect of one's spiritual duties. *(CCC 1866, 2094)*

social doctrine of the Church   The Church's social teaching is a body of doctrine, on economic and social matters, articulated by the Church as it encounters events in the course of history. The Church makes moral judgment about these matters when the salvation and rights of the person demand it. *(CCC 2420–2425)*

social justice   A part of the cardinal virtue of justice; according to Catholic social teaching, it is that aspect of justice which urges the individual member of a social group to seek the common good of the whole group rather than just his or her own individual good; it presumes, in the explanation of Pope Pius XII, "a social conscience that calls individuals to their social duties, urges them to take into account in all their activities their membership in a community, to be preoccupied with the welfare of their neighbors and with the common good of society." Social justice strives to bring authentic moral values to the organization of society and to the social institutions (educational, economic, political) by which society functions. *(CCC 2426–2436)* See **unions, labor; wage, just; work.**

society of apostolic life   A group of people who live together in common and who pursue some apostolate.

society   A body of individuals living together as a community. Society is essential to the fulfillment of the human vocation. To attain this aim, respect must be given to interior and spiritual values. *(CCC 1897–1899)*

solidarity   This term refers to the principle of social charity as a direct result of the unity of humankind before God. Solidarity implies that special attention be given to those who are powerless, excluded from a fair share of distributed goods, and who are facing unjust conditions. *(CCC 1942)*

sorcery   A kind of magic that invokes evil spirits in order to attain some end. Such occult intervention is against the first commandment. *(CCC 1852, 2117)*

soul   That part of the human person that animates the body; the principal of spiritual activities such as thinking and willing; according to Catholic teaching, the human soul is individually created for each person by God and infused at the time of conception and is immortal. *(CCC 365–367)*

speculation   The practice of buying lands, goods, commodities, and so on, in the expectation of a rise in price so that the speculator can sell at an advantage. Speculation is unlawful if the buyer manipulates the market through fraud or if the speculator corners such large quantities that others thereby suffer. *(CCC 2409)*

speed   Those who exceed the normal safety limits of a vehicle and endanger their own life and those of others show intemperance and lack of reasonable care for the common good. *(CCC 2290)*

spiritism   Also called spiritualism, it is the belief that the living can communicate with spirits and with the deceased by way of a human medium or inanimate objects, such as a Ouija board; practices derived therefrom are a violation of the first commandment of the Decalogue and opposed to the virtue of religion. *(CCC 2117)*

Spiritual Exercises   See retreat.

spiritual life   A term used by Christians to refer to the interior life of sanctifying grace, by which one shares in the life of the triune God (see John 14:23) and becomes a temple of the Holy Spirit, and to describe the efforts of the individual Christian to cultivate that life by participating in the sacraments, prayer, works of penance, and charity.

spiritual works of mercy They are to counsel the doubtful, instruct the ignorant, admonish sinners, comfort the afflicted, forgive offenses, bear wrongs patiently, and pray for the living and the dead.

stational churches Churches in the city of Rome where the early popes would celebrate the liturgy on at least one special day. Examples of stational churches include St. Mary Major at Midnight Mass on Christmas and St. John Lateran for Easter.

Stations of the Cross A popular devotion (also called Way of the Cross) in honor of the Passion and death of Christ; it consists of meditating on fourteen "stations" or "stages" in the Passion of Christ, such as his condemnation by Pilate, his scourging, his journey to Calvary, and the tomb. The stations are wooden crosses, often inserted in paintings or sculptures, and may be attached to the walls of a church or oratory or erected outdoors. The stations must be lawfully erected and blessed by one who has the authority to do so. *(CCC 2669)*

sterility The inability to generate children because of some physical defect; according to the Code of Canon Law, "Sterility neither prohibits nor invalidates marriage" (Canon 1084, §3). *(CCC 2374–2377)*

sterilization Depriving a person of the reproductive function; according to Catholic moral teaching, it is morally justified when necessary for life or health; but as a contraceptive measure it is a grave violation of the moral law. *(CCC 2297)* See **contraception.**

stewardship The religious conviction that every gift of nature and grace comes from God and that the human person is not the absolute master of his or her gifts and possessions but, rather, the trustees (stewards) of them (see 1 Peter 4:10); they are given "in trust" for the building up of the kingdom of God. *(CCC 2417)*

stigmata The term designating the wounds suffered by Christ and which have subsequently appeared on holy individuals in different shapes and forms. The most famous stigmatic is Saint Francis of Assisi.

stipend, Mass An offering made to a priest on the occasion of requesting a Mass to be offered for one's personal intentions; according to the Code of Canon Law, "In accord with the approved usage of the Church, it is lawful for any priest who celebrates or concelebrates Mass to receive an offering to apply the Mass according to a definite intention" (Canon 945, §1), but at the same time priests are urged to "celebrate Mass for the intention of the Christian faithful, especially of the needy, even if no offering has been received" (Canon 945, §2); the faithful who make such an offering "contribute to the good of the Church and by their offering take part in the concern of the Church for the support of its ministers and works" (Canon 946); the Code of Canon Law also insists that "any appearance of trafficking or commerce is to be entirely excluded from Mass offerings" (Canon 947) and has strict regulations governing this entire matter (see Canons 948–958).

stole See **vestments.**

stole fee Offerings given to a priest for the performance of a sacrament. This kind of fee is voluntary as canon law requires priests to provide these services free of change.

stoup A vessel for holding holy water.

strike An organized work stoppage on the part of employees for the purpose of obtaining values and benefits that employees believe they are entitled to; according to Catholic social teaching, a strike is morally justified provided that there is a just cause for it, that there is proper authorization by a free decision of the employees or those who represent them, that it is a last resort (after every other reasonable means has been exhausted), and that only just means are used in carrying it out. *(CCC 2435)*

subsidiarity An article of Catholic social teaching first proclaimed by Pope Pius XI in 1931. This principle cuts two ways. First, that a larger institution should not interfere with a smaller institution. Second, larger institutions have an obligation to support smaller institutions in positive ways. *(CCC 1883–1885)*

substance A philosophical term that designates the pure existence of a thing considered separately from the accidents, or outward appearances. The Church uses the term substance to designate the divine Being in its unity and to describe the transubstantiation of the bread and wine into the body and blood of Christ. *(CCC 252)*

suffering Emotional, physical, spiritual, or mental pain. Seen by the Church as a consequence of original sin. *(CCC 1521)*

suicide Intentionally causing one's own death; objectively speaking, suicide is a serious violation of God's law, a rejection of God's sovereignty and loving plan; subjectively, however, suicide often seems to result from profound psychological disturbances or mental imbalances and thus may not be the result of a free and deliberate act. *(CCC 2280–2283)*

Sunday; Sunday rest   See **holy days of obligation.**

supererogation   Actions which develop one's spiritual life but which exceed the demands of morality.

superstition   Either the worship of God in an unworthy manner (for example, by bizarre cultic practices) or attributing to persons or objects a power which belongs to God alone (for example, astrology, spiritism); superstition is a violation of true religion. *(CCC 2110–2111)*

support of the Church   One of the Precepts of the Church rooted in the biblical principle of stewardship and based on the fact that the Church, in both its local and worldwide dimensions, depends upon the voluntary contributions of the faithful to carry on its ministry. *(CCC 2043)*   See **stewardship.**

surrogate motherhood   The practice of carrying another couple's child to term. This practice infringes on a child's right to be born to a mother and father known to him or her and intrudes on the marriage bond. *(CCC 2376)*

swearing   Calling on the name of God to witness to the truth of a statement or promise; according to Catholic teaching, swearing is justified only in support of the truth and in favor of justice. *(CCC 2150)*

Syllabus, the   The series of eighty propositions condemned by Pope Pius IX in *Quanta Cura* in 1864. This encyclical condemned the liberal and modernistic errors of the age.

symbolon   A Greek word designating half of a broken object. When the broken parts were placed together, they verified the bearer's identity. Thus a symbol of faith is a sign of recognition and communion. This same Greek word means a "collection" or "summary." Thus a gathering of the principal truths of the faith, as in a creed, is a symbol of faith. *(CCC 188)*

symbols   Things or signs by which another reality can be experienced. In the theological sense, a symbol allows us to look behind just the messages of our senses to a belief in a greater and more mysterious reality not readily apparent. *(CCC 1146–1149)*

synagogue   The Jewish meeting place or center, less sacred and formal than the Temple, used for religious worship, biblical readings and study, prayer, and other community affairs.

Synod of Bishops   According to the Code of Canon Law, "The synod of bishops is that group of bishops who have been chosen from different regions of the world and who meet at stated times to foster a closer unity between the Roman Pontiff and the bishops, to assist the Roman Pontiff with their counsel in safeguarding and increasing faith and morals and in preserving and strengthening ecclesiastical discipline, and to consider questions concerning the Church's activity in the world" (Canon 342).

synoptic Gospels   Synoptic is from a Greek word meaning "seeing the whole together" and is applied to the Gospels of Matthew, Mark, and Luke because they present a similar view of the life and teaching of Jesus. *(CCC 515)*   See **Gospels.**

T

tabernacle   A receptacle for the exclusive reservation of the Most Holy Eucharist; according to the Code of Canon Law, it "should be placed in a part of the Church that is prominent, conspicuous, beautifully decorated, and suitable for prayer" (Canon 938, §2); moreover, it should be "immovable, made of solid and opaque material, and locked so that the danger of profanation may be entirely avoided" (Canon 938, §3); a special lamp (often called the sanctuary lamp) "to indicate and honor the presence of Christ is to burn at all times before the tabernacle in which the Most Holy Eucharist is reserved" (Canon 940). *(CCC 1183, 1378)*

Talmud   The Jewish compilation containing the Mishnah or oral interpretations of the law in written form; Jews (and some Christians too) still consider it an authoritative guide and aid to the spiritual life.

tax evasion   A tax is revenue collected by a governing body for the support of the common good. It is a moral duty to pay legitimate taxes. *(CCC 2436)*

teaching office of the Church   See **magisterium.**

technology   A word referring to the application of science to industrial and money-making objectives. It also refers to a view of the world dominated by machines, computers, and standardization. *(CCC 2293–2294)*

temperance   One of the cardinal virtues; it moderates and regulates the desire for pleasure, especially but not exclusively in regard to the pleasures of eating, drinking, and sex. *(CCC 1809)*   See **virtue**.

temporal punishment   The punishment still due to venial or mortal sins already forgiven; it is "temporal" as opposed to "eternal," that is, the punishment of hell; temporal punishment may be remitted in this life by the practice of penance and other virtues, in the next life in purgatory. *(CCC 1472–1473)*   See **indulgence; purgatory**.

temptation   An attraction or enticement to sin, arising from within a person or from without (that is, "from the world, the flesh, or the devil"); it is not of itself a sin but an opportunity or occasion of proving one's fidelity to God: Catholic moral teaching encourages the Christian to deal with temptation by prayer for grace and prudent action. *(CCC 405, 409)*

terrorism   A system that aims at spreading fear among people in order to discourage certain ideas or activities. The methods of terrorism may include threats, spying, police states, kidnapping, torture, random acts of violence, and so forth. *(CCC 2297)*

testament   See **covenant**.

theft   The secret taking of another's goods against his or her reasonable wishes; it is a sin against the seventh commandment, a violation of commutative (person-to-person) justice. *(CCC 2408, 2454)*

theological virtues   The three virtues of faith, hope, and charity that are God-given (infused with the gift of sanctifying grace) and God-directed (that is, God himself is their direct object); these virtues enable us to know and love God in himself and lead to union with him in mind and heart. *(CCC 1812–1813)*   See **faith; hope; charity**.

theology   The science that treats of God, the things that relate to God, and God's relations with the world; it is, according to an ancient definition, "faith seeking understanding," that is, a systematized and organized study of what God has revealed and what believers have accepted; this science has historically been divided into a number of branches, such as dogmatic theology, moral theology, pastoral theology, and the like. *(CCC 236)*

Thomas Aquinas, Saint   Born in Italy around 1225, he joined the Order of Preachers (Dominicans) and became one of the greatest theologians in the history of the Church; his genius was the ability to relate faith and reason, theology and philosophy; he wrote many books, the chief of which was his *Summa Theologica*, a broad exposition of theology as related to philosophical principles; he died in 1274, was canonized in 1323; he is considered one of the greatest Doctors of the Church and a sure guide in Catholic theology.

time   A reckoning of events; God exists outside of "time"; whatever that ultimately is proven to be. *(CCC 338)*

tithing   The biblical mandate that one should contribute one-tenth of one's income to support the works of religion and charity; sometimes used to describe any fixed pledge of income, even if less than one-tenth.

tobacco   Tobacco is a drug; it is legal, socially acceptable, and highly addictive. As evidence mounts that smoking tobacco, especially in the form of cigarettes, is dangerous to health, good stewardship demands that this danger to health be confronted by the Christian person. *(CCC 2290)*

Torah   A term commonly used to refer to the Mosaic Law as contained in the Pentateuch or first five books of the Bible, namely, Genesis, Exodus, Leviticus, Numbers, and Deuteronomy. *(CCC 1961)*

torture   The use of physical or moral violence to obtain confessions, punish the guilty, frighten opponents, and to satisfy hatred. These cruel practices are unnecessary to preserve public order and are offenses against human dignity. *(CCC 2298)*

tradition   According to Catholic teaching, one of the sources (together with Sacred Scripture) of divine revelation; it is, as Vatican II, points out, the Word of God which has been entrusted to the apostles by Christ the Lord and the Holy Spirit; unlike many Christian communities that teach Scripture alone is the source of divine Revelation, the Catholic Church professes that "sacred tradition and sacred scripture form one sacred deposit of the word of God, which is committed to the Church" (Dogmatic Constitution on Divine Revelation, §10). *(CCC 80–83)*

Transfiguration of Christ   The appearance in glory of Jesus Christ during his earthly life, as recorded in Matthew 17:1–3, Mark 9:2–13, and Luke 9:28–36; a significant event that showed the Lord to be the Messiah, reaffirmed his sonship with the Father, and foreshadowed his future glory; this event is commemorated on the first Sunday of Lent each year, and there is a special feast of Transfiguration on August 6. *(CCC 554–556)*

transubstantiation   In Catholic theology of the Eucharist, a technical term that describes the change of the whole substance of bread and wine into the whole substance of the body and blood of Christ while only the accidents (taste, smell, and so on) of bread and wine remain. *(CCC 1373–1377)*

Trent, Council of The nineteenth ecumenical council of the Catholic Church held in twenty-five sessions between 1545 and 1563; its primary work was a defense of Catholic teaching against the attacks of the Protestant reformers: in presenting this defense it also offered a comprehensive treatment of Catholic teaching on the nature of justification, original sin, grace, faith, the seven sacraments (especially the Eucharist), the veneration of saints, purgatory, and indulgences. Trent set in motion a number of Catholic reforms in regard to the liturgy, the religious education of the faithful, the training of candidates for the priesthood, and the devotional life of the Church. Its influence was, for the most part, widespread and positive, and it is considered one of the most important of the Church's ecumenical councils. *(CCC 884)* See **ecumenical council.**

triduum A three-day series of public devotions, similar to a novena except for the shorter time period. See **novena.**

Trinity, Holy See **Holy Trinity.**

truth From the moral point of view, truth is an accurate representation of one's self and one's thoughts in our relations with others. *(CCC 2465–2466)*

"two ways," parable of The two ways referred to in this parable are the way of Christ which leads to life everlasting; and the other way which leads to destruction. *(CCC 1696)*

U

unbaptized, fate of If, as the Church professes, baptism is necessary for salvation (see John 3:5), what can be said of the salvation of those who die without baptism? This theological question has been pondered for centuries. Briefly, Catholic teaching holds that, in the case of adults, there are two possibilities: (1) baptism of blood or martyrdom and (2) baptism of desire. In the case of infants, a rather common theological opinion has been that infants who die without baptism are excluded from heaven but spend eternity in a state of natural happiness called limbo. This theological explanation has never been explicitly taught by the Church. Another fairly common theological explanation has been that God in his mercy can supply for the lack of baptism in a way that has not been revealed to us. In a document from the Vatican's Congregation for the Doctrine of the Faith (1980) it is said that the Church "knows no other way apart from Baptism for ensuring children's entry into eternal happiness"; but in regard to children who die without baptism, the Church "can only entrust them to the mercy of God, as she does in the funeral rite provided for them. *(CCC 1257–1261)* See **baptism of blood; baptism of desire.**

understanding One of the gifts of the Holy Spirit which disposes one to be readily open to divine inspirations and to the living Word of God. *(CCC 1830–1831)*

unions, labor Catholic social teaching has long defined the right of workers to form associations to protect their vital interests, while at the same time insisting that unions should pursue their goals only in morally acceptable ways. A recent authoritative statement of these principles is to be found in the encyclical letter of Pope John Paul II, On Human Work *(Laborem Exercens)*, especially in paragraph 20. After discussing various rights of workers within the context of basic human rights, the pope points out: "All these rights, together with the need for workers to secure them, give rise to yet another right: the right of association, that is, to form associations for the purpose of defending the vital interests of those employed in the various professions. These associations are called labor or trade unions...." These unions should always strive "to secure the just rights of workers within the framework of the common good of the whole of society...." *(CCC 2430)*

United States Catholic Conference (USCC) A service agency for the National Council of Catholic Bishops; its purpose, as described in the Official Catholic Directory, is to assist "the Bishops in their service to the Church in this country uniting the people of God where voluntary collective action on a broad interdiocesan level is needed" and to provide "an organizational structure and the resources needed to insure coordination, cooperation, and assistance in the public educational and social concerns of the Church at the national or diocesan level."

unity, Christian See ecumenism.

Urbi et Orbi Literally, this Latin phrase means "to the city and the world"; specifically, it refers to the solemn blessing of the pope given to his visible audience in the city of Rome and also to the entire invisible audience of the faithful throughout the world.

usury   In moral theology, the taking of excessive or exorbitant interest on the loan of money. It is a violation of the virtue of justice.

V

validation of marriage   The making valid of a marriage contract that was originally invalid for one of three reasons: (1) because of the presence of a diriment (invalidating) impediment; (2) because of a defect of consent; (3) because of a defect of form. The procedures for validation in these cases are given in the Code of Canon Law, Canon 1156 through Canon 1160.   See **annulment; impediments to marriage.**

validity   This term entered the vocabulary of the Church with the Council of Trent. Validity concerns the conditions that have to be followed for some act to be effectual or legal. For example, reception of baptism is a prior condition for validly receiving any of the other sacraments.

validity of sacraments   When applied to sacraments, validity refers to the minimal requirements of matter, form, and circumstances needed for valid administration and to recognize that an action or celebration has resulted in a true sacrament. For example, the minister must resolve to do what the Church intends in celebrating a sacrament. Since the spouses minister the sacrament to each other in marriage, their intention to celebrate the sacrament is an absolutely necessary condition for validity.

values, moral   The things that are essential to appropriate human living include, for example, the capacity for love. Other moral values consist of such virtues as chastity, fortitude, justice, and temperance.

Vatican, the   A name used to describe a number of different realities: for example, the residence of the pope built upon the Vatican Hill in the city of Rome; the various congregations or tribunals through which the pope governs the Church; the basilica of St. Peter; the sovereign state of 109 acres, established in 1929 by an agreement between the pope and the Italian government, ruled as an independent territory by the pope.

Vatican Council I   The twentieth ecumenical (general) council of the Catholic Church held in Rome during the pontificate of Pope Pius IX, from December 1, 1869, to October 20, 1870. This council dealt at length with questions of faith, revelation, and the relationship between faith and reason; it is best known for its definition on the universal jurisdictional primacy of the pope and his infallibility when proclaiming by a definitive act some doctrine of faith or morals. See **infallibility.**

Vatican Council II The twenty-first ecumenical council of the Catholic Church held in Rome for four sessions: the first during the pontificate of Pope John XXIII, October 11 to December 8, 1962; the other three during the pontificate of Pope Paul VI, September 29 to December 4, 1963, September 14 to November 21, 1964, and September 14 to December 8, 1965. This was the largest (2,800 members) and most productive (16 significant documents) of all the ecumenical councils. The teaching of Vatican II had an enormous impact on the Church in all parts of the world. Of the 16 documents enacted by the council 4 were constitutions of major importance for the whole Church, 9 were decrees on particular topics for particular groups within the Church, and 3 were declarations. Space permits only a brief description of each of these documents.

- Dogmatic Constitution on the Church sets forth the Church's understanding of her own nature. Its first chapter, "The Mystery of the Church," presents the vision of the Church at once divine and human, embracing all people of good will, namely "the People of God" (second chapter). The third chapter describes the bishops of the world as a "college" collectively responsible, under the leadership of the pope, for the work of the Church. The fourth chapter deals in a very positive way with the role of the laity in the Church; the fifth with the universal call to holiness; the sixth with religious communities; the seventh with the relationship between the pilgrim Church on earth and the "Heavenly Church." Chapter eight, the final chapter, describes the role of the Blessed Virgin Mary.

- Dogmatic Constitution on Divine Revelation sets forth the Church's teaching on how God reveals himself to humankind. The transmission of this revelation is recorded in written form in the Scriptures; its transmission by word of mouth is part of the tradition of the Church. Both Scripture and tradition spring from one and the same source.

- Constitution on the Sacred Liturgy sets forth the Church's teaching on worship as the heart of her life. It instructed that the sacred texts and rites should be drawn up so that they express more clearly the holy things which they signify and that the Christian people, as far as possible, should be able to understand them with ease and take part in them fully, actively, and as befits a community.

- Pastoral Constitution on the Church in the Modern World sets forth the Church's sincere effort to speak to all men and women, to shed light on the dignity of the human person and to cooperate in finding solutions to the outstanding problems of our time.
- The nine decrees addressed the following subjects: the pastoral office of bishops, ecumenism, the Oriental Catholic Churches, the ministry and life of priests, education for the priesthood, the renewal of religious life, the missionary activity of the Church, the apostolate of the laity, and the instruments of social communication.

(The three declarations dealt with religious freedom, the Church's attitude toward non-Christians, and Christian education.)

veil   Part of the habit of women religious consisting of a covering over the head and shoulders. The form and fabric of the veil varies. The color was usually black for professed and white for novices. Today in many of the active orders of women religious, the veil is optional.

The bride at the marriage ceremony often wears a veil of lace or similar material. In many parts of the world the veil is commonly worn by the married women as a symbol of marital fidelity.

veneration of the cross   In this devotional, a deep reverence and respect is directed toward the cross. In the Good Friday service, the veneration of the cross involves the procession with the cross through the congregation with the invitation to come forward to show some sign of respect for it. The faithful often bow and/or kiss the cross as a sign of reverence.   See **Good Friday.**

veneration of images   Devotion to icons or images is not against the first commandment which forbids idols. Rather honoring the images and symbols of God and the saints venerate the person portrayed rather than the image itself. *(CCC 2132)*

vengeance   The imposing of punishment on someone who has done a moral wrong is a right that belongs to God alone. *(CCC 2302)*

venial sin   In contrast to mortal (grave, serious) sin, a venial sin may be described as a less serious rejection of God's love, not a fundamental choice against God, not a complete turning away from him. It is a failure to love God and others as much as we should, a transient neglect of God and his law. Saint Thomas describes it this way: "Although a person who commits a venial sin does not actually refer his or her act to God, nevertheless he or she still keeps God as his or her habitual end. The person does not decisively set himself or herself on turning away from God, but from overfondness for a created good falls short of God. He or she is like a person who loiters, but without leaving the way. *(CCC 1854, 1862–1863)*   See **sin; mortal sin.**

Veni Creator Spiritus   This hymn addressed to the Holy Spirit has long been connected with the sacraments of confirmation and orders and special Church elections and meetings. Its seven verses are sung for Evening Prayer on Pentecost Sunday.

Veni Sancte Spiritus   The Latin opening words and name of the sequence in honor of the Holy Spirit that is said at the Mass of Pentecost. It has also been called "The Golden Sequence." It is sung at Mass between the second reading and the Gospel.

vernacular   The mother tongue or common spoken language of the people is used in liturgical worship. Ordinarily liturgies are in the local languages, except when another language was originated from missionaries or dictated by a conquering nation. The Second Vatican Council officially approved the vernacular for Catholic liturgy in the Roman rite.

Veronica's veil   Tradition has it that a woman who had compassion on Jesus on his way to Calvary gave him her veil that he might wipe the perspiration from his face. The imprint of Jesus' face was miraculously made on this veil. It is now a relic in St. Peter's Basilica in Rome. This event is celebrated in the sixth station of the cross.

Vespers   The evening service of the Divine Office is also known as Evening Prayer or Evensong. It is one of the two principal hours of prayer. In structure it has an introductory verse; a hymn appropriate for the day, feast or liturgical season; two psalms and a New Testament canticle; a reading from Scripture followed by a responsorial hymn; the *Magnificat*; intercessions, followed by the Our Father, the prayer of the day, and a final blessing.

vestibule   The part of a Catholic church between the outer church door and the inside through which people must pass in order to reach the interior worship space is known as an entrance hall or antechamber. Today the vestibule is often an area which displays books and pamphlets, church bulletins, and parish announcement boards. It is also the place where the procession to begin the celebration of the Eucharist originates and where it returns after it is ended to greet the faithful.

vestments   Garments used in the celebration of the Eucharistic Liturgy and other sacraments. The vestments have their origin in the ordinary dress of the Roman Empire in the first centuries of Christianity, but they have taken on a symbolic meaning also. The principal vestments now in use:

Amice: a square or oblong piece of linen (or similar material) to which two long tapes are attached at the upper corners. It is worn over the shoulders and is symbolic of "the helmet of salvation."

Alb: a long, white (*albus* is Latin for white) garment, symbolic of the total purity that should cover one's approach to God.

Chasuble: a long, sleeveless outer garment worn over the alb by a priest or bishop. Traditionally, the chasuble is a symbol of charity.

Cincture: a cord worn around the waist to keep the alb neatly in place.

Humeral veil: a rectangular shawl worn around the shoulders and used to cover the hands. It is used in Eucharistic processions and devotions for holding the ciborium or the monstrance.

Stole: a long, thin band of appropriate material worn around the neck and shoulders, symbolic of "the yoke of the Lord"; it is worn by the priest in solemn celebration of all the sacraments (the deacon wearing it over the shoulder only).

Surplice: a waist-length, lace-decorated, wide-sleeved, white, alblike vestment worn over the cassock outside of Mass.

Viaticum The reception of Holy Communion when there is probable danger of death. According to canon law: "The Christian faithful who are in danger of death, arising from any cause, are to be nourished by Holy Communion in the form of Viaticum" (Canon 921). It is important that Viaticum not be delayed too long but that the sick be nourished with this "food for the journey" while they are still conscious. *(CCC 1524–1525)* See **anointing of the sick.**

vicar general The priest or bishop appointed by the bishop to assist him in the government of his diocese. The duties of the vicar general are specified in canon law. His office ends with that of the bishop.

Vicar of Christ The pope is the representative of Christ on earth and the visible spiritual head of the Church. The title is used exclusively for the Bishop of Rome as the successor of Peter. *(CCC 882)*

vice A bad habit that leads a person into sin is called a vice. This habitual inclination to do evil is the result of repeated sinful actions. Qualities that characterize a vice are spontaneity, facility, and pleasure in doing what is morally wrong. The capital sins typify these sinful patterns of pride, sloth, lust, envy, anger, gluttony, and covetousness. The opposite of vice is virtue.

vigil   The word *vigil* comes from the Latin *vigilia* which means "a watching." A vigil is a prayer watch kept the night before the feast. The mother of all vigils is the Easter Vigil which begins after nightfall on Holy Saturday and ends before dawn on Easter Sunday. Other important vigils during which Mass is celebrated preceding the feast are Christmas, Pentecost, birth of John the Baptist, Saints Peter and Paul, and the Assumption. The day and evening before certain feasts have a special Office in preparation for the feast day. *(CCC 1281)* See also **Easter Vigil**.

vigil lights   Small candles placed in glass cups often burn before a shrine or replica of a saint as an act of devotion or for a particular intention. Vigil lights are Catholic sacramentals and are symbols of the deep hope of the faithful that their prayers will be answered and that their special needs will be met. These vigil lights symbolize the light of prayer and may burn for only a few hours or as long as a week. It is believed that the flame "keeps vigil" when the person cannot be present.

It is customary for persons lighting these votive candles to leave a small donation to support the church's ministry and to defray the basic costs associated with the vigil lights.

violence   Physical or psychological force that is used to coerce individuals to act against their will or against the preference to choose in a certain way. Violence is one of the greatest obstacles against freedom of the will.

virgin birth   The basic Christian doctrine that Jesus Christ was conceived and born of Mary while she remained a virgin; this belief is included in all the creeds ("I believe in Jesus Christ, his only Son, who was born of the virgin Mary..." and is an article of Catholic faith. *(CCC 499)*

virginity   The observance of perpetual sexual abstinence. In the Christian context its motive is "for the sake of the kingdom of heaven" (Matthew 19:12). In speaking of the evangelical counsels, Vatican II teaches that "towering among these counsels is that precious gift of divine grace given to some by the Father to devote themselves to God alone more easily with an undivided heart in virginity or celibacy (see Matthew 19:11; 1 Corinthians 7:32–34). This perfect continence for love of the kingdom of heaven has always been held in high esteem by the Church as a sign and stimulus of love, for as a singular source of spiritual fertility in the world" (Dogmatic Constitution on the Church, §42). *(CCC 1618–1619)*   See **celibacy; chastity**.

virtue A good habit that enables a person to act according to right reason enlightened by faith and to do so with relative ease and with perseverance despite obstacles. The Christian tradition distinguishes especially between theological virtues and moral virtues. Theological virtues are powers infused by God with sanctifying grace, enabling the person to act on a supernatural level; they are faith, hope, and charity. The moral virtues are powers which are acquired by repeated human acts aided by the grace of God; there are many moral virtues, but the chief ones are prudence, justice, fortitude and temperance. *(CCC 1804–1809, 1812–1813)* See **theological virtues; faith; hope; charity; prudence; justice; fortitude; temperance.**

virtue, infused Some virtues are called *infused* because they are not acquired as the result of continual practice but are given directly by God. Infused virtues may be either theological or moral. The theological virtues of faith, hope, and charity and the moral, or cardinal virtues, of prudence, justice, fortitude, and temperance are infused virtues given to a newly baptized person. These virtues bring to fulfillment the gifts the person has, help the individual act in a supernatural way, and incline the person toward good.

visions A gift through which a person sensibly experiences God, angels, or saints. Visions are physical when something is seen, psychological when they occur in the inner imagination, and intellectual when the person receives a sudden and unmediated grasp of divine truth or deeply experienced intuitive understanding. Because visions are a charism, they are for the spiritual good of persons. Visions are not necessary for salvation or holiness. *(CCC 707)*

Visitation Mary paid a visit to her cousin Elizabeth at Ain Karim after the angel announced to her that she was to become the Mother of God. When Elizabeth saw Mary she was filled with the Spirit and proclaimed "Blessed are you among women, and blessed is the fruit of your womb." Mary responded with the *Magnificat*. (See Luke 1:39–56.) The second Joyful Mystery of the rosary recalls the Visitation. The feast is celebrated on May 31.

visitation, canonical The official inspection of a religious house made by a bishop, the superior of a religious community or order, or someone delegated by either, to ensure the observance of canon law or for some other purpose is a visitation. The bishop in a diocese makes an official visit to all diocesan institutions under his jurisdiction every five years.

vocation In a general sense, a call from God to salvation and holiness; thus, Vatican II speaks of the universal call (vocation) to holiness for all the members of the Church. In a specific sense, a call to a particular way of life in the Church: to priesthood, religious life (as a priest, nun, or other religious), Christian marriage, or the single life in the world. *(CCC 825)*

vow   As defined in the Code of Canon Law: "A vow is a deliberate and free promise made to God concerning a possible and better good which must be fulfilled by reason of the virtue of religion" (Canon 1191, §1). A vow is public if it is accepted in the name of the Church by a legitimate superior; otherwise, it is private. A vow is solemn if it is recognized as such by the Church; otherwise it is simple. *(CCC 2102–2103)*

voyeurism   The practice of achieving sexual gratification by the secret observance of sexual acts. Voyeurism contradicts the purity of heart essential for a vision of God. *(CCC 2523–2525)*

Vulgate   The Latin version of the Bible translated by Saint Jerome from the Greek and Hebrew in the fourth century is the one commonly used in the Catholic Church and was declared authentic by the Council of Trent in 1546.

W

wage, just   According to Catholic social teaching, the matter of the just wage is one of the most important elements in the relationship between employer and employee. The most recent expression of this teaching is found in Pope John Paul II's encyclical entitled On Human Work *(Laborem Exercens)*: "The key problem of social ethics in this case is that of remuneration for work done. In the context of the present there is no more important way of securing a just relationship between the worker and the employer than that constituted by remuneration for work" (§19). It is true that many complex questions arise about the working out of this moral obligation, but the moral teaching of the Church insists on several basic principles, among which are the following:

- The minimum just wage should be determined by the very reason why a person works—namely, to earn a livelihood.

- The just wage must take into consideration the requirements of the family. In the words of Pope John Paul II: "Just remuneration for the work of an adult who is responsible for a family means remuneration which will suffice for establishing and properly maintaining a family and providing security for its future" (§19).

- Women employees have a right to receive equal wages for equal work. *(CCC 2434, 2409)* See **social justice.**

wake This term describes the custom of remaining awake and on watch with a deceased person; it is usually a period of one or two days before the funeral when mourners may pay their respects to the deceased and offer their condolences to the bereaved. According to Catholic custom, the wake should also be a time of prayer for the repose of the soul of the deceased and for strength and courage on the part of the bereaved. It is customary in the United States to have a liturgical wake service (a "vigil for the deceased") and/or the praying of the rosary. See **funeral rites.**

war, morality of In view of the fact that war involves many evils, including the maiming and killing of other human beings, the question about its morality arose early in the Christian community: Is it possible to justify war from a Christian viewpoint? The answer to this question gradually developed into what is commonly called "the just-war theory." Briefly, this theory held that four conditions were necessary for a war to be just: (1) a war must be declared by lawful authority; (2) there must be a just cause, a serious grievance, for going to war; (3) there must be a right intention, such as true self-defense, not mere vengeance; (4) there must be a right use of means, that is, the war must be carried out in a moral manner. In modern times, Pope Pius XII (who was pope during the Second World War) frequently turned his attention to the just-war theory. His views were adopted and expressed by Vatican II in what might be called an updated version of the just-war theory. The following points are emphasized: (1) the only "just cause" for modern war could be as a means of self-defense against a very grave injustice that touches a free community of people, and provided that this injustice cannot be halted by any other means; (2) the "right use of means" demands that all weapons be subject to moral control, that indiscriminate destruction of whole cities or areas is morally wrong, that the rights of the innocent and noncombatants must be carefully safeguarded.

In the nuclear age, the question arises: Can this updated just-war theory be applied to nuclear war? There are many people who believe that the just-war theory cannot be applied to nuclear war; the moral safeguards simply cannot be observed. There are others, however, who maintain that even nuclear war may be conducted in a moral manner. In May 1983 the American Catholic bishops issued a comprehensive pastoral letter on peace and war, The Challenge of Peace: God's Promise and Our Response. The letter acknowledges the diversity of opinion among people of good will on the morality of using nuclear weapons in any form, but the bishops insist that, if nuclear weapons may be used at all, they may be used only after they have been used against our country or our allies, and, even then, only in an extremely limited, discriminatory manner against military targets. The bishops seriously challenge the assumption that nuclear war can in fact be limited in this way. Moreover, they insist that every effort must be made to reduce and limit the arms race, that deterrence must not be seen as an end in itself but only as a temporary justification on the way toward a progressive disarmament. *(CCC 2307–2317)*

water, liturgical use of   A few drops of water are mingled with the wine to be consecrated at the Mass. This action symbolizes the union of the two natures in Jesus, the unity of Jesus with the people of God, the pain and toil of our lives which become one with the blood of Jesus, or the commingled water and blood that came from Jesus' side at the crucifixion.

Other liturgical uses of water occur at baptism, blessing of bells, consecration of a church, washing of hands after the Offertory, and Mandatum. Holy water is used in fonts at the entrances of the church, for blessings, and in homes.

Water is essential to human life and has many natural qualities: it cleanses, refreshes, purifies, cannot be confined, is flexible, is everywhere. Water is a symbol of exterior and interior purity of life and sometimes for chaos.

Way of the Cross   See Stations of the Cross.

ways of the spiritual life   There are three stages of the spiritual journey of the Christian. Traditionally, the three phases were described as the purgative, the illuminative, and the unitive way. The purgative involved conversion from sin and disengagement from the senses or material things. The illuminative phase entailed a deepening of one's knowledge and love of God through contemplation. In the unitive phase, desire is overshadowed by love of God and prayer consisting of loving attentiveness in which the person experiences an intense union with God.

These phases are not rigid, distinct, or successive and are governed by the uniqueness of the person and the ability to respond to God's grace. As persons mature in their spiritual journey they may be at different points in their prayer life and have distinctive needs. It is helpful for a spiritual director to be familiar with the process of prayer so that the directee might be properly companioned.

Whitsunday In England this is the name given to the feast of Pentecost. Whitsunday means white Sunday and is believed to refer to the white garments worn by the baptized on that day.

will A person seeks that which is or seems to be good through this spiritual power of the human soul. The will tends toward good or away from evil when recognized by the intellect. This faculty or power which enables a person to make a free choice has the capability to intend, choose, consent, desire, hope, hate, love, and enjoy. *(CCC 1734)*

will of God God has an infinite capacity to desire the good and hence all human beings should let their lives be guided by this sovereign principle. Because God's will is a mystery, persons who want to conform their lives to it have to search for ways to discover what it is for them. The will of God is ordinarily understood as the apparent designs of God for a person's entire life or for any segment of that life. The will of God can be known to some degree through natural reason, revelation, and the teachings of the Church. Regular prayer, daily reflection, and the help of a spiritual companion are all part of God's ordinary way in showing his will to those who are serious about their spiritual journey. The will of God is not always easy to discern in practice and, at times, it can call for painful sacrifice.

There are varied proven approaches to this process of discovery. Christians have prayed daily since the time of Jesus that the will of God be realized "Your will be done, / on earth as it is in heaven" (Matthew 6:10).

wine, Eucharistic The wine consecrated during the Eucharistic Prayer must be pure grape juice which has been naturally fermented. The wine may be white or red. A few drops of water are added to the wine at the Offertory. The consecrated wine is distributed to the faithful during the Communion rite. *(CCC 1332–1334)*

wisdom One of the gifts of the Holy Spirit that enables a person to have a right appreciation (or "taste") for the things of God and to have right judgment in discerning what is true and good. *(CCC 1831)*

witchcraft The exercise of supernatural power with the assistance of evil spirits often includes the casting of spells, sorcery, and so on. Witchcraft is gravely sinful for those who engage in it because of cooperation with evil spirits and because it is often employed with the intention of causing harm to others.

witness, Christian As a Christian idea, this word means that the believer gives testimony to his or her faith in Jesus Christ and his

Gospel in all of his or her thoughts, words, and deeds, even at the cost of personal sacrifice or hostility on the part of others.

Word of God　An expression used to describe several different realities: notably, Jesus Christ as the Word of God (see John 1:1, 14); and the Bible as containing "the Word of God in the words of men."　See **Bible.**

work　Catholic social teaching has long emphasized that human work or labor, whether of a physical or mental nature, is of great importance to human dignity and to Christian spirituality. This teaching was expressed clearly in the encyclical of Pope John Paul II, On Human Work (*Laborem Exercens*): "Work is not only good in the sense that it is something to enjoy; it is also good in the sense of being something worthy, that is to say, something that corresponds to man's dignity, that expresses his dignity and increases it. If one wishes to define more clearly the ethical meaning of work, it is this truth that one must particularly keep in mind. Work is a good thing for man— a good thing for his humanity—because through work man not only transforms nature, adapting it to his own needs, but he also achieves fulfillment as a human being and indeed becomes 'more a human being'" (§9). Moreover, work can be a means of sanctification and a way of bringing the spirit of Christ to one's ordinary activities. *(CCC 2427–2428)*　See **wage, just.**

works of mercy　See **mercy, corporal works of.**

worker priests　The idea of worker priests seems to have started with priests who had performed forced labor in Germany during World War II. These priests joined the workforce to evangelize alienated workers.

　　The secular employment of priests is left to the discretion of the local ordinary. "Unbecoming" employment is forbidden by the Code of Canon Law (§285).

world, responsibility for　The expression reflects both an expanded perception of the vulnerability of creation to human actions, as well as a deepening understanding of human reliance on the natural world. Every person is called to a commitment to and a moral accountability for the welfare of the planet.

　　Responsibility for the world is a call to moral accountability on the part of both individuals and corporations for the negative consequences on the planet. The Church calls us to reclaim our stewardship and interdependence with nature.　See also **creation; stewardship.**

worship The adoration given to God expresses itself in praise, thanksgiving, self-offering, sorrow, and petition. Private worship of God can occur anywhere and at any time (John 4:21–24). Public worship is liturgy centered on Christ.

The reverence and adoration paid to God is called *latria*. Sometimes the word *dulia* is used for the esteem paid to the saints, but this is better distinguished by the word *veneration*.

Worship is an interior activity which often expresses itself in bodily gestures or postures: singing, kneeling, prostrating, dancing, and other forms of movement. Worship is also expressed in rites and ceremonies. See also **adoration; Book of Hours; liturgy; Office, Divine**.

Wounds, the Five Sacred During the Passion and Crucifixion, Jesus incurred the four nail marks in his hands and feet and the wound in his side from the soldier's spear (John 19:34). Devotion to the Five Wounds has entailed explicit emphasis on Jesus' endurance of the pain of the cross and on the symbolic implications of the blood and water pouring from his side.

wreath The Advent wreath is a symbol of preparation for Christmas. See also **Advent wreath**.

wrath of God The ancient Israelites used this metaphor of anger to describe God's attitude toward sin. This is an anthropomorphism which occurs in the Old Testament to describe God as punishing sinners (Psalm 2:11). Jesus employs this anthropomorphism when he says "You brood of vipers! Who warned you to flee from the wrath to come?" (Matthew 3:7). Paul describes the Day of Judgment as the "day of wrath" (Romans 2:5). The author of Revelation refers to "the wrath of the Lamb" and "the wrath of God the Almighty" (6:16; 19:15).

X, Y, Z

Xavier, Saint Francis Born at Xavier (Navarre), Spain, in 1506, Francis was one of the first members of the Society of Jesus. Though he suffered from ill health, he went willingly to the Far East. For eleven years he preached the Gospel in India, Ceylon, and Japan. He had a strong desire to preach the Gospel in China, but before he could begin his missionary work there he died. His death came in 1552, when he was only forty-six years of age. He is an outstanding example of missionary zeal and a patron of missionaries.

Yahweh A Hebrew name for God meaning, approximately, *I AM WHO*

AM (see Exodus 3:13–14); it especially designates God as creator of the universe and the source of all life. Sometimes translated into English by the word *Jehovah.* See **God.**

year, liturgical   The liturgical year, in the words of Vatican II, "unfolds the whole mystery of Christ." The liturgical year begins with the First Sunday of Advent, a season of approximately four weeks, with emphasis on the coming of Christ both at the end of time and into human history. The Christmas season, celebrating the Incarnation of Jesus Christ, begins with the Vigil of Christmas and lasts until the Sunday after January 6. The period between the end of the Christmas season and the beginning of Lent belongs to Ordinary Time of the year. The season of Lent, with special emphasis on conversion and penance, begins on Ash Wednesday and lasts until the Mass of the Lord's Supper on Holy Thursday. The Easter Triduum begins with evening Mass of the Lord's Supper on Holy Thursday and ends with evening prayer on Easter Sunday. The Easter season lasts from Easter until Pentecost, a period of 50 days, with emphasis on our sharing in the Resurrection of Christ. Ordinary Time resumes on the Monday following Pentecost and continues until the beginning of Advent, comprising 33 or 34 weeks. Throughout the liturgical year, the holy Church honors with special love the Blessed Mary, Mother of God (for example, on December 8, feast of the Immaculate Conception), and includes days devoted to the memory of the martyrs and other saints. *(CCC 1168–1173)*   See **Advent; Lent; Easter.**

youth ministry   A pastoral ministry in the Christian community that tries to discern, address, and respond to the particular needs and challenges encountered by young people and their families in contemporary society. The goal is to help these persons become mature followers of Jesus who live out their baptismal commitments to witness to a Christian way of life. The team entrusted with youth ministry tries to build relationships with the young people, supports their personal and spiritual growth, seeks to address their real-life needs and questions, and invites the youth and their families into the ministry of the people of God.

zeal   The love of God in action. Zeal is characterized by intense passion and eagerness. Zeal in God's service comes from a realization of the great blessings received through faith and it communicates itself in a desire to proclaim and live the Catholic faith in its fullness. Zeal is the charity and resulting attempt that enables one to serve God and others in the furthering of the kingdom of Christ, the sanctification of souls, and the furthering of the glory of God by making

God better known and loved and thus more faithfully served. *(CCC 2750)*

Zechariah, Book of One of the prophetic books of the Old Testament; written in 520 B.C., it is noteworthy especially for its many prophecies concerning the Messiah and the messianic kingdom.

Zephaniah One of the prophetic books of the Old Testament; written in the second half of the seventh century before Christ, it contains strong prophecies of punishment for Jerusalem and its people because of their idolatry and superstition; it also predicts, however, that a holy remnant of the people will be spared.

Zionism A Jewish nationalist movement that began in the late 1800s. The major goal of early Zionism was the establishment of the state of Israel which was realized in 1948. The goals of modern Zionism include the intensifying of Jewish national unity, reinforcing the Israeli identity and welcoming Jews from the diaspora around the world who wish to have a national home.

zucchetto The small skullcap worn since the thirteenth century by bishops or other prelates. The color varies according to the rank of the wearer. The pope wears a white zucchetto made of watered silk. The cardinals wear scarlet and bishops use purple. Priests of monsignorial rank may wear black with purple piping. A small brown skullcap is worn by Capuchins. All others may wear simple black, including abbots who do not have episcopal dignity.

A Calendar of Catholic Saints

"Exactly as Christian communion between men on their earthly pilgrimage brings us closer to Christ, so our community with the saints joins us to Christ, from whom as from its fountain and head issues all graces and the life of the People of God itself. It is most fitting, therefore, that we love those friends and co-heirs of Jesus Christ who are also our brothers and outstanding benefactors, and that we give due thanks to God for them, humbly invoking them, and having recourse to their prayers, their aid and help in obtaining from God through his son, Jesus Christ, Our Lord, our only Redeemer and Savior, the benefits we need. Every authentic witness of love, indeed, offered by us to those who are in heaven tends to and terminates in Christ, 'the crown of all the saints,' and through him in God who is wonderful in his saints, and is glorified in them."

Dogmatic Constitution on the Church, §50.

1   Mary, Mother of God
    Clarus, abbot (tailors)
2   Basil "the Great," bishop and doctor
        (hospital administrators)
    Gregory of Nazianzus, bishop and doctor
3   Genviève, virgin (Paris)
4   Elizabeth Ann Seton, religious
5   John Nepomucene Neumann, bishop
    Simeon Stylites (shepherds)
6   André Bessette, religious
7   Raymond of Peñafort, priest (lawyers)
8   Gudula, virgin (Brussels, invoked against toothache)
9   Adrian, abbot

10 Agatho, pope
   William of Bourges, bishop and confessor
11 Theodosius the Cenobite
12 Benet Biscop (architects, glass workers)
13 Hilary of Poitiers, bishop and doctor,
   (invoked against snakebite)
14 Felix of Nola (invoked against perjury)
15 Ita, abbess
16 Priscilla (widows)
17 Anthony of Egypt, abbot (butchers, basket weavers,
   invoked against eczema)
18 Margaret of Hungary, nun
19 Canute IV (Denmark)
20 Fabian, pope and martyr
   Sebastian, martyr (archers, athletes, police officers)
21 Agnes, virgin and martyr
22 Vincent of Saragossa, deacon and martyr
   (roofers, wine makers)
23 Emerentiana, virgin, martyr (invoked against stomachache)
24 Francis de Sales, bishop and doctor
   (editors, journalists, writers)
25 Dwyn, abbess (invoked against sickness in animals)
26 Timothy, bishop (invoked against stomachache)
   Titus, bishop (Crete)
27 Angela Merici, virgin
   John Chrysostom, bishop and doctor (orators)
28 Thomas Aquinas, priest and doctor (students, theologians)
29 Gildas the Wise, abbot (invoked against dog bites, rabies)
30 Martina, virgin, martyr (nursing mothers)
31 John Bosco, priest (apprentices, editors)

1   Brigid of Ireland (fugitives, newborns)

2   Jeanne de Lestonnac, widow

3   Blaise (wild animals, invoked against throat disease)

    Ansgar, bishop (Denmark, Iceland, Norway)

4   Andrew Corsini, bishop, confessor
      (invoked against sudden death)

5   Agatha, virgin, martyr (jewelers, nurses,
      invoked against fire)

6   Paul Miki and companions, martyrs

    Dorothy (brides, florists)

    Amand (hotel workers)

    Raymond Nonnatus, confessor (obstetricians)

7   Moses, desert monk (Saracens)

8   Jerome Emiliani (orphans)

    Meingold, martyr (bankers, miners)

9   Apollonia, virgin, martyr (dentists)

10 Scholastica, virgin

11 Commemoration of the apparitions of Our Lady of Lourdes

    Caedmon (poet)

12 Marina, virgin

13 Stephen of Rieti, abbot

14 Cyril, monk, and Methodius, bishop (Czechoslovakia)

15 Euseus, hermit (shoemakers)

16 Juliana, martyr

17 Seven Founders of the Servants of Mary

18 Simeon, bishop, martyr

19 Conrad of Piacenza (invoked against famine, hernia)

20 Eleutherius of Tournai, bishop

21 Peter Damian, bishop and doctor

22 Margaret of Cortona
23 Polycarp of Smyrna, bishop and martyr
    Milburga, virgin (birds)
24 Matthias, apostle (alcoholics)
25 Wallburga, virgin (invoked against coughs)
26 Victor of Plancy, hermit
27 Gabriel Possenti (college students)
28 Romanus, abbot (invoked against insanity)
    Oswald of Worcester, monk

MARCH

 1 David (Wales)
 2 Agnes of Bohemia
 3 Aelred of Rievaulx, abbot
 4 Casimir, confessor (Poland)
 5 Phocas of Antioch, martyr (invoked against snakebite)
 6 Fridolin, abbot (optometrists)
 7 Perpetua and Felicity, martyrs
 8 John of God, religious (booksellers, printers, invoked
       against alcoholism, heart disease)
 9 Frances of Rome, religious (motorists)
    Catherine of Bologna
10 Kessog, bishop (Scotland)
11 Eulogius of Cordova, martyr (carpenters)
12 Seraphina, virgin
13 Ansovinus, bishop (harvests)
    Roderic and Solomon, martyrs
14 Lubin, bishop
    Matilda, widow
15 Louise de Marillac, widow (social workers)
    Clement Mary Hofbauer

16   Herbert or Heribert, bishop (invoked for rain)

17   Patrick, bishop (Ireland)
      Gertrude of Nivelles (cats, gardeners)

18   Cyril of Jerusalem, bishop and doctor
      Edward, martyr

19   Joseph, husband of Mary (fathers, house hunting,
         workers; invoked for a happy death)

20   Cuthbert, bishop (sailors)

21   Enda, abbot

22   Nicholas von Flüe (Switzerland)

23   Turibius of Mogrovejo, bishop (native rights)

24   Catherine of Sweden (miscarriage)
      Gabriel the Archangel (diplomats, postal workers, telephone
         workers)

25   Dismas (criminals)
      Lucy Filippini, virgin

26   Ludger, teacher

27   Alkelda (invoked against eye disease)

28   Gontran, king

29   Cyril of Heliopolis, martyr, and Mark, bishop

30   John Climacus, abbot

31   Balbina (invoked against lymph-gland diseases)
      Benjamin, martyr

APRIL

1   Catherina of Palma, virgin
   Hugh of Grenoble, bishop

2   Francis of Paola, hermit (naval officers, seafarers)

3   Richard of Chichester, bishop (coach drivers)

4   Isidore of Seville, bishop and doctor

5   Vincent Ferrer, priest (builders)

6   Notker Balbulus (invoked against stammering)

7   Jean-Baptiste de La Salle, priest (teachers)
     Henry Walpole, priest, martyr

8   Walter of Pontnoise, abbot (prisoners)

9   Casilda (invoked against bad luck)

10   Hedda, abbot of Medeshamstede

11   Stanislaus of Cracow, bishop and martyr (Poland)
     Gemma Galgani (hospital pharmacists)

12   Zeno of Verona, bishop (anglers)

13   Martin I, pope and martyr

14   Lydwina of Schiedam, virgin (skaters)

15   Hunna (laundry workers)

16   Benedict Labre (the homeless)
     Bernadette of Lourdes, virgin

17   Stephen Harding, monk

18   Aya (invoked against lawsuits)

19   Expiditus (emergencies; invoked against procrastination)
     Adjutor (swimmers; invoked against drowning)

20   Agnes of Montepulciano, virgin

21   Anselm of Canterbury, bishop and doctor

22   Theodore of Sykeon, bishop (for/against rain)

23   George, martyr (England, equestrians, horses)
     Adalbert of Prague

24   Fidelis of Sigmaringen, priest and martyr

25   Mark, evangelist (Egypt, cattle breeders)

26   Paschasius Radbertus, monk

27   Zita (invoked in the search for lost keys)

28   Peter Chanel, priest and martyr (Oceania)

29   Catherine of Siena, virgin and doctor (invoked against fire)

30   Pius V, pope

1   Joseph the Worker
2   Athanasius, bishop and doctor
    Zoe and Hesperus, martyrs
3   Philip and James, apostles
    Timothy and Maura, martyrs
4   Florian (fire fighters, soap makers)
5   Judith, widow (Prussia)
6   Ava (children learning to walk)
7   Domitian, bishop (invoked against fever)
    John of Beverley, bishop
8   Wiro of Ruremonde (Holland)
9   Pachomius, abbot
10 John of Ávila, priest
11 Gengulf or Gangulphus (invoked against unhappy marriage)
    Walter of L'Esterp, abbot
12 Francis Patrizzi (reconciliations)
    Pancras, martyr (treaties)
13 Servatius of Maastricht (invoked against foot trouble)
14 Mary Mazzarello, virgin
15 Isidore the Farmer (ranchers, piety, love of the poor,
        animals)
16 Honoratus of Amiens, bishop (bakers, millers)
    John of Nepomucen (bridges, invoked against detraction)
17 Madern (invoked against lameness)
    Robert Bellarmine, bishop and doctor (catechists)
18 Eric of Sweden, martyr
    John I, pope and martyr
19 Celestine V, hermit (bookbinders)
    Dunstan, bishop (goldsmiths, locksmiths)

20 Bernardino of Siena, priest (advertising,
   invoked against hoarseness)

21 Hospitius, confessor

22 Julia, martyr (Portugal)

   Rita of Cascia, widow (desperate cases; invoked against
   infertility, loneliness, tumors)

23 Desiderius, bishop (invoked against perjury)

24 Vincent of Lérins, monk

25 Venerable Bede, priest and doctor (scholars)

   Gregory VII, pope

   Mary Magdalen Dei Pazzi, virgin

26 Philip Neri, priest (Rome)

27 Augustine of Canterbury, bishop

28 Bernard of Montjoux (mountain climbers, skiers)

29 Bona of Pisa, pilgrim (flight attendants)

30 Ferdinand III (engineers, governors, rulers)

   Joan of Arc (France, the military)

31 Petronilla, virgin, martyr

JUNE

1 Justin Martyr (philosophers)

2 Elmo (invoked against seasickness)

   Marcellinus and Peter, martyrs

3 Charles Lwanga and companions, martyrs (young Africans)

   Kevin, abbot

4 Quirinus, bishop, martyr (invoked against earache)

5 Boniface of Mainz, bishop and martyr (brewers)

   James Salomonius (invoked against cancer)

6 Claud, bishop (toymakers, invoked against bad luck)

   Norbert, bishop

7 Meriadoc, bishop (invoked against deafness)

8   Médard, bishop (harvests)

9   Columba of Iona, abbot

10 Olivia of Palermo

11 Barnabas, apostle

12 Antonina, martyr
    Leo III, priest

13 Anthony of Padua, priest and doctor
        (the poor; invoked to find lost objects)

14 Dogmael (babies learning to walk)

15 Germaine of Pibrac
    Vitus, martyr (comedians, dancers, invoked
        against lightning, oversleeping)

16 John-Francis Regis, missionary (lace makers, marriage)

17 Harvé, abbot (invoked against blindness, demons)

18 Ephraem the Syrian, poet and theologian

19 Boniface of Querfurt, bishop, martyr (Prussia)
    Romuald, abbot

20 Florentina of Seville, nun

21 Alban of Mainz, martyr (refugees)
    Aloysius Gonzaga, religious (young men)

22 John Fisher, bishop and martyr
    Thomas More, martyr (civil servants, lawyers)

23 Audrey (invoked against throat pain)

24 Birth of John the Baptist (Quebec,
        roadworkers, health spas)

25 Frebronia, martyr

26 Anthelm, bishop

27 Lazlo (Hungary)

28 Irenaeus, bishop

29 Paul, apostle (Greece, tentmakers, upholsterers)
    Peter, apostle (boatmakers, clockmakers, fishers;
        invoked against fever, foot trouble)
    Emma or Hemma, widow

30 Theobald of Provins
    Basilides (prison guards)

1   Oliver Plunkett, bishop, martyr
2   Processus and Martinian, martyrs
        (invoked against infirmity)
3   Thomas, apostle (architects, builders, construction workers,
        masons; invoked against doubt)
4   Bertha of Blangy, widow
    Elizabeth of Portugal
5   Anthony Zaccaria, priest
6   Maria Goretti, virgin and martyr (teenage girls)
7   Palladius, bishop
8   Kilian (Austria)
9   Veronica Giuliani, virgin
    Goar of Trier (potters, innkeepers)
10 Seven Brothers
11 Benedict of Nursia, abbot (the dying, monks, those who
        break things, invoked against gallstones,
        kidney disease, poison)
12 John Gualbert (foresters, park rangers)
13 Mildred, virgin
14 Camillus of Lellis, priest (nurses, invoked against
        compulsive gambling)
    Blessed Kateri Tekakwitha, virgin
15 Bonaventure, bishop and doctor
    Donald of Ogilvy
16 Mary Magdalene Postel, foundress
17 Alexis, "the man of God"
18 Arnulf of Metz, bishop (music)

19   Justa and Rufina, virgins, martyrs (Seville)

20   Margaret (childbirth)

21   Lawrence of Brindisi, priest and doctor
     Victor of Marseilles

22   Mary Magdalene (hairdressers, perfumers)

23   Bridget of Sweden, religious

24   Boris (Moscow)
     Christina the Astonishing, virgin (psychiatrists)

25   James the Great, apostle (furriers, veterinarians,
       invoked against arthritis)

26   Joachim and Anne, parents of Mary

27   Pantaleon, martyr (doctors)
     Seven Sleepers of Ephesus (invoked against insomnia)

28   Samson of Dol

29   Martha, virgin (dieticians, wives)

30   Peter Chrysologus, bishop and doctor

31   Ignatius of Loyola, priest (religious retreats)

AUGUST

1   Alphonsus Liguori, bishop and doctor (moral theologians)

2   Eusebius of Vercelli, bishop

3   Lydia (cloth dyers)

4   Jean-Baptiste Vianney, priest (parish priests)

5   Nonna

6   Justus and Pastor, martyrs
     Sixtus II, pope and martyr

7   Albert of Trapani (invoked against earthquakes)
     Cajetan, priest

8   Dominic de Guzman, priest (astronomers)

9   Emygdius of Ancona

10   Lawrence, deacon and martyr (cooks, librarians)

11 Clare of Assisi, virgin (embroiderers, television)
12 Porcarius and companions, martyrs
13 John Cassian, martyr (teachers)
   Concordia (babysitters)
14 Maximilian Kolbe, priest and martyr (drug addicts)
15 Arnulph of Soissons, bishop (brewers)
   Joseph of Calasanz (Christian schools)
16 Stephen of Hungary, king
   Roch (dog lovers, invoked against contagious diseases)
17 Hyacinth (Lithuania)
18 Helena, empress (archeologists)
19 John Eudes, priest
20 Bernard of Clairvaux, abbot and doctor (beekeepers)
21 Bernard Tolomei, founder (olive growers)
22 Symphorian, martyr
23 Rose of Lima, virgin (Peru, florists)
24 Bartholomew, apostle (cheese merchants, plasterers,
      invoked against nervous ticks)
25 Genesius of Arles (actors, comedians, secretaries)
   Louis of France, king, confessor (masons, sculptors)
26 Teresa of Jesus, founder (older people)
27 Monica (mothers)
28 Augustine of Hippo, bishop and doctor (printers)
29 Sabina, martyr
30 Felix of Rome
31 Aidan of Lindisfarne, bishop

SEPTEMBER

1 Giles, abbot (invoked against lameness, leprosy)
2 Agricolus of Avignon, bishop (invoked against bad luck)
3 Gregory the Great, pope and doctor (music, singers)

4   Rose of Viterbo, virgin (florists)
    Laurence Giustiniani, bishop, confessor (Venice)
5   Bertinus, abbot
6   Donatian, bishop
    Magnus of Füssen (invoked against hail, vermin)
7   Cloud or Clodoald
    Gratus of Aosta (fear of insects)
8   Corbinian, bishop
9   Peter Claver, priest (African Americans, race relations)
10 Nicholas of Tolentino, confessor (seafarers, holy souls)
11 Protus and Hyacinth, martyrs
12 Guy of Anderlecht (cabdrivers)
13 Amatus, abbot
    Notburga, virgin (servants)
14 Maternus, bishop
15 Catherine of Genoa, widow (nurses)
16 Cornelius, pope and martyr (invoked against twitching)
    Cyprian of Carthage, bishop and martyr
17 Hildegard of Bingen, mystic
18 Joseph of Cupertino, confessor (astronauts, pilots)
19 Januarius, bishop and martyr (blood banks)
20 Andrew Kim Taegon, priest and martyr,
        Paul Chong Hasang and companions, martyrs
    Eustace (hunters, invoked against family troubles)
21 Matthew, apostle and evangelist (accountants,
        customs officials, security guards, tax collectors)
22 Maurice, martyr (hat makers, infantry soldiers,
        invoked against gout)
23 Cadoc (invoked against cramps)
24 Gerard of Csanrd, bishop, martyr (Hungary)
25 Albert of Jerusalem, bishop
26 Cosmas and Damian, martyrs (barbers, chemical workers)

27 Vincent de Paul, priest (charitable giving)
28 Wenceslas, martyr (Bohemia)
   Lawrence Ruiz and companions, martyrs
29 Michael, Gabriel, and Raphael, archangels
30 Jerome, priest and doctor (librarians)

OCTOBER

1 Thérèsa of Lisieux of the Child Jesus, virgin (florists,
   pilots, invoked against tuberculosis)
2 Guardian Angels (police)
3 Gerard of Brogne, abbot (invoked against jaundice)
4 Francis of Assisi, confessor (animals, ecology, merchants)
5 Placidus (invoked against chills)
   Maurus (invoked against colds)
6 Bruno Hortenfaust, priest
      (invoked against demonic possession)
   Marie-Roe Durocher, virgin
7 Our Lady of the Rosary
8 Pelagia the Penitent (actresses)
9 Denis, bishop and martyr (invoked against frenzy)
   John Leonardi, priest
10 Francis Borgia, confessor
11 Gomer or Gummarus (unhappy husbands,
      invoked against hernia)
   Kenneth or Canice, abbot
12 Wilfrid of York, abbot
13 Comgan, abbot (Austria)
14 Callistus I, pope and martyr
15 Teresa of Ávila, virgin and doctor
      (Spain; invoked against heart attacks)

16 Gerard Majella (childbirth, mothers)

    Hedwig, religious

    Margaret Mary Alacoque, virgin

17 Ignatius of Antioch, bishop and martyr

18 Luke, evangelist (doctors, artists)

19 Isaac Jogues and John de Brébeuf, priests and martyrs, and companions, martyrs

    René Goupil (anesthesiologists)

20 Contardo Ferrini (universities)

    Irene, virgin (peace)

21 John of Bridlington (invoked against complications in childbirth)

    Ursula (orphans, teachers; invoked against the plague)

22 Donatus of Fiesole, bishop

23 John Capistrano, priest (military chaplains)

24 Anthony Claret, bishop (weavers, savings banks)

25 Crispin and Crispinian, martyrs (shoemakers)

26 Bonaventura of Potenza

27 Frumentius, bishop

28 Jude, apostle (hopeless cases)

29 Baldus (invoked against family problems)

30 Dorothy of Montau

31 Quentin, martyr (locksmiths; invoked against coughs and sneezes)

NOVEMBER

1 All Saints

    Marcellus of Paris, bishop

2 All Souls

3 Hubert of Maastricht (dogs, hunters, trappers)

    Martin de Porres, religious (public-health workers)

4   Charles Borromeo, bishop (seminarians,
      invoked against ulcers)

5   Elizabeth, mother of John the Baptist

6   Leonard of Noblac (invoked against robbery)

7   Willibrord, bishop (invoked against convulsions)

8   Four Crowned Martyrs

9   Benen, bishop

10 Leo "the Great," pope and doctor (choirs, musicians)

11 Martin of Tours, bishop (innkeepers, the military)

12 Josaphat Kuncevych, bishop and martyr

13 Frances Xavier Cabrini, virgin (immigrants)
      Homobonus of Cremona (businesspeople)

14 Lawrence O'Toole, bishop (Dublin)

15 Albertus Magnus, bishop and doctor (scientists)

16 Gertrude the Great, virgin
      Margaret of Scotland

17 Elizabeth of Hungary, religious
      Gregory Thaumaturgus (Wonderworker),
        bishop (desperate situations)
      Hugh of Lincoln, bishop (sick children, swans)

18 Rose Philippine Duchesne, virgin

19 Narses

20 Edmund, martyr

21 Gelasius I, pope

22 Cecilia, virgin and martyr (composers, music)

23 Clement I, pope and martyr (stonecutters, tanners)
      Columbanus, abbot (invoked against depression, floods)

24 Colman of Cloyne, bishop

25 Catherine of Alexandria (lawyers, librarians, nurses,
        universities; invoked against diseases of the tongue)

26 John Berchmans (altar servers)

28 Stephen the Younger, martyr

29   Sernin, bishop

30   Andrew, apostle (invoked against neck problems)

1   Edmund Campion, martyr (printers)

2   Viviana or Bibiana, virgin, martyr

3   Francis Xavier, priest (missionaries, tourism)

4   Barbara (architects, fire fighters)
John of Damascus, priest and doctor

5   Sabas, abbot

6   Nicholas of Myra, bishop (brides, dockworkers, travelers)

7   Ambrose of Milan, bishop and doctor (beekeepers, orators)

8   Immaculate Conception

9   Leocadia, virgin, martyr

10   Eulalia (invoked for calm waters)

11   Gentian or Fuscian (innkeepers)

12   Our Lady of Guadalupe (Mexico)
Jane Frances de Chantal, religious

13   Lucy, virgin and martyr (invoked against eye disease)

14   John of the Cross, priest and doctor (poets)

15   Valerian, bishop (invoked against exposure to cold)

16   Adelaide, widow

17   Lazarus (lepers)

18   Flannan, bishop

19   William of Fenoli

20   Dominic of Silos, abbot (captives)

21   Peter Canisius, priest and doctor

22   Chaeremon, martyr

23   John Cantius, priest

24   Adela, widow and abbess

25 Eugenia, virgin, martyr
26 Stephen, first martyr (bricklayers)
27 John, apostle and evangelist (writers)
28 Holy Innocents, martyrs (babies)
29 Thomas Becket, bishop and martyr (blind)
30 Catherine Labouré
31 Sylvester I, pope